Publisher's note 2017

Mention the 1960s and most people probably think of The Beatles, psychedelia, Vietnam, the mini-skirt. This book corrects the error of focussing too heavily on the end of that decade: things were very different when the Sixties dawned, only six years after the end of rationing. Here is a book which captures the spirit of women who still knew how to make do and mend, who made their own cleaning products, who revelled in bottling and preserving, and eating food in season.

Two generations have been born since the 1960 publication of *The Countrywoman's Year.* Many of the contributors to that first and only previous edition are probably no longer with us: not only most of the contributing WI members, but also the eminent illustrators of the day, and the publishing houses and magazines who gave permissions. After all that time, and all the changes which have occurred in the countryside since 1960, and in the lives of women, as publishers we wondered: beyond the social history or the nostalgia, was there anything left of relevance in this book for women today?

At first glance it might not seem so. In her fascinating Introduction on page 11, Dame Shirley Paget, Marchioness of Anglesey and former chairman of the National Federation of Women's Institutes, wrote that women in the countryside were spared 'the dreary sameness that threatens a semi-urban life' and that the 1960 countrywoman is fortunate in that she can instead 'enjoy the special country pleasures – the farm butter, the elderberry wine, the lavish flowers and the fresh herbs... she is spared the polluted sky, the clatter, the distraction, the unknown crowds of city life. Instead she enjoys this country scene in the company of friends, or at any rate well-known foes, and with leaves that are green to look at, and sounds that are separate to hear'.

The book proceeds to take us, at a good pace, through the seasons of the rural year, enjoying the bounty of them all. Some of the suggestions seem unlikely hobbies for the majority of modern women. Who owns a butter churn today? Who would trouble to smock nylon? But cumulatively, it all starts to inspire. How satisfying it could be to make your own furniture polish or the Queen Charlotte's Almond Paste for Chapped Hands, to bake bread or make a lovely holly wreath for the front door. One step further and readers might find that they had always wondered how to make corn dollies, patchwork, Durham quilts, how to make a rug or paint watercolours. The expected WI strengths are all here – how to make Old-fashioned Seed Cake, easy horse-radish sauce, the basics of flower arranging, how to make crystallised flowers and candied fruits.

But what surprises today, perhaps, is the strong sense of the women's fun and the happiness which emanates from this book. In the darkest winter nights, the WI games recommended in *The Countrywoman's Year* sound like the best antidote to depression imaginable and I for one can't wait to play Write to Aunt Agatha or Happy Family Musical Chairs in which Master Baker has to have Mrs Baker and the two children all sitting on his knee. On the section dealing with honey alone, there are no fewer than seven different step-by-step alcoholic drinks to be made. These are spirited ladies! Pounding a mound of bread-dough begins to sound like a much more appealing prospect than watching another box-set. And these resourceful, happy women might have taken old-fashioned pride in their spring-clean or their herb-growing activities, but they also knew, as set out in this yearbook, how to market their produce professionally, how to speak in public, and serve on a committee. These country women who could hang wallpaper and keep bees also knew when the chairman could use her casting vote and the precise meaning of 'ex-officio' and 'quorum', as well as the chemical processes involved in alcohol production...

Karen McCall
Merlin Unwin Books, 2017

THE WI COUNTRYWOMAN'S YEAR 1960

Edited by
The Marchioness of Anglesey

MERLIN UNWIN BOOKS

This edition published by Merlin Unwin Books, 2017
First published by Michael Joseph Ltd, 1960

Merlin Unwin Books Ltd
Palmers House, Corve Street
Ludlow, Shropshire SY8 1DB

www.merlinunwin.co.uk

The editor of this book, the late Elizabeth Shirley Vaughan Paget,
has asserted her moral right to be identified with this work.

ISBN 978-1-910723-45-6

Typeset in 12 point Bembo by Merlin Unwin Books
Printed by Nutech Print Services

Merlin Unwin Books would like to thank Linda and Robert
Yeatman for bringing *The Countrywoman's Year* to our attention.

Acknowledgments

The Country Wife mural which appears on the dust jacket [of the original 1960 edition of this book] was designed and made by Constance Howard for the Festival of Britain in 1951.

Two members of the National Federation of Women's Institutes saw the preliminary sketches and W.I. craftswomen contributed towards the mural which is worked in many different materials, the figures being threequarters life-size and padded. The mural was seen at the Festival of Britain, where it hung in the Land Pavilion. It was there suggested that it be given to the Women's Institute movement. So at the close of the Festival in 1951 the Country Wife was moved to Denman College where it is now displayed to the great enjoyment of all members.

The Country Wife mural, Festival of Britain 1951

The Eric Ravilious engravings that decorate the book throughout are reproduced by kind permission of the Trustees and also the BBC, *Country Life*, the Golden Cockerel Press, the Kynoch Press, London Transport Executive, Josiah Wedgwood, and the Yorkshire Rural Community Council.

Generous help was also given with additional engravings, drawings and diagrams by Joan Hassall, Roger Nicholson, Freda Nichols, G. D. McKerrow, J. Green, P. Bangs, Herefordshire County Federation of Women's Institutes, B. T. Batsford, Mills & Boon and *The Times*. Finally I am indebted to the following people and Associations who have contributed to the text of this book and whose advice has been so readily given: Beryl Ash, F. W. Beech, B.Sc., Ph.D., A.R.I.C., Rita Bandy, M. Pauline Bigland, R. A. Burtt, M. K. Cardwell, Jeanetta Cochrane, Averil Colby, Vera Cox, M. J. Dunn, V. B. Denbigh, Leslie Ferguson, Dorothy Gullick, Phyllis Hosking, D. F. Hutton, Margaret Hutchings, Atherton Harrison, Gwen Jones, Gwynedd Lloyd, Norah Lambourne, J. M. MacFarlane, Sybil Matthews, Olivia Parr, E. Ramsay Harvey, N. F. Tripp, Viola Williams, Rose Walker, Boosey & Hawkes, British Beekeepers' Association, British Nylon Spinners, Edinburgh and East of Scotland College of Agriculture, Herefordshire County Federation of W.I.s, Ministry of Agriculture, Food and Fisheries, Natural Rubber Development Board, Oxford University Press and many W.I. County Federations for recipes from their County Cookery Books.

Contents

Summer

Autumn

Winter

Introduction

The woman whose home is in the country in England or Wales today [1960] is trebly fortunate. She is fortunate because she can now share nearly all the interests – whether it be music or the theatre or debate – that recently were only readily available to the town housewife and for this she has largely wireless and television to thank. She is still more fortunate because in the country are cherished the particular local skills, the local festivals and history, and the local dishes that save us from the dreary sameness that threatens a semi-urban life; most fortunate of all because she can enjoy the special country pleasures – the farm butter, the elderberry wine, the lavish flowers and the fresh herbs. As a background to such great variety, she is spared the polluted sky, the clatter, the distraction, the unknown crowd of city life. Instead she enjoys this country scene in the company of friends, or at any rate well-known foes, and with leaves that are green to look at and sounds that are separate to hear.

An idyllic picture? Perhaps; but not so very far from the truth for the 450,000 members of the Women's Institutes who belong to more than 8,000 Institutes all over England and Wales. From large meetings of a hundred or more in mining villages in County Durham or in new housing estates in Bucks or Berks to the meetings of twelve or more old friends in a Welsh-speaking 'pentref' or in a hamlet on top of Dartmoor, there is this same infinite variety. The subject of the monthly meeting will be as varied as the members themselves: talks, demonstrations, discussions; accents, tastes and talents.

This book brings together some of the literature that is already available to Women's Institute members. It also includes many articles specially written for this book by W.I. members or friends. Most of the illustrations are by the late Eric Ravilious whose family have close ties with the Women's Institute movement and through whose generosity these engravings have been made available. I must also

11

here record special thanks to Jacqueline MacFarlane, of the National Federation of Women's Institutes, who has been responsible for the production of many of the publications used here and who has been my adviser throughout.

Each section begins with a contribution from out-of-doors which leads, almost inevitably, into the kitchen; then into the rest of the country home and to the parlour to use needle, and scissors and paste; after that, leisure or a venture to be shared with friends; and finally local recipes, skills and festivals to be made known to others. This pattern has been repeated in Spring, Summer, Autumn and Winter; but I have made the most arbitrary divisions between the seasons, contrary to all official definitions. By the end of January, in the west at least, spring has begun – the snowdrops are out, the moles visibly at work, the evenings lighter. It is a long season, as long as I can make it, till the roses confirm that full summer has come. By the end of August, autumn has begun; and winter is the shortest season of all – a couple of months or so centred on the great climax of Christmas and very soon after, spring begins again. This may be an unorthodox distribution, but, for many countrywomen at least, it is the right one.

All those who have contributed to this book, as well as the great body of Women's Institute members who have already enjoyed much that it contains, will share my belief that there is much here that others will want to know, whether they live in the town or in the country, in England or abroad. It is our hope in fact that this *Countrywoman's Year* may give something of value to everybody's year.

Shirley Paget
The Marchioness of Anglesey
1960

Spring

Take weapon away of what force is a man?
Take huswife from husband and what is he than?

As lovers desireth together to dwell
So husbandry loveth good huswifery well.

Though husbandry seemeth to bring in the gains
Yet huswifery labours seeme equall in pains.

Some respit to husbands the wether may send
But huswives affairs have never an end.

The Preface to *The Book of Huswiferie*
Thomas Tusser 1557

Of course January is really midwinter; but not for me. Living surrounded by the Gulf Stream, it may well be that the first of the camellias are in flower and the aconites are open. The mountains will be white and possibly, not probably, the Island will be covered in snow. But in any case by the end of January when the evenings are longer and green shoots are showing, I am sure that spring has begun however many the unfortunate lapses to winter. This is no time for the countrywoman to plan to go far afield; away from the Gulf Stream she may be snowed up and her own village become the limit of her existence. If she can get as far as the Village Hall for her W.I. monthly meeting, it will provide the ideal opportunity to see all her friends in one evening. So it is that many January meetings become the annual W.I. parties when members and their husbands and friends have the perfect excuse to play again all the gay, ridiculous games they enjoyed as children. Certainly for any country mother these paper games and quizzes are staple evening diet until the children go back to school.

It is in fact the time for falling back on our own resources. We may provide our own entertainment; we may copy the farmer's wife who still makes her own delicious butter and cheese; or we may join the increasing number of housewives who have rediscovered the incomparably better taste of warm, home-made bread and stone-ground flour.

This change from winter to spring is very gradual and very tentative. The first crinkly double daffodils, ugly I think, give way to the perfect Lenten lily; the brilliant stark red sticks of dogwood begin to blur as the leaf buds grow; the gulls forget the bird table.

The earth, though still horribly cold to the planting fingers, is soft again. The keen gardener, if she is also a keen cook, may be replenishing her herb garden with balm, rosemary and sorrel, excellent flavours that the poor city cook can seldom find at all or, if she does, only as the desiccated, tasteless remains of their real selves.

Busiest of all are the house-proud. The migration from room to room has begun as each succumbs to spring-cleaning fever. The barer each room becomes, as pictures are taken down and rugs are removed to the garden to be beaten, the more horribly evident – in harsh spring sunshine – is the need for new wallpaper, new covers, new lamp-shades. It's a thoroughly uncomfortable time for everyone, thought by husbands to be quite unnecessary and merely extravagant, immensely satisfying to the housewife alone. A spotless, shining house is her justification for those long, lazy, imaginary days of the summer to follow.

From the Garden

CULINARY HERBS

Herbs, in the culinary sense, are plants which provide flavouring or garnishing for our food, through the use of either the root, stem, leaves, flowers, or seeds. In times past, when there was less variety in cookery and materials and in methods of preserving foods, herbs were much more widely grown and used than they are today, but there is still a big demand for the better-known herbs. The value of freshly gathered produce from our gardens cannot be over-emphasised.

Household requirements of any one herb are usually moderate, so a small piece of suitable ground, easily accessible to the kitchen, would provide a useful and interesting Herb Garden.

BALM

An easily-grown perennial herb – about two feet high, which can be raised from divisions in March, or seeds or cuttings in April or May. It does best in a light soil. Its strong lemon flavour makes it especially useful for stuffings (particularly veal), cooling drinks and as an ingredient of pot-pourri.

Balm Sauce

Try using the finely chopped leaves of Balm, whether fresh or dried, instead of Mint for sauce. Make in the same way as Mint Sauce and serve it with lamb.

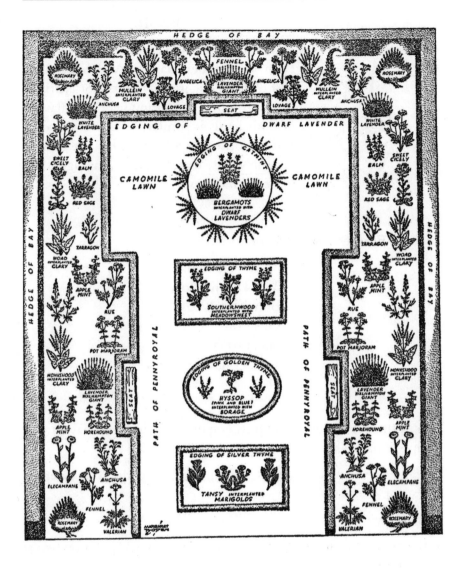

In this symmetrical garden the herbs on the right and left are identical. They are as follows: top – Rosemary, Anchusa, Mullein interplanted Clary, Lovage, Angelica, Fennel, Lavender; sides – White Lavender, Sweet Cicely, Balm, Red Sage, Tarragon, Woad interplanted Clary, Apple Mint, Rue, Pot Marjoram, Monkshood interplanted Clary, Lavender, Apple Mint, Horehound, Elecampane, Anchusa, Fennel, Valerian, Rosemary.

BASIL

(Bush and Sweet). Half-hardy annuals sown from seed under glass in March or April and planted out in May, one foot apart, in a well-drained and sunny bed. The flavour of both basils is similar, being very strong, and reminiscent of cloves. They are used to flavour soups, tomato dishes, sausages, and in herb mixtures.

Summer Basil & Tomato Soup

5½lbs ripe tomatoes
3 or 4 garlic cloves
Bunch fresh basil
Olive oil
Sugar to taste
1 pint vegetable stock

Method

This is the perfect quick soup to conjure up when you have a glut of ripe tomatoes.

1 Halve the tomatoes, sprinkle with chopped garlic, black pepper and sugar

2 Brush with oil

3 Roast cut side up on a greased baking sheet until well browned at Gas 4 180C.

4 Cool then puree.

5 Add chopped basil and vegetable stock

6 Chill for at least 4 hours before serving and seasoning to taste.

BAY

An evergreen, laurel-like shrub which is likely to suffer winter damage if grown in exposed situations. Plant in April. The fresh or dried leaves are used to flavour boiled salmon, pickled fish and meat, stews, soups, milk puddings and custards.

Marinated Pilchards

Thoroughly clean and wash as many pilchards as will fill an earthenware jar or pan. Put a bay leaf inside each fish and season well with pepper and salt. When the pan is full of fish, pour in sufficient vinegar to cover them, tie down with brown paper and put into slow oven. Leave all night. It is usual to put this into an oven after the baking is finished, and if the bones of fish are dissolved by next morning, it is ready to serve. If not, return to oven until done. Must be eaten cold.

BORAGE

A member of the forget-me-not family, with bright blue flowers, this easily-grown annual attains a height of about eighteen inches. Sow in the garden in April. The young leaves and flowers are well known as an ingredient of several beverages, especially claret cup, to which they impart a flavour of cucumber.

Claret or Cider Cup

To 1 large bottle of sound Claret (or a slightly larger amount of cider) add 1 sherry glass of Cognac, the rind of half a lemon in thin slices and the pulp, a sprig of borage, ice and powdered sugar to taste, but at least one tablespoonful of sugar. Stir twice and then pour in 1 large bottle of soda water. Stir again, and according to season, drop in two or three gently pinched strawberries, or half a dozen pinched raspberries or grapes, or a thin slice of melon. Leave for 20 minutes, and stir again before use.

N.B. – No cucumber, and no lacing with any liqueur but Cognac. A glass jug should be used, any touch of silver or other metal being fatal to wine.

CARAWAY

A biennial grown from seed sown in the open ground in April, and later thinned to one foot apart. Fairly heavy, but well-drained soil in semi-shade is suitable. The plants grow the first year, die right down for the winter, reappear the following spring and flower in May or June. The seeds are gathered before they fall, dried off and used for 'seed' cake, and in confectionery.

Old-Fashioned Seed Cake

½lb sugar	A little grated nutmeg
¾lb butter	4 eggs
1lb flour (sifted)	½ teaspoon baking powder
½oz caraway seeds	A little milk, if necessary

Cream the butter and sugar, add alternately flour (to which caraway seeds and nutmeg have been added), and beaten eggs and milk to make a not too soft consistency, adding baking powder last of all. Pour into a prepared tin and bake in a moderate oven for 2 hours.

CHERVIL

A hardy annual which is best sown several times in the year to provide a succession of fine parsley-like leaves useful for soups, salads, egg and fish dishes. As it withers quickly, it is not so useful for garnishing as parsley. The plants should be spaced six to eight inches apart, as un-thinned, they tend to run to seed very quickly.

Cream Salad Dressing (without vinegar)

3 tablespoons olive oil
2½ tablespoons lemon juice
3 tablespoons cream
½ teaspoon salt

1 tablespoon chopped
onion, parsley, chives
chervil and tarragon

Mix all together, and add the cream last of all before serving.

CHIVES

'The Infant Onion'. The plants are collections of little bulblets providing grass-like tops which can be cut again and again from March to October. Best grown in moist situations, the clumps should be divided every three or four years, and small portions replanted in fresh ground, about nine inches apart, in spring. The finely chopped tops give a mild onion flavour to salads, soups and egg dishes.

Herby Pie

Take two handfuls of parsley leaves, one of spinach, mustard, cress, white beet leaves, and one handful of finely sliced lettuce hearts, three or four borage leaves and a dozen chives. Wash these herbs well, and boil them for three or four minutes. Drain the water from them, chop them small, season with salt and pepper and spread them in a buttered dish. Make a batter with five tablespoons of flour and a pinch of salt, mixed smoothly with two eggs and as much milk as will bring it to the consistence of thick cream. Pour this over the herbs, stir all well together and bake in a moderate oven. If liked, the edges of the dish can be lined with good pastry.

DILL

An annual growing two to three feet high and bearing yellow flowers in July. Sow in ordinary well-cultivated soil in rows one foot apart and thin the seedlings to nine inches. Although the chopped leaves can be used like parsley in a white sauce, the plant is chiefly grown for its seeds, which are harvested and dried when ripe and used in pickling vinegar. Soak seeds in vinegar for a few days for Dill Vinegar.

FENNEL

This attractive-growing perennial, with its finely-cut leaves, reaches a height of about four feet when grown in ordinary soil in a sunny position. Seed can be sown outside in April and the plants thinned to eighteen inches apart, or roots can be obtained and planted in autumn or spring.

Fennel sauce is served with fish (particularly boiled salmon and mackerel). The seeds can be used to flavour soups and pickles. The wild fennel is very inferior in flavour to the cultivated strains.

Roast Mackerel

Roast them with fennel; after they are roasted open them and take out the bone; then make a good sauce with butter, parsley and gooseberries, all seasoned; soak your mackerel a very little, with your sauce, then serve them hot.

GARLIC

Used very sparingly to give an onion flavour to soups, stews and salads. The bulbs are collections of bulblets called cloves, and single cloves should be planted in sunny enriched ground in February or March, setting the cloves two inches deep and six inches apart in rows nine inches apart. Dry off the mature bulbs in August and store in a dry, cool and frost-proof place. Select the best bulbs to plant the following year.

Vegetable Soup

2 large carrots	A small piece of garlic
2 large onions	Salt
2 leeks	A little fine tapioca, if liked
A bunch of fresh parsley	

Prepare and cut up vegetables, cover with cold water, bring to the boil and allow to simmer for 4 hours. Strain and serve.

HORSERADISH

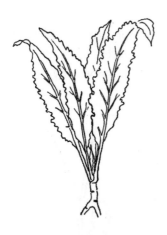

There may be doubt as to the wisdom of introducing this herb to the garden as it can become a real nuisance if uncontrolled. By planting straight four-inch lengths of root bearing only one growing crown or bud, in dibbled holes one foot deep and one foot apart in March, and lifting these grown roots again the following early winter, with any resultant side roots, the horse-radish should be kept well controlled. The grated root has a 'hot' flavour and is used for sauces for meat and fish.

Horseradish Sauce

> 2 tablespoons grated horseradish
> 1 teaspoon freshly made mustard
> Salt and vinegar to taste
> ¼ pint cream

1. Mix the horseradish and seasonings, add vinegar. 2. Stir in the cream. 3. Serve with roast beef.

MARJORAM

Sweet Marjoram (a half-hardy perennial best treated as an annual) is usually considered superior to Pot Marjoram (hardy perennial) for culinary purposes. The first should be sown outdoors in April (or under cloches in March to produce an earlier harvest) in any ordinary light soil in an open position. Thin to nine inches apart. The Pot Marjoram grows in any ordinary soil, attaining a height of about one foot. It is propagated by division or seeds in April. Both Marjorams are used either fresh or dried for flavouring many dishes, particularly forcemeats and for a soup 'bouquet'.

MINT

A popular herb of many uses and usually easy to grow. Plant pieces of root laid two inches deep and about nine inches apart in a shady bed of good soil in February or March. In the autumn cut all the stems off to ground level and top-dress the bed with compost or rotted manure. If 'Mint Rust' (recognised by abnormally thick and distorted stems and leaves) is present, spread some dry straw among the withering stems in autumn and set light to it. This should destroy any spores on the old stems or ground surface. It is a wise precaution to do this annually before top-dressing. 'Bowles Variety' is a good early round-leaved mint more immune to rust than the ordinary Spearmint. A few roots boxed up in December or January and forced, will provide an early cutting.

Mint Jelly

1 pint apple juice	2 heaped tablespoons chopped mint
¼ pint vinegar	1¾lb moist sugar

Boil together juice, vinegar and sugar until it begins to set. Add mint, boil up, skim, try sample. When done, pot up into small jars.

PARSLEY

Two sowings of this useful herb should be made each year in April and July. The seed, which is usually very slow in germinating, should be sown in good soil and thinned to ten inches apart. A protection of leaves, straw or cloches in frosty weather, will ensure fresh parsley all the year round. Rich in vitamin C, parsley should be eaten raw as well as in cooked dishes. The many varieties vary in length of stem and curl of leaf.

Parsley Bread Sauce

This recipe dates from 1586, and though rarely seen nowadays, makes an excellent sauce served with roast or baked rabbit or chicken.

1. Take a large handful of parsley, wash and chop finely. 2. Boil with 2–3oz butter and a little sieved cooked spinach for colour. 3. Season with ½ teaspoonful salt and pepper to taste. 4. When ready, add sufficient fine white bread crumbs and boil until it thickens.

ROSEMARY

An attractive shrubby herb which grows best against a sunny wall in a well-drained soil containing lime. It is propagated by soft cuttings in May or heeled cuttings in autumn, in sandy soil. Seed can be sown in April or May. The chopped leaves can be sprinkled over mutton before roasting, added to rabbit stew, and used in home–cured lard.

SAGE

A woody evergreen plant growing best in light soil with plenty of sun. Plants should be renewed every three or four years as young plants produce more and better leaves. Heeled cuttings taken in April and shaded for a few weeks will provide new plants easily, as will seed sown under protection in March. Sage is very strong in flavour and is used with onions for pork, duck and goose stuffings, and in sausages.

Duck Stuffing

Take 3 large onions, peel them, put them into boiling water, boil for a quarter of an hour, take 12 leaves of sage and chop them fine, put them into a basin with half a pint of bread crumbs, a teaspoon of salt and pepper, drain off the onions, chop them up, and put them in the basin with the bread crumbs. Mix well together and it is ready for use.

SAVORY

Winter Savory is an almost evergreen perennial, growing about one foot high. It thrives best in poor soil in a sunny position. New plants are raised from divisions or heeled cuttings or seeds in April. Trim established plants in October and top-dress with soil and leaf-mould. Summer Savory is a low-growing annual, sown in April and thinned to six inches. Both herbs are similar in flavour and are used in stuffings, soup, and cooked with broad beans.

Pork Sausages

3lb lean fresh pork	1lb stale bread crumbs
1½ tablespoons salt	1 tablespoon black pepper
Sage and savory to taste	Ground mace, cloves and
1½lb chine fat [next to	nutmeg to taste
backbone]	

Wash and soak skins. Soak bread and press dry in sieve or cloth. Finely mince the lean meat and fat. Beat up bread with a fork and add seasoning. Mix all ingredients very thoroughly. Fill skins and tie into suitable lengths. If not used at once, sausages should be hung.

SORREL

The French Sorrel is the best to grow, as it provides bigger and better leaves than other varieties. Sour or acid soils suit the sorrels which can be raised from seed sown outdoors in April or by divisions of roots in early spring. Set the plants about one foot apart and if flowering stalks are regularly removed, the plants will last several years. The acid-tasting leaves are cut up for use in omelettes, soups and salads.

Sorrel Soup

Wash a good ½lb sorrel. Cut up fine. Add 1½ pints good stock and simmer for 20 minutes. Thicken. Put to one side. Beat 2 yolks of eggs. Stir these with a little cream into soup at last minute. It must not boil. Add diced fried bread just before serving.

TARRAGON

Perennial plants growing two to four feet high, the Tarragons are not altogether hardy. It is wise to grow them in a sheltered position and to protect some of the roots in winter. Propagate by divisions or cuttings in spring, and grow in light, good soil. The variety known as True French has a better flavour than the Russian Tarragon, but is not so hardy. The chief use of this herb is for making Tarragon vinegar, but a few leaves can be added to a salad.

Tarragon Vinegar

1 quart bottle of white vinegar in 2 bottles. Pick just before it blooms and fill the bottles with long sprays of tarragon. Strain off after one month; but fresh vinegar can be added to the bottles.

THYME

Of the many thymes grown in gardens, the Common and Lemon Thymes are best for culinary purposes. Sunshine and a well-drained position suit these herbs which should be renewed every few years by divisions or cuttings or seeds in March or April. The plants should be frequently trimmed to prevent legginess and are best if not allowed to flower. Much used in stuffings, stews and in jugged hare.

Jugged Hare

1 hare (skinned)   ¼lb butter
1 carrot   1 pint stock
1 onion   1 tablespoon red currant jelly
1 small turnip   Port can be added
2 teaspoons chopped sweet herbs★
Forcemeat balls (if liked)
3oz flour

★Thyme, Parsley, Marjoram, Bay Leaf.

1. Slice the onion, carrot and turnip and fry in butter with the herbs in a saucepan.

2. Joint the hare into neat pieces and add them to the vegetables.

3. Simmer for ½ hour.

4. Mix the flour to a paste with a little stock, stir into the contents of the pan, add the stock, bring to the boil and cook slowly for 1 hour.

5. Add the red currant jelly and dish up, straining the sauce on it.

Drying of Herbs Most herbs can be used either fresh or dried. As a general rule, herbs for drying should be gathered on a dry day, when the plants are well developed, but just before they flower. Rinse the cut plants in cold water, shake thoroughly, tie in small bunches (big bunches are apt to go mouldy in the middle) and hang in a dry, airy place. When dry and crisp, remove the leaves from the stems and rub the leaves through a fine sieve. Store in airtight jars fully filled in a dark place. Parsley should be dried quickly in a fairly hot oven to keep its bright green colour.

Bouquet Garni A bunch of fresh herbs, usually two or three stalks of parsley, a sprig of thyme and of marjoram and a bay leaf, tied with thread and added to foods cooked in stock or water. If dried herbs are used, tie in a little piece of muslin. Remove the herbs before serving.

Fines Herbes A mixture of equal quantities of chopped fresh parsley, chervil and chives and (if liked) tarragon. To be sprinkled on salads and in omelettes and scrambled eggs.

Mixed Herbs Usually consist of sage, parsley, thyme and marjoram, with others added if desired. Used fresh or dried for flavouring meat and fish dishes, stuffings, etc.

In the Kitchen

BUTTER-MAKING

People who keep a cow or two for their own use sometimes have more milk than they can use and may wish to make a few pounds of butter to eat themselves.

Butter is made from the cream or fat globules in milk. This can be obtained either by setting the milk in shallow pans and leaving until the cream has risen to the surface when it can be skimmed by hand, or by using a mechanical separator.

EQUIPMENT

For separating cream from milk

Either a series of pans for setting milk and a hand skimmer, or a separator. There are several good makes available.

For butter-making

Pails (stainless or galvanised steel, not plastic)
2 crocks for cream (glazed earthenware)

31

Dairy thermometer
Scotch hands [wooden butter beaters]
Pint measure: long-handled one is the best
Wooden butter scoop
Hair sieve
Muslins
Dairy salt
Churn
Butter worker or board or slab on which to make up butter
Paper for wrapping
Scrubbing brush for cleaning churn, etc.
Small squeegee for cleaning down sides of crock, etc.

RIPENING OF CREAM

To ripen cream naturally, add each day's cream to that of the previous skimming or separating, taking care to stir thoroughly. On the day of churning, do not add the morning's cream, but start a fresh crock. The best temperature in which to keep the cream is 58° to 60°F. In summer it will probably be necessary to churn twice a week, in winter once a week will probably do.

Cream can be churned or made into butter by one of several different methods, but the keeping quality depends very largely on being able to get rid of the butter-milk and the most satisfactory way to do this is to use an end–over–end churn. There are also on the market small glass churns with inside beaters which can be used for butter to be eaten at home, and it is even possible to make butter for immediate use in an electric mixer or by merely beating up the cream with Scotch hands. Instructions for making butter with an end–over–end churn follow.

PREPARATION OF CHURN AND UTENSILS

Before use, the churn should be thoroughly scalded and then cooled. In the churn lid is a ventilator and a small glass window. When scalding, care should be taken to see that the ventilator is pressed in so that steam may escape. Near the bottom of the churn is a bung-hole for escaping water and butter-milk; be careful to see that the bung is in firmly before turning the churn.

All Scotch hands, scoops, measures, cloths, and sieves should also be scalded.

PREPARATION OF CREAM FOR CHURNING

Thin the cream until it runs off a Scotch hand in a fairly thick stream. The temperature of the cream should be 56°F when the atmosphere outside is 56°F. In hot weather the cream may be cooled to 52°F and in cold weather raised to 58°F. This can be done by varying the temperature of the water used to thin the cream.

CHURNING

Pour in cream through top (remembering to see bung is in firmly). Fix lid.

Turn the churn smoothly and fairly slowly, pressing ventilator frequently to allow gas to escape.

Increase the speed slightly to about fifty revolutions to the minute.

Watch small glass window. When it begins to clear and the cream has a slightly gritty look, it means that breaking water should be added to prevent the cream churning into a solid mass of butter. Ideally, it should churn into small grains, as it is then easier to get rid of the butter-milk, but only practice and experience will normally achieve this. Should the butter come in a more solid mass, extra care is needed in the later processes.

Take off the lid. Add breaking water using a measure and taking care to wash down the lid and sides of the churn. The temperature of the water is usually slightly lower than the churning temperature, but sometimes in cold weather when the butter is taking a very long time to come, it can be slightly warmer. The amount of water added is a little more than the original amount of thinned cream.

Fix lid. Turn a few quick turns, ventilating and watching

glass. Directly glass clears, stop churning.

Undo lid. Put pail with sieve under bung-hole. Take out bung, let butter-milk drain, catching any grains in sieve.

Return bung, shake grains into churn. Pour in clean water (washing down sides and lid).

Fasten lid. Turn twice, undo lid. Drain water into bucket, catching grains in sieve.

Repeat until water is quite clear of butter-milk, usually three washings.

Replace bung.

SALTING

The addition of salt to butter brings out the flavour and improves the keeping quality. The salt can either be added at this stage as brine or later as dry salt. The former has the advantage of giving a more even salting and preventing streakiness in the butter, the brine also tends to harden the butter, an advantage in hot weather or where the butter has been over-churned.

If dry salt is used, it is sprinkled evenly on the butter after it is removed from the churn and before it is worked.

Brining is strongly recommended. Good dairy salt should always be used, 1lb of salt to 1 gallon of water.

ADDING BRINE

Strain the brine through muslin into the churn. Replace lid. Churn a few times and leave for 10-15 minutes.

MAKING THE BUTTER

Remove butter from brine by lifting out grains with a scoop into a sieve. Empty the sieve completely either on to a butter worker where this is available or on to a board, or slab, on which the butter is to be made.

A butter worker is an oblong table with a roller at one end and a hole for draining at the other. It can be slightly tilted while the butter is being worked to help drainage and put flat while the butter is being made up.

If a worker is used, the roller is run over the butter three or four times until the surplus moisture is squeezed out. If no worker is available, then the moisture is squeezed out by beating and turning with the Scotch hands.

Butter for use in the home can be made into any shape or size, but for sale it is usual to make the butter up into oblong bricks, although in the West Country butter is still marketed locally in plain rolls.

It needs practice to make up butter properly: the sides should be straight and the corners sharp. There are traditional patterns which can be made on the top of the brick with the Scotch hands. A simple one is to start at the one corner making an imprint across then reversing the process from the other corner.

All butter should be stored in a cool place, preferably on a stone, slate, or marble surface.

Milk, cream, and butter should always be kept away from smells, otherwise all three may become tainted.

CLEANING OF CHURN AND UTENSILS

The churn, worker, scoop, Scotch hands, etc, should all be well scrubbed with lukewarm water, and when thoroughly cleaned, should be scalded. Care should be taken to see that the rubber ring on the churn lid is properly washed. All muslins must be washed, boiled, and hung out to air. For providing water for sterilising equipment, an electric, gas, or bottled gas boiler is useful.

If the floor is stone or tiled, this should be washed and, if possible, scalded; a squeegee helps to get rid of surplus water.

Where no dairy is available for making butter or setting milk, a separate room facing north with a stone floor and a water supply is advisable. Care should be taken to see that windows are covered so that flies are kept out. Drains should be trapped outside.

PRESERVING BUTTER FOR WINTER USE

Where butter is made in large quantities during the summer, it is sometimes useful to preserve some of it for winter use. A most satisfactory method of doing this is to immerse the butter in a brine made in the following way:

> 4lb salt, ½lb demerara sugar, and 1oz saltpetre per gallon of water. Boil and cool.

Make the butter as usual, paying special attention to washing out all traces of butter-milk. Make it up into 1lb or ½lb bricks, wrap in good quality parchment and then submerge in brine. The butter should be kept submerged and be taken out as and when required.

COTTAGE CHEESE OR CROWDIE

This cheese can be made from ripened, separated or skim milk, or even good buttermilk. Cottage cheese is eaten fresh; no ripening is necessary. If properly made, it will retain its flavour for 5-8 days.

Method

Heat skimmed or separated milk to 90°F and add some good soured buttermilk or starter, also a few drops of rennet in water; stir well, and leave in a warm place for 12 hours, when it will be coagulated and should split clean over the finger when inserted under the surface, or the curd should come clean away from the side of the tin.

Cut the curd into 1-inch cubes with a long knife, cutting horizontally with the skimmer.

Heat curd to 90°F after cutting to facilitate separation of whey. Settle for 10 minutes, then run off the whey and spread the curd on a cloth on the draining rack and tie cloth – tightening as draining takes place. This is usually complete in 4-6 hours. When ready it should hold together when pressed in the hand. Add ¼ ounce salt per pound of curd. If desired, some nicely ripened cream can be added and thoroughly mixed into the curd, then spread in a 2-inch layer and press lightly with a board. In 3 hours the cheese is ready for use and can be cut into squares and packed if for sale.

BUTTERMILK CROWDIE

This can be made by raising the temperature of buttermilk to 140°F, holding at this for 15 minutes, stirring continually. Cool to 90°F. Settle for 20 minutes, then run off the whey. Ladle the remaining curd into a cloth and treat as above. Drainage takes 6–8 hours.

Mix with a small quantity of good cream and add ¼ ounce salt per pound. This is ready for immediate use.

If the buttermilk is of good quality, this cheese should prove delicious.

YEAST COOKERY

Yeast is a non-flowering plant consisting of a single cell, which is so minute that it can only be seen under the microscope. Nearly 2,500 of these single cells would fit along one inch of a ruler. Most plants and animals are made up of a large number of individual cells, each with special functions to perform but working together. The yeast has an independent existence and all the functions of a living plant, ie breathing, feeding, growing and reproducing, are carried out by the single cell. For these natural functions warmth, moisture and the right food are necessary, and when they are not available the yeast cells are dormant.

In bread-making, the aim is to provide the most satisfactory conditions for yeast cells to live and reproduce, because in doing this, they produce a gas – carbon dioxide – in steady and increasing amounts. The gas acts as a raising agent to stretch the dough.

Yeast will flourish best at a temperature of 80-85°F. Sudden cooling or draught will inhibit growth, and heat will kill the cells. Therefore for success in yeast cookery, even and correct temperature of ingredients, utensils and the atmosphere are of fundamental importance in preparing the doughs for baking.

During mixing, kneading and proving, the carbon dioxide produced as the yeast breathes and feeds is distributed and trapped in the elastic dough. When sufficient gas has been produced, the dough is baked at a high temperature. This causes the gas to expand and raise the dough, it kills off the yeast cells, and changes the nature of the constituents of flour to give a firm spongy texture. Alcohol produced by the yeast cells as they feed on the starch and sugar, is driven off by heat.

YEAST SUITABLE FOR BREAD-MAKING

1. Compressed baker's yeast. This is pale fawn in colour with a fresh, fruity smell.

2. Dried yeast. Pellets or flakes of dried yeast can be kept in cool dry conditions for long periods. They are useful for those living in rural and isolated areas, and can be used in place of compressed yeast in all recipes, but it is important to remember:

(a) normally half as much dried yeast as fresh is required in any recipe;

(b) the dried yeast needs reconstituting before use, by soaking in lukewarm water (85°F) containing ½oz sugar to ½ pint reconstituting water. The liquid and sugar used for the reconstitution are part of the quantities specified in the recipe. If the recipe does not require sugar, the dried yeast can be reconstituted without sugar, but will be slower in action;

(c) to get results comparable with fresh yeast, a longer proving time is necessary. The effective action of dried yeast varies and information upon the correct quantity to use should be obtained from the suppliers for their particular product.

These two types of yeast are suitable for bread-making and yeast cookery because they give rapid fermentation at moderate temperatures and have a pleasant flavour. Brewers' yeast ferments much more slowly, it is dark in colour, and the flavour of hops tends to persist. It is therefore not suitable.

Compressed bakers' yeast can be obtained from bakers who make the bread they sell; dried yeast from large grocers and health stores.

39

STORAGE OF YEAST

Yeast can be stored for long periods in aluminium kitchen foil, or for a short time in a screw-capped jar, in a cool place such as a cool larder or the cool part of a refrigerator. Yeast can be stored in a deep freeze or icebox, but loaves made with it tend to have rather a close texture. The actual storage life varies from days to a month depending on the freshness of the yeast when bought. The smell of the yeast, which should be mild, slightly acid and free from staleness or putrefactive flavours, is an indication of its freshness and the flavour it will give to the baked product.

Supplies of dried yeast when opened should be stored in a dry cool place in a screw-capped jar. It is not necessary to keep dried yeast in a refrigerator. The keeping period of dried yeast varies with the different brands.

INGREDIENTS USED IN YEAST COOKERY

Flour contains starch, protein and fat (these three are the source of energy in flour), minerals and vitamins of the vitamin B group. Wheat before it is made into flour is usually described as either 'hard' or 'soft' wheat; hard wheat has a higher protein content than soft wheat and is more suitable for bread-making. In practice, a blend of flour from hard and soft wheats is usually chosen. The flour from soft wheats makes excellent pastry, biscuits and cakes.

Flours with a high extraction rate are strongly recommended, as this means that a high proportion of the nutritive value of the original wheat has been retained in the flour.

Salt gives flavour to bread, and prevents the yeast from fermenting too quickly. Too much salt will kill the yeast cells, and salt in the dry form draws the natural moisture from the yeast cells, and should therefore not be allowed to come in contact with yeast. It should be dissolved in water and added to the yeast in liquid, then the mixture immediately added to the dry ingredients. The usual proportions, unless otherwise stated, are 2 level teaspoons of salt to 1lb flour. Free-

running (table) salt should not be used in yeast cookery. Table salt
has added chemicals to keep it free-running, which will affect the
yeast. Salt-free bread can be made but extra mixing and kneading
are required.

Sugar is a food for yeast. Too much sugar will kill some of the yeast
cells and so delay fermentation, so creaming the sugar and yeast is
not recommended. Yeast is able to convert starch in the flour to
sugar.

Fat enriches the dough and gives improved silkiness and moisture
to the crumb. It reduces the elasticity of the dough and retards
slightly the action of the yeast.

Liquid may be milk, water or a mixture of both. The amounts vary
according to the recipe but approximately ½ pint to 1lb of flour is
a useful guide. In plainer mixtures water alone often gives a lighter
texture.

> 20 fluid oz = 1 pint
> 10 fluid oz = ½ pint
> 5 fluid oz = ¼ pint or 1 gill

Malt added to the dough increases the gas produced by the yeast.

Other ingredients, including eggs, sieved potatoes, dried fruit
and various flavourings, can be added to doughs to make richer and
varied yeast goods.

STEPS IN BREAD-MAKING

1. Mixing

Prepare the ingredients in the correct quantities, sieve the flour and warm to 80°F. Whisk the yeast in half the warm water and dissolve salt in the other half. Mix together and add to the warm flour. If it is not possible to take the temperature of the water, approximately the correct temperature can be reached by adding 1 part *boiling* water to 7 parts cold tap-water. The water should be at 80-85°F when added to the yeast. This is below blood heat. Using the hands with fingers stretched open, mix the dough and work it with a firm tearing action.

2. Kneading

Remove the flour from the basin on to a floured board to knead. This means folding it over on itself and pushing with a firm rocking motion until it becomes smooth and shiny.

3. Proving or rising

Put the dough into a warm basin, cover it with muslin wrung out in hot water and a tea towel to keep out the draughts and stand it in a warm place (80°F). Suitable places include the rack over a cooker, a *very* low oven, in front of a fire or over a pan of warm water. Direct heat or steam is too hot and will destroy the yeast cells.

The dough should be allowed to double its size; it should then be removed and 'knocked back', ie handled roughly so that some of the gas is forced out of the dough; the subsequent kneading distributes larger pockets of gas into smaller ones, evens the temperature throughout the dough and prevents the dough from overflowing the container.

Some housewives knead and prove three times, but care should be taken not to over-ferment the dough.

4. Shaping

After the last proving, the dough is ready for shaping or moulding. Scale off the dough to a suitable size, knead well and mould into oblongs which will half fill the loaf tins. Cover and leave to 'rest' for 5 minutes. Re-mould and put into warm, greased, floured tins.

5. Rising

Place the dough in a warm place, covered to protect it from draught, and leave until it has risen to the top of the tin.

6. Baking

The loaves can be brushed with milk or water or left untouched. Bake in a hot oven at 425°F. A container of water placed in the oven before baking, and left there throughout the cooking, gives an atmosphere of steam which produces a crisp top crust. The heat makes the gas expand causing the dough to rise, it sets the gluten and browns the outer crust. The dough above the level of the tin is in contact with the hot air and the first quick rise of the loaf can easily be seen in the finished bread. This is called 'oven spring' and is a characteristic of well-fermented bread. Bread is sufficiently baked when a hollow sound is heard on tapping the underneath of the loaf with the knuckles.

OVEN TEMPERATURES

Oven temperatures suggested in the recipes given here are based on the following scale:

Oven Heat	°F at Centre of Oven
Moderate	350–375°F
Moderately hot	375–425°F
Hot	425–450°F

Stages 1–6 outlined for bread-making are used in most plain yeast recipes. In the richer types of doughs containing fat, sugar and eggs which delay the action of the yeast, the main dough is

often preceded by a thin batter containing liquid, yeast, a little flour and a small quantity of sugar. This 'sponge' rises rapidly and gives the yeast a start before being introduced into the main dough. All mixtures should be proved until the dough doubles in size.

QUALITIES OF A GOOD LOAF

1. Good even shape with a fine 'oven spring'.
2. Fine even grain.
3. Silky texture when the hand is passed over the cut surface.
4. Even light-brown colour outside. The inside colour will depend on the flour used.

Common faults in bread	Cause
White pimples or spots on top of the loaf.	Dough had a skin on it before being placed in oven due to chilling or evaporation. A damp muslin covering the dough will help to avoid this.
Coarse honey-combed structure.	Too much liquid.
A 'flying top' when the top breaks away from the rest of the loaf.	The top crust bakes hard before there is full expansion of dough, due to under proving or chilling – or dough too tight because not well worked.
Lack of volume, uneven texture.	Under-proving and kneading or baking at too high a temperature.
Lack of volume – open texture and crumbly.	Over-proving and weakening of gluten; or baking at too low a temperature.
Smell of alcohol.	Over-proving.

REFRIGERATED DOUGHS

When yeast dough is placed in a refrigerator the action of the yeast is slowed down. This is useful to the housewife for she can prepare the dough in advance and bake bread or rolls as required.

The bread dough is prepared as normally, kneaded, proved and kneaded again. It is then placed in a bowl, covered with damp muslin 2-3 layers thick (or brushed with melted fat) and covered with a cloth. It should be placed in the refrigerator quickly to slow down the action of the yeast. Each day the dough should be pressed down and the muslin damped if necessary. The layer of fat may also need renewing. The dough should be torn off as required and the exposed surface covered. After kneading and proving it is baked as usual. The dough can be kept 2-3 days but the type of dough and the temperature of the refrigerator must determine the length of time a dough will keep. A rich dough mixture will last longer than plain dough.

Yeast doughs can be placed in the deep freeze. Allow several hours for the dough to thaw, and only thaw the amount of dough required.

★★★★★

RECIPES

PLAIN BREAD DOUGH

Bread Rolls

1lb flour	½ pint lukewarm milk or water
2 level teaspoons salt	
½oz yeast	Milk to glaze

Sieve flour; dissolve salt in half liquid; whisk yeast in remaining liquid, mix the two and add to flour. Mix to a dough; knead; prove. Knead lightly and cut into 16 even pieces; form each piece into a roll or fancy shape, place on a greased baking sheet, leaving room to rise; prove. Brush over with milk and bake in oven at 425°F for approximately 20 minutes.

If a soft crust is preferred, brush rolls with milk or margarine immediately after removing from oven.

Shapes for bread rolls:

(a) Plain round – with or without knife cut.

(b) Parker House rolls: Roll out dough on lightly-floured board to ½-inch thickness. Cut into rounds with 3-inch cutter. Crease each round deeply a little to one side of centre with dull side of knife. Fold larger half over smaller half – press along fold. Place just touching each other on a greased baking sheet. Brush tops with melted butter or margarine. Prove.

These can be used instead of bridge rolls, the sandwich fillings being put in the 'crack'.

(c) Cottage-type roll: Divide the dough according to the number and size of roll required. Reshape, placing one-third of each piece on top, with two-thirds at the base.

(d) Plait. Three equal pieces of dough, make into sausage shapes and plait.

(e) Two or three ovals, place side by side just touching.

(f) A horseshoe.

(g) A wheatsheaf.

PASTRY-TYPE DOUGH

Yeast Pastry

> White bread dough from 8oz flour, 3oz lard; *or*
> 12oz proved bread dough, 3oz margarine

Roll dough into oblong shape and spread quarter of the fat down two-thirds of length, fold and roll as for rough puff pastry. Repeat process four times in all.

Wrap dough in greased paper and then in a cloth, leave in refrigerator or cold place overnight.

Roll out and cut as required. Leave in a warm place to prove before baking at 450°F.

Use as flaky pastry for sweet and savoury dishes.

Eccles Cakes

8oz yeast pastry	4oz currants
2oz demerara sugar	2oz mixed peel
2oz margarine	¼ level teaspoon mixed spice

White of egg and caster sugar for brushing over.

Roll out pastry ¼-inch thick, cut in rounds with 4-inch cutter. Warm sugar, fat, currants, finely chopped peel and spice. Place a teaspoon of mixture in centre of each round of pastry. Wet edges and seal down centre. Turn over, roll out to required size, marking three cuts down centre. Prove. Brush over with water or white of egg and caster sugar. Bake at 450°F for 20 minutes.

CREAMED FAT MIXTURE

Yule Cake

8oz margarine	½ level teaspoon nutmeg
8oz moist brown sugar	½ level teaspoon ground cloves
5oz golden syrup	½ level teaspoon ground mace
3 large eggs	½ level teaspoon cinnamon
1lb flour	½ level teaspoon salt
1¼oz yeast	1¼lb currants and raisins
8oz lukewarm milk or	5oz mixed peel
milk and rum	

Cream margarine and sugar, add syrup and beat together. Add beaten eggs teaspoon by teaspoon, beating continuously. Add sieved flour, spices and fruit. Whisk yeast in half milk, dissolve salt in remaining milk and add to dry ingredients

Bake at 375°F for approximately 1 hour in 8-inch cake tin.

MELTED FAT MIXTURE

Doughnuts

8oz flour	¼ pint lukewarm milk
1 level teaspoon salt	½oz margarine
2 level tablespoons sugar	Jam
½oz yeast	Fat for frying

Sieve flour, mix in sugar. Whisk yeast in half the milk, melt margarine in remainder and add salt, cool until lukewarm. Add the two liquids to flour, mix and knead well; prove. Knead lightly, cut into 16 portions; form into balls, flatten, place jam in centre of round, fold edges of round together enclosing jam, press together. The doughnuts can be cut into rings if preferred. Prove. Fry in deep hot fat turning frequently, holding doughnuts below surface of fat to obtain even browning. Fry to a deep golden colour. Drain on paper and toss immediately in caster sugar (and cinnamon if liked).

The fat is the correct temperature for frying doughnuts when a piece of bread turns brown immediately in the fat.

RUBBING FAT INTO PLAIN AND FRUIT MIXTURES

Muffins

1oz yeast	½oz salt
1 pint lukewarm water	½oz sugar
2½lb flour	

Whisk yeast in half water, sieve flour, add sugar; mix yeast and rest of water containing dissolved salt with dry ingredients. Prove; knead well; prove. Divide into 2½-oz pieces. Make into rounds ½-inch thick; cook on greased oven plates, both sides evenly.

Hot Cross Buns

8oz flour	1½oz fat
½ level teaspoon salt	1½oz raisins
1oz sugar	½oz yeast
1 level teaspoon ginger	4oz lukewarm
milk	
½ level teaspoon cinnamon	1 egg
2 level teaspoons mixed spice	Pastry crosses
(optional)	

Sieve flour, rub in fat, add sugar, spices and raisins; whisk yeast with half milk, dissolve salt in remaining milk, add egg (reserving a little for brushing buns). Place yeast mixture in centre of flour, allow to sponge through. Mix to a light consistency with rest of milk, knead and prove. Knead, roll out, shape. Put on a greased baking tray and prove. Brush with egg, cut a cross on buns with a knife, then put on a pastry cross. Do not make pastry too short in texture. Bake at 425°F.

About the House

POLISH AND SHINE

Most of us are as house-proud in the twentieth century as were our predecessors of several generations ago. We achieve our aims by less devious and exacting means perhaps, but a comfortable, cheerful and well-run home is still our ambition.

The recipes which follow should be of help to the spring-cleaning housewife.

LINOLEUM

Take half a tin of polish, and fill it up with paraffin. Set in a safe place to dissolve and stir until smooth. Used on linoleum, tiled or polished floors, this will both clean and polish, and make the surface less slippery.

TILES AND STEPS

If red ochre or white hearthstone is mixed with a little thin starch (left over from washing day) the tiles will keep clean much longer and the colour will not wash off during a shower of rain.

MARBLE FIREPLACES

8oz whitening	8oz shredded soap
2oz washing soda	2oz powdered pumice

Put the ingredients in a jar; mix them well. Pour over them two pints of boiling water. Stand the jar in a pan of boiling water and simmer for twenty minutes to half an hour, stirring at intervals. Spread this paste, while it is still hot, over the stained marble, getting it well into any cracks or carving. Leave for twenty-four hours. Wash off with soapy water. This quantity is sufficient for two mantelpieces, unless they are very elaborate; the same mixture may be used to clean a badly stained tombstone.

PAINT ON WOODWORK AND WALLS

2 tablespoons soft soap   ¼lb glue

Put soap and glue in a 2-lb jam jar almost filled with water. Stand jar in a pan of hot water until the glue is melted. Stir well. Use on high-gloss paint.

FOR PAINTED WALLS

One tablespoon of bicarbonate of soda to 1 quart of warm water.

BATHS

Mix some whiting with water and rub all over the bath. Rinse out with warm water. This has been used with success for baths discoloured by brown water from springs or streams.

CHIMNEYS

Burn potato peelings mixed with salt at least once a week in your grate. Such a glaze will form on the inside of your chimney that it cannot get clogged with soot, so is not likely to go on fire.

WINDOWS

Paraffin and vinegar (or water) in equal parts. About 1 tablespoon of butter of antimony to the pint and a little methylated spirits. Shake well and apply with small pads of butter muslin. This mixture may also be used for polishing mirrors, brass, silver and highly polished furniture.

A crack in a window-pane can be mended by painting it with waterglass.

FURNITURE CREAM

1oz Castile soap	1 pint genuine turpentine
1oz beeswax	½ pint rainwater
1oz white wax	

Dissolve shredded soap in the rainwater in one pan. Shred the waxes into the turpentine in another pan, but do not let it get too hot. Pour warm soapy water into the turpentine, stirring until cool. Pour, when creamy, into wide-necked bottles. This makes 1½ pints of excellent polish.

TO REMOVE WHITE RINGS CAUSED BY HEAT OR WATER FROM POLISHED SURFACES

Sprinkle with a little salt. Rub vigorously with a soft rag moistened with olive or salad oil. Polish with a soft dry cloth.

TO REMOVE SCRATCHES FROM FURNITURE

Rub with a cork of nitre in 2 teaspoons of water. Apply with a camel-hair brush and afterwards polish with a good furniture cream

TO CLEAN RUGS AND CARPETS

Take sufficient Fuller's Earth and mix it to a paste with boiling water. Spread this thickly over the stain and allow it to remain for twenty-four hours. Brush the paste off with a whisk and in most cases the stain will have disappeared. An old carpet that needs a thorough cleaning can be treated on the floor it occupies. Thoroughly brush all the dust and dirt out; shred half an ounce of soap into half a pint of boiling water with a teaspoon of ammonia and a small lump of soda; a small brush should be lightly dipped into this mixture and the carpet well scrubbed; rinse by means of a cloth constantly wrung out in clean, warm water. Finally rub with a dry cloth.

TO CLEAN AND PRESERVE LEATHER UPHOLSTERY

Boil half a pint of linseed oil for one minute. Stand until nearly cold. Pour in half a pint of vinegar and stir well. Bottle and shake before using. Apply a little on a flannel and rub well into the leather. Rub with a soft duster until the polish is restored. This treatment softens the leather and prevents cracking.

HANGING WALLPAPER

Wallpaper gives a room a 'dressed' look. To those who have never undertaken it, wallpapering appears to be a mysterious and possibly messy art, but those who practise it affirm that it is quite straightforward. It is best for two people to work together, preferably by daylight, and to set about the job when they have enough free time to be able to finish it within a short period, perhaps a week-end.

EQUIPMENT

Paperhanger's or trestle-table, step-ladder, paste brush, galvanised bucket with string tied across to prevent brush falling in, paperhanger's brush, stout string and bunch of keys to make a plumb line, rule and pencil, cold-water paste and size (one proprietary product will serve both purposes), soap and water or detergent, a couple of clean towels or rags.

HOW MUCH PAPER IS NEEDED

Measure the width of your walls, allow – but be very careful not to underestimate – for your doors and windows and divide the total by 21 inches, which is the standard width of all English wallpapers. The rolls are approximately 11½ yards long, so divide your figure by 2 if the height to be papered is over 10 feet; by 3 if it is between 10 feet and 8 feet, and by 4 if it is between 6 feet and 8 feet. Remember that it is better to overestimate than run short and that some extra allowance should be made for matching patterned papers.

PREPARATION OF THE WALLS

Time spent on preparing is well spent – it saves labour and worry later. Begin by covering the floor with newspapers.

If the walls have been papered before: Provided the old paper is tight and smooth, simply brush it down. If it is in bad repair, strip it off, smoothing the edges of any irremovable pieces with sandpaper and also any overlapping edges.

If the walls have been painted before: Wash them down with soap and water or detergent and let them dry out thoroughly. Smooth any flaking paint with glass-paper; fill in any cracks or holes with filler and smooth this down before sealing with primer.

If the walls have been oil-distempered: Scrape this off as far as possible, then coat with alkali-resisting primer.

If the walls have been soft-distempered: Scrape off any loose flakes and then wash them down with warm water.

If the walls are old bare plaster: Either line them with paper or coat them with size.

Size every type of wall for easier working and sure results. A thin coat is all that is needed and it only takes about an hour to dry.

HANGING THE WALLPAPER

1. Trim off the selvedges on both sides if this has not been done by the retailer.

2. Cut a length of paper equal to the height of the wall plus about 6 inches.

3. Cut several additional lengths, taking great care to match the pattern; remember however to keep back some paper for panels interrupted by doors and windows.

4. Begin papering by a door or window so that any variation in matching the pattern on the first and last strips will not be noticeable.

5. Drop the plumb-line from a tack placed in the picture rail or cornice about 15 inches to the right of the door or window. This will ensure the first strip of paper being hung straight, irrespective of the woodwork which is frequently not 'true'.

6. Place the first strip of paper, pattern-side down on the table; near edge to the edge of the table. Paste about half the length of the paper, leaving a couple of inches unpasted at the top and on the far edge. Move the strip over to the far edge of the table and paste this edge. Fold the end towards the middle (paste to paste) and draw along the table to enable the bottom half to be pasted, again leaving the end unpasted. Fold this towards the centre, paste to paste; continue folding (paper to paper) until the strip can be carried over to the wall.

Before actually hanging the paper leave the paste to soak in for a few minutes.

Wipe the edges of the table.

7. To hang the paper: take the strip by the top dry edge, lift it high and into position with the dry edge above the cornice or picture rail and place in position with the right-hand edge parallel to the plumb line. The pasted sides of the paper will unfold with their own weight – or you can pull them out. Press the top down and smooth it firmly with the paperhanger's brush. Work towards the bottom,

making sure that the paper is going on straight and using downward and sideways sweeps with the brush to take out creases and bubbles.

At the top and bottom, crease the join with the closed scissors; then pull away and cut before replacing and brushing back into position.

Continue round the room matching each piece to its left-hand neighbour.

8. *At the corner*: Measure the distance from the last strip to the corner and cut the next strip to this width plus ½ inch (or a little more if the corner is not straight).

Paste the paper to the wall and carry it on round the corner for ½ inch. (Do not try and turn the corner with the full paper width.) Next paste on the remainder of the strip, matching in the usual way.

9. *Special pieces over fireplaces, etc:* Where the paper has a strong pattern, it should be centred. Therefore cut and paste this first and work outwards to left and right.

10. *Windows and doors*: As for corners, measure the distance from the last strip and add ½ inch. Use the remainder of the strip for the wall above or below the window and above the door.

In The Parlour

LATEX FOAM UPHOLSTERY

Latex foam sheeting can be purchased from many departmental stores, furnishing stores and handicraft shops.

When buying, it is desirable to specify first-quality, new latex foam. Care should be taken to see that the foam is smooth and of an even grey colour throughout.

Adhesives

The following adhesives are suitable for use with latex foam:

>Batesman's Non-Flam Rubber Solution
>Bostick D or 299
>Dsp. L. 107 Upholstery Solution
>Gripso Rubber Solution
>Holdtite Upholstery Solution No. 9A. or 27
>Phillisol Rubber Cement
>Stycco Rubber Solution

These solutions are obtainable from departmental stores, handicraft shops, principal ironmongers, leather merchants and upholsterers' suppliers.

The instructions on the container regarding the application of the adhesive should be carefully followed. There is, however, no need to roughen the surfaces of the latex foam.

Some of these adhesives are inflammable and where this is indicated on the container suitable precautions should be taken.

Care of Latex Foam

Under normal conditions latex foam gives a very long life of comfort.

It is resistant to mould, mildew, moths and vermin and therefore requires no special care in this respect.

There are only two precautions to observe. It should not be cleaned with solvents such as petrol and dry-cleaning fluids, and it should not be exposed to sunlight or strong light for long periods when uncovered.

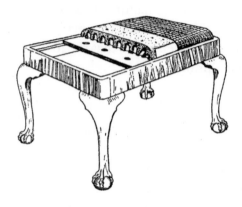

A Drop-In Stool Seat

Materials

Wooden stool frame (rebate to take loose seat to be ½ inch deep).
Loose-seat base (½-inch plywood with ½-inch holes bored 3 inches apart, for ventilation).
Piece of cavity sheet latex foam, medium density (2 inches thick and ½ inch larger all round than plywood base).
⅜-inch upholstery cut tacks.
3-inch wide strips of calico. The width can be varied if required but should never be less than 2 inches.
Rubber adhesive.
French chalk or talcum powder.
Outside covering material.

Tools

Scissors. Ball-point pen. Hammer.
Old kitchen knife or palette knife for spreading
adhesive.

Instructions

1. The plywood base must be made small enough to allow for the thickness of the covering material when the loose seat is fitted into the stool frame.

2. Latex foam can be marked to size (½ inch larger all round than the plywood base) with a ball-point pen, and then cut with ordinary scissors (kitchen scissors with serrated blades cut well). Keep the cut as vertical as possible and try not to twist the latex foam too much when cutting, as this can give an uneven edge.

3. Cut back the sides of the latex foam at an angle of about 45 degrees on the cavity side. Fit 3-inch wide strips of calico to the outside edges of the top surface of the latex foam. These should extend 1 inch each end to allow for fitting the corner. Do this by spreading a 1-inch band of rubber adhesive along one edge of the four strips of calico. Now spread a 1-inch band of rubber adhesive round the outside edges of the top of the latex foam. Allow the adhesive to become tacky before pressing the tapes firmly on to the latex foam. (Where particular instructions are given with an adhesive, these should be followed carefully.) Dust over with french chalk or talcum powder to dry off surplus adhesive.

4. Lay the latex foam, cavity side down, on the plywood base so that there is an even ½-inch overhang all round. Now, starting from the centre on a long side and working outwards, pull the calico over and temporarily tack to the underside of the plywood base with tacks driven in (the tacks should be a sufficient distance from the edge of the plywood base so as not to ride on the bottom of the rebate of the stool, and should be 1 inch to 1½ inches apart all round the seat). See that the pull on the tapes is even when finally driving in the tacks,

so that the latex foam edge has an even contour and is pulled down to the edge of the wood and not lapping over.

5. The final cover can now be put on. Measure over the top of the seat and cut the cover 1½ inches larger all round than the seat size to allow for tacking.

Lay cover in correct position on seat, then holding the two together, turn over so that the seat is upside-down. The cover is now temporarily tacked in position, straining the cover slightly. (Note remark about rebate in point 4.)

The cover is now finally tacked off, the temporary tacks being removed as this proceeds. The last 2 inches at the corners are left untacked until last. When finally tacking off, the cover should be strained and smoothed into position with the left hand as each tack is driven in. Do not over-strain the cover over the latex foam as this only reduces the resiliency.

Corners are now finished off. The corner of the cover is strained and tacked first, then the cover pleated and tacked. If the cover is fairly thick, a piece cut from inside each pleat can help to give a clean corner.

A dining-room chair with a drop-in seat can be reupholstered in the same way.

MAKING LAMPSHADES

FIRM MATERIAL LAMPSHADES

Lampshade-making is a delightful and popular craft. Shades are made on one of two foundations – two rings or a frame.

Points to consider beforehand:

1. Size and shape suitable for purpose.
2. Material.
3. Colour.
4. Trimming.

Neat and trim binding of rings and frames is all-important. Tape or bias binding should match material and be as inconspicuous as possible. Accuracy in measuring and fitting shades and neatness of stitching and fixing trimming are essential if a good result is to be achieved.

1. Some consideration must be given regarding the *size and shape* of the shade in relation to the position it is to occupy, ie hall, passage, bedroom, living-room or dining-room. Is it desired to spread the light or to concentrate it on one particular spot? The shape for the shade should be chosen accordingly.

2. The following are some of the *materials* suitable for firm lampshades:

(a) Paper (b) Parchment (c) Embossed parchment
(d) Buckram (e) Acetate: matt, embossed, flocked,
linen-backed (f) Perforated board (g) Coated board.

Adhesives: (a) Mistic, (b) Copydex (white, rubberised);
(c) Bateman's (d) Uhu, clear, non-staining glue.

Most materials will stand a certain amount of heat, but commonsense must be exercised to avoid a too highly powered lamp bulb discolouring or burning the shade.

Material ironed on to Buckram. This involves a simple method and is entirely satisfactory. Suitable materials are cotton, silk, lace and net (not nylon). The material should be thoroughly saturated, squeezed dry and spread over the buckram, right side up. With a fairly hot iron the material should be pressed on to the buckram, working from centre outwards. There is sufficient glue in the buckram to hold the material firmly in position. N.B. – It is wise to experiment first with a small piece.

3. *Colour.* The lampshade should form part of the decoration of the room and should look right, whether in daylight or at night. The best effect is often obtained by using ivory, oyster, pink, or soft

yellow. Red and other strong colours can also be very attractive.

4. *Trimming.* Braid, ruching, cord, fringe, bobbles, ribbon.
Trimming should tone with the material, darker if anything, but a contrasting colour can be introduced. Many shades are spoilt by the use of too ornate trimming. Simple trimming gives a more satisfying result and proportion to size and shape should be considered carefully. Hard, bright-coloured trimming is usually unsatisfactory. An individual touch can sometimes be added to advantage by a hand-made trimming or other decoration on the lampshade, but care must be taken not to overdo this.

Fixing Trimming. Stitches damage and weaken firm materials. It has been found that a better method is to stick the trimming into position. This must be done neatly and firmly.

The Cone Shade

This shade is usually made on two loose rings. A graph has to be drawn to obtain the pattern. The shade can be made any depth, but a good general proportion is obtained by adding together the diameters of the top and bottom rings and dividing by two. For example:

Top ring	5 inches diameter	} = 15 ÷ 2 = 7½
Bottom ring	10 inches diameter	
Depth	7½ inches diameter	

A tall cone or a coolie can be drawn by this method, the depth being altered to suit requirements.

Absolute accuracy in drawing the graph is essential, and this cannot be stressed too strongly. Variation of as little as ⅛ inch will give a lopsided appearance to the finished shade. A graph can never be adjusted to suit another set of rings; a new graph must always be drawn, even for a second set of rings supposedly the same size. Graph paper, 10 squares to 1 inch, is helpful to the beginner.

Holes can be punched top and bottom and the shade thonged to rings with cord or narrow ribbon, or trimming can be stuck on after the shade has been sewn to rings. Overlap can be stuck or stitched, but the former gives a neater finish.

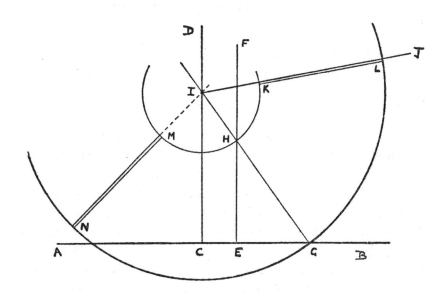

METHOD FOR DRAWING PATTERN

1. Draw a straight line AB across the paper about 3 inches from the bottom.

2. Mark a point C on AB slightly to the left of centre. Draw a line CD at right angles to AB and running to the top of the paper.

3. Measure the diameter of the top and bottom rings which have not been taped.

4. From C mark off CE along AB equal to half a diameter of the top ring. From E draw a line EF at right angles to AB and parallel to CD.

5. From C mark off CG equal to half diameter of bottom ring on AB.

6. Having decided the depth of the shade (see above) mark off from G this depth on to EF cutting it at H. Draw GH to cut CD at I.

7. From I draw a line out to the side of the paper IJ.

8. Using I as the centre, draw two arcs, one with radius IH and the other radius IG, cutting the line IJ at K and L respectively. Take the top ring and mark it at one point. Place this ring with the mark on point K, roll the ring round the smaller arc until the mark is once again touching the paper, mark this point M. Take the bottom ring and starting at L, work in the same manner on the larger arc ending at N. Join NM and extend the line to cut at I. It will do this only if the graph is accurate: unless it is accurate the shade will be lopsided. Cut out the section KL, NM allowing an extra ¼ inch overlap at each end. This is the pattern.

PLEATED SHADE

Any material that will hold the pleat is suitable, e.g. coloured paper, wallpaper or buckram. Material required is six times the diameter of the bottom ring of a straight Empire frame and 2 inches deeper than the struts; ¾ inch or 1 inch is a suitably sized pleat for a table-lamp. Pleats should be measured and folded accurately. On the inner fold of each pleat, a semi-circle ¾ inch from the top edge should be punched. A complete hole, 1 inch down from the top edge and in the centre of each fold should be punched to accommodate a cord. Ends of material should be joined together and a cord threaded through the complete holes. The pleats should be drawn together and the shade slipped on to the frame, so that the semi-circles fit on to the top ring. The cord should be tied sufficiently tightly to hold the shade in position.

SOFT MATERIAL LAMPSHADES
SECTIONAL SHADE

After the frame has been taped, a paper pattern must be made and fitted on *each* section before material is cut. This process is necessary as frames are never absolutely perfect. Bulldog clips or small clothes pegs are useful for holding pattern when fitting and for holding material to section when stitching. Materials should

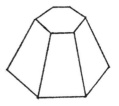

be sewn neatly and firmly to taped frame. Edges should just meet. No stitches should show on inside of shade. Joins should be covered with trimming, stuck on, struts first, then top and bottom.

A STRETCHED SILK LAMPSHADE

Materials required

A Bow Empire Frame, strong, 10-inch base diameter, 5-inch top diameter, 6 struts; approximately 6 yards ½-inch tape or fine bias binding to match materials; 12 inches of material (colour is optional, but pastel shades are recommended). Sewing silk to match; steel pins.

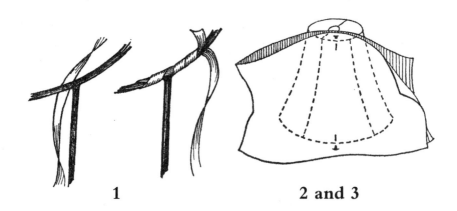

1   **2 and 3**

Method

1. Tape frame tightly in 1-yard lengths. To finish, tie a knot or stick with an adhesive.

2. Take a straight piece of material, 12 inches by 36 inches wide and double it, right side outwards.

3. Mark centre of double material and pin to top and base centres of frame, equidistant from two side struts. Always use steel pins.

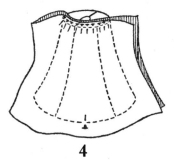 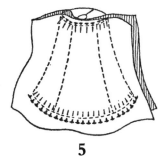

4   **5**

4. Pin double material half-way round top of frame.

5. Stretching double material slightly downwards, pin half-way round base of frame. Numerous pins should be used and should be placed not more than ½ inch apart.

6. Stretch material sideways and pin to opposite side struts. Half of the frame should now be covered. Stretch and re-pin until material is drum tight and fits the frame perfectly, both outside and inside.

7. Make a faint pencil mark on the material down the centre of opposite struts. Pin double material either side of struts to ensure that it does not slip.

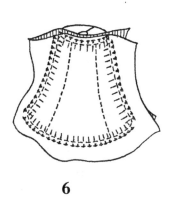 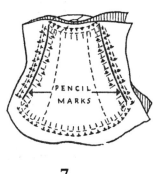

6   **7**

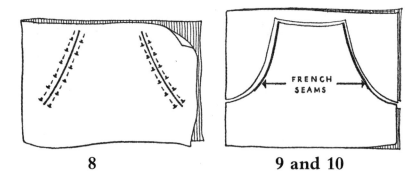

8   **9 and 10**

8. Remove all pins attaching material to frame, but not the ones holding double material together.

9. Machine narrow French seams down the pencil lines. The first row of stitching should be just outside the pencil mark.

10. Turn right side out.

11. Slip over frame, making sure that the seams coincide exactly with opposite side struts.

12. Pin material all round top of frame and all round base, stretching and re-pinning where necessary until the material fits snugly on to the frame. No gaps must be left inside the shade between the struts and the material.

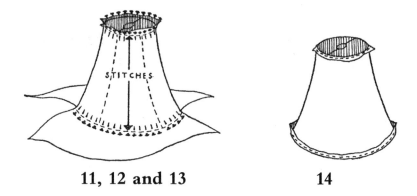

11, 12 and 13   **14**

13. When the material fits the frame exactly and is drum-tight, sew to tape on outer edge of top and base, but *not* down struts, removing pins as work proceeds.

14. Cut away surplus material, leaving sufficient for a narrow turn on to outside of frame. Neatly stitch to the frame and trim raw edges.

15. Sew trimming (gimp or braid) round top and base with invisible stitches, taking care that all raw edges of material are covered. Fringe can be used for trimming the base, with a braid added, if necessary.

16. All stitching should be as invisible as possible. Accuracy and neatness will give a satisfactory result.

17. If a 'balloon' lining is required, this should be measured and made up in the same way as described above, but slightly smaller. Cover and lining need single seams only. After the outer covering has been stitched to the frame, the lining should be slipped inside, pinned, stretched and sewn before the shade is trimmed.

N.B. This method can be applied to any size of Bow Empire Frame.

15 and 16

With Our Friends

PARTY GAMES

WRITE TO AUNT AGATHA

Each person writes (in not more than 100 words) an imaginary problem similar to those found in women's magazines. The papers are then collected, shuffled up, and redistributed. Each person then writes an answer to the problem she has been given. The most amusing answer wins the prize.

TELEGRAMS

Choose one or more titles (such as the title of a magazine or the name of your village) and ask each person to write a telegram in which each word begins with the letters (in correct sequence) of the chosen title. A prize may be given for the best, or the most amusing, telegram read out.

DRAWING GAME

Everyone is given a card with the name of an animal on it. On the reverse side of the card she draws the animal, after which all the cards are collected and spread on tables, or pinned round the wall. A second piece of paper is given to everyone and they have to write down the names of the animals or birds from the drawings.

RUSSIAN SCANDAL

Four or six people are sent out of the room. The remainder of the people think of a subject to be mimed, such as bathing the baby, setting the breakfast, going for a bathe in the cold sea, going to bed, etc. One person from outside is then called in and told what to do. She brings in another person from outside, who watches her as she does the mime. When she has finished she sits down, and a third person is called in, who in turn watches the mime done by the second one. This goes on until each person from outside has been called in, seen the mime and copies it to the best of her ability. This final mime bears little or no relation to the original choice. If the miming of the last people is very wide of the mark, the leader should then be asked to repeat the original mime.

WHISTLING STORY

A short story is made up to include a number of well-known song titles. The story is read aloud, but when a title is reached, it is not read but is whistled by the reader (and probably a small choir of competent whistlers) and members are asked to guess the name of the song.

READING *THE TIMES*

Divide people into two teams of six, each sitting opposite each other, very close together, with knees touching, as in a crowded railway carriage. Give each person a copy of *The Times* thoroughly muddled with some pages upside-down. The first team of six to re-arrange all their papers correctly wins.

POTATO PEELING

Give each competitor a large potato and a knife. Tell them to peel it as quickly, and in as few pieces as possible. When this is done, give them each a handful of pins and tell them to pin back the peel. (Don't tell them about pinning it back until they have peeled their potato!)

HAPPY FAMILY MUSICAL CHAIRS

For this game the number of players must be divisible by four (12, 16, 24, etc).

For easy explanation we will assume that twenty-four people are playing. From a pack of Happy Family cards remove sufficient complete families for the players (six families, making twenty-four cards).

Put five chairs down the centre of the room, and line up the players round the chairs. Give each player a card (having well-shuffled the cards first). Players must not divulge which card they have got.

As the music is played they go round the chairs. When it stops everyone shouts loudly who she is, and endeavours to collect the rest of her family.

When the complete family has assembled, they must sit down on a chair in the following order: Mr Bun, Mrs Bun on his knee, Master Bun on his mother's knee, and Miss Bun on her brother's knee.

As there are only five chairs for six families, one family is 'out' and a chair is removed, also one 'family' from the cards – after which the game continues until the last two families fight for the last chair.

Local Festivals

Dancing, mock battles, fairs, mock trials, all come in the spring, with only very few of the local festivals retaining a religious significance. The Blessing of the Fishermen and the nets is one of these. People come from far and wide to a sheltered spot near the woods at Norham in Northumberland. The ceremony itself is held at one of the fisheries called Pedwell (St Peter's Dell) on the night of February 14th. The service ends as the church clock strikes midnight, the first net is 'shot' and the Vicar is given one of the first fish to be caught. The Pedwell prayer is:

> *Good Lord, Lead us,*
> *Good Lord, Speed us,*
> *From all perils us protect,*
> *In all darkness us direct,*
> *Fresh nights to land our fish*
> *Sound and big to fill our wish.*
> *Keep our nets from snag and break,*
> *For every man a goodly take*
> *God grant us.*

Another springtime religious ceremony is the building of Penny Hedge at Whitby on Ascension Eve. The garth or yard is originally supposed to have been some sort of an enclosure made with staves, cut with a knife costing a penny. The enclosure was made by the tenants of Whitby Strand before the port of Whitby was granted to the Abbey. The tenants were summoned to their task by the blowing of a horn. Even when the Abbey had stouter enclosures, the abbots, jealous of their rights, kept up the custom though in time the origin was forgotten and a legend concerning the hunting of a wild boar which sought refuge in a hermitage was invented. In defending the boar the hermit was mortally wounded and demanded as penance from the hunters that each year they build a penny hedge early on Ascension Day that would withstand three tides. The hedge is still built each year on the east side of the river.

The Kiplingcotes Derby is run each year in the spring and has been run without a break ever since 1519 – so claiming to be the oldest horse-race in Britain if not in the world. The course for this race, held between noon and one o'clock on the third Thursday in March, runs from the outskirts of South Dalton, Yorkshire, through three or four parishes to a point near Kiplingcotes Farm on the wolds.

Dating from medieval times and said to be the original of present-day football is the Haxey Hood Game played every year on the afternoon of January 6th at Haxey in Lincolnshire. Legend has it that in the thirteenth or fourteenth century Lady Mowbray, gay and charming in a scarlet hood, went out walking one blowy January day, when a sudden gust lifted the hood from her head and billowed it right away. Village men working in the neighbouring fields gave chase, but the hood would not be caught. After a long chase, at last it was retrieved, and Lady Mowbray, it is said, was so amused that she gave a piece of land to the village with the request that a mock hood might be thrown up on January 6th every year, and the pursuit continued.

The hood nowadays has become 13 hoods, or rather 13 little bolsters, 18 inches or so long, twelve of them of canvas and one of dark-brown leather; scarlet, however, still appears on the hats and shirts of the men. These, still a round dozen of them, are called boggarts, a title whose origin is obscure. With them is a fool with a black face and strips of paper on his back, while over the lot, 13 in all, is a King boggart. This position seems to be more or less hereditary. The King leads the procession down the full length of the village street until it reaches an old stone in front of the church. Here the fool is hoisted and told to make a speech, but while he tells the story of the first Haxey Hood a paper fire is lit beneath his feet. Then the papers on his back are set alight. This is a custom which is said to have been prevalent all over England in pre-Conquest days, but it survives in very few places. The procession next moves out of the village and up the hill to a barren common. Here the game proper starts. The boggarts range themselves at points outside an immense circle, with the King, the villagers and any strangers in the centre. A canvas hood is thrown up, the crowd surges forward and whoever extricates the canvas from the struggling crowd dives out of the mass and makes for the outer circle. If he can get beyond this, victory is his, and that particular hood is dead, but if a boggart catches him before he is over the boundary, the ruse has failed, and the hood is returned to the King who throws it up again. The same happens with all thirteen hoods, but for the final tussle with the leather hood the boggarts close in and activities are no longer confined to the common, but spread through the whole of the little town.

Here are three rival inns and these form goals. Each inn has its own band of supporters, whose business it is to see that the prize goes in the right direction. They tussle for the hood, lie on it, race with it, dodge with it, always pursued by rival factions. Finally the hood reaches the 'Duke William', 'King's Arms', or 'Carpenters Arms' as the case may be, and once across the threshold, victory is acclaimed. The hood is placed on the mantelpiece in a position of safety and honour until the next 'Hood Day'.

Other somewhat unorthodox games of football are played on Shrove Tuesday in many towns and villages including Sedgefield in County Durham, and Ashbourne in Derbyshire. At Ashbourne the ball is made by a local craftsman and is kicked off by a brook, the two teams being 'up'ards' and 'down'ards'. It is a free-for-all scramble continuing until a goal is scored and often ending up in the brook itself. The scorer of the goal keeps the ball.

In Sedgefield the game is even more strenuous. According to custom the parish clerk is obliged to furnish a football on Shrove Tuesday which he throws into the marketplace where it is competed for by the mechanics against the agriculturalists of the town and neighbourhood.

At one o'clock promptly the ball is put through the bull ring. It is at once apparent that the liberal use of sheet-iron leg guards is not merely a precaution but an absolute necessity for no sooner does the ball touch the ground than the most indiscriminate kicking begins and continues throughout the game, which often does not end until late afternoon.

This very ancient custom is kept alive with much vigour on the part of both old and young who turn out in large numbers to take part in the yearly struggle for holding the ball either as tradesmen or countrymen. Law, like the rest of the institutions in the town, seems to take a holiday for this day, for trespassing must be tolerated without reserve as the contestants are now in the road and next in the fields, wherever the ball may be. There being no restriction or limit to the arena, the ball has been as far as Thorpe over four miles away, and Middleton and Ferryhill have also been visited during the progress of the game.

Another game played on Shrove Tuesday is Hurling at St Columb in Cornwall. It is said that the game may go back a thousand years, and might be called a sort of 'hard rugby'. The two goals – one Town and one Country – are a mile east and west of the small town. The ball made of apple wood covered with silver is engraved 'Town and Country do your best, For in this Parish I must rest.'

The first 'hurl' is the ball in each case being 'thrown up' by an invited guest. Shop fronts and windows are barricaded for the game, as there are sometimes hundreds of players in the streets. A fierce battle rages between Town and Country before the ball reaches a final goal and becomes either Town or Country Ball until the following year.

Another Shrove Tuesday celebration is the Pancake Race at Olney in Buckinghamshire. 'Toss your pancakes – are you ready?' is the cry as the starting bell rings and the women of Olney, dressed as housewives in apron and headcovering, run with their pancakes to the Church porch, where the winner receives a kiss from the bellringer. This race, which was first run in 1445, probably formed part of the last fling celebrations before the long Lenten fast, and with some lapses has continued to take place on Shrove Tuesday through the centuries.

In 1947 the custom was revived by the vicar of Olney. In 1950 a challenge was accepted from a town called Liberal, Kansas, U.S.A., and now the race is not only for a kiss but for the Transatlantic Pancake Trophy, as the women of Olney compete against the women of Liberal. After the race, the winner and a large congregation go into the Church for a shriving service, during which it is now customary to sing hymns composed by Cowper and Newton who lived at Olney in the eighteenth century.

Contests of a different kind are egg and cheese rolling. At Preston in Lancashire they keep up the six-hundred-year-old tradition of Egg Rolling on Easter Monday. The dyed and painted eggs are rolled down the slopes of Avenham Park.

In other parts of the north, eggs are rolled along flat surfaces until their shells break, or are rolled between wickets in the contest. There was also a Pace-Egging Play, but this no longer appears to be performed, though in some parts of Cheshire children with their eggs go round the village with the threatening rhyme 'your hens shall lay all addled eggs' unless presumably the villager gives them pennies and cakes.

At Birdlip in Gloucestershire the cheese-rollers gather at the foot of a maypole on Whit Monday each year. The starter in ancient smock and white beaver hat drops a rope and Double Gloucesters – now only imitation – roll down the hill. When the starter fires a pistol, the men and girls set off in pursuit to catch their cheeses. The custom is centuries old and is thought to go back to the claiming of common-land rights.

Rights of different kind are upheld by the Hock-Tide Tutti-men of Hungerford in Berkshire on the Tuesday after Easter. The annual Jury, or Hock-tide Court, assembles at the Town Hall at 9am, having been summoned by the blowing of the horn from the balcony at intervals from 8am. The Tutti-man also stands on the steps of the Town Hall and summons the Hock-tide Jury, who after they have held their court, together with the Constable, send the Tutti-men on their way. The Tutti-men start on their rounds to collect tithes, and in default of which they claim a kiss from the ladies of the house. The men are smartly dressed in tails and top hats and carry long poles beautifully decorated with flowers and ribbons. At the top of each pole is a spike on which is stuck an orange. Following behind is the orange man who throws oranges to the dozens of children who also scramble for 'hot pennies' thrown by Tutti-men. Lunch is taken at the 'Three Swans' hotel where there is a large party, and a secret punch is served from an ancient bowl. More visits to houses at the lower end of the town, and then tea is served at 'The Bear'.

As regards the far-famed kissing, it is much more frequently evaded now than was the case in days gone by, when a lady refusing to accept it was almost guilty of an insult to authority. A kiss can be asked for at each house visited and the lady presented with the orange from the top of the pole, which is then replaced.

Finally an old practice with a £10 prize for the winner: this is the Candle Auction at Old Bolingbroke in Lindsey, Lincolnshire. Originally it was for the distribution of ancient doles on St Thomas's Day, but the Pin and Candle auction now deals with the grazing on a village playing field. The auction is held in the Village Hall and the bidding starts when a pin is stuck into a lighted candle about half an inch from the top. The Chairman opens the proceedings by saying 'Don't dilly-dally. The pin is in. Help yourselves.' The last bid made before the pin falls from the melting wax secures the grazing rights for sheep and cattle from April 6th to November 14th, a prize worth £10.

Local Skills

SURREY STITCH RUG-MAKING

The Surrey Stitch Rug was worked out by a W.I. member living in Surrey, and might be said to be the only true W.I. craft in that it was invented by a W.I. member. Through the Women's Institutes the craft has become widely known and is extremely popular since it has considerable hard-wearing qualities.

MATERIALS

The choice of these and their use in relationship to each other is one way in which individuality can be expressed and there is now a large selection of both canvas and wool available.

Foundation. (a) Double-mesh canvas: this can be obtained to give 3, 4, 5, 7, 8, 9 or 10 holes to the inch. (b) Single strand canvas: the evenly woven jute is recommended although coastguard canvas or a good hessian are also possibilities. Where the single-strand canvas is used, two threads equal one double weft or warp bar of the double-mesh canvas; with the jute 8 threads, ie 4 stitches = 1 inch. The rough edges of single-strand material fray easily so they should be machined before working.

Wool. Good quality mixed wool thrums (the 'left-overs' from carpet factories) produce an ideal pile, using one, two or three threads according to the size of the holes in the canvas. Thrums can be bought at varying prices according to the lengths of wool in the bundles and the numerous shades in any such bundle are an inspiration for producing patterns. For work on fine canvas, Brussels thrums are excellent.

Needles. These should be blunt-pointed and large-eyed, numbers 14 or 16 for coarse and 20 or 22 for fine canvas.

Method

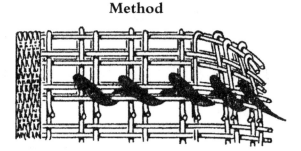

Fig 1

Preparation of canvas: The cut ends should be turned over (2 to 2½ inches for canvas giving up to 5 holes to the inch; 1 to 1½ inches for finer canvases) and the work begun through double canvas. When double-mesh canvas is used, the narrow double bar of 2 close-weft threads dividing the holes forms the top edge, in the single-strand foundations 2 weft threads of the material.

The rough edge should be over-sewn securely to the canvas, each hole lying exactly over the hole beneath it. Work with this fold uppermost as the rough edge is hidden by the pile. If single-strand canvas is used it is somewhat difficult to work through the double but it can be done.

Treatment of edges: To ensure long life for rugs it is essential that the edges be covered securely. Closely worked blanket stitch or double crochet are possible methods, though a plaited edge wears far longer.

With the right side of the canvas (ie the rough-edge side) uppermost, and remembering that in working this edge the needle should always pass from the back to the front of the canvas, the needle is:

1. Brought from the back of the canvas through the right-hand corner hole, leaving the loose end of the wool lying along the top edge to be covered by subsequent stitches;

2. Carried through the next hole to the left;

3. Taken back to the corner hole a second time (thus forming a cross stitch over the top edge of the canvas);

4. Carried forward 4 holes, counting the original corner hole as 1;

5. Taken back 3 holes to hole 2.

The plait is then continued – always on 4 holes and back 3 holes.

It is, of course, possible to work this plait from left to right as long as it is remembered that, when starting, the bottom half of the first cross always lies in the direction in which the plait is to travel.

When a new thread is needed, the old one is brought out at the long stitch (the 'on 4' hole), the new one is threaded along the back of the worked plait for a short distance, and brought out at the same (long stitch) hole, then the plait is continued as usual. The 'tail' of the old thread is carried along the top of the canvas until covered.

The obvious difficulty regarding any edging is how to cover the extremely sharp points at the four corners and here individual ingenuity should be exercised. One suggestion is to work a separate cross stitch right over the point (before starting on the plait) as an extra cornering.

On approaching the corner the plait is shortened until it becomes a single cross stitch, the corner is neatly oversewn across the 'point' cross stitch and the plait down the selvedge edge started in the original way, ie with a single cross stitch, the bottom half of which goes the way the plait is to be worked. When using coarse canvas, a narrower and neater edge results if the selvedge is doubled back on itself when working along it. Three strands of wool are sometimes advisable when working the selvedge sides.

To keep the rug in good shape it is advisable to work the top edge first, from right to left, carrying the plait a short way down the left-hand selvedge, then to start again at the right-hand top corner and carry the plait a short way down the right-hand selvedge. This makes a strong framework for the pile and the plait can be continued down the sides of the rug so that it is always a short way in front of the pile.

The Pile Stitch or Knot is made with two movements of the needle, the first being towards the worker and the second from right to left.

1st Movement. The needle is brought under a double-weft bar of the canvas towards the worker from hole A to hole B, and the wool drawn through until ¾ inch is left. (This length is determined by the length of pile required.) The needle is then carried up to the left and the ¾-inch end brought down over the bar, the left thumb being placed on it to hold it firm. (Figs. II and III.)

2nd Movement. The needle is inserted at hole C, and brought out at hole A, passing over the loop of wool. The needle is then drawn down and pulled towards the worker, when it will be found that a knot has been made on top of the canvas. The long end of wool is cut to the required length of the pile (say ¾ inch) unless the same colour is to be used in the next stitch. In this case, the needle is passed under the bar of canvas between holes C and D and through the loop of wool which will thereby have been produced. The needle is drawn through until the loop is the same length as the

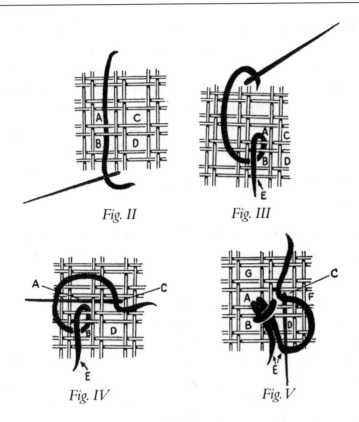

Fig. II   Fig. III

Fig. IV   Fig. V

previous stitch, the loop is held down firmly with the left thumb, the wool is carried upwards and the second movement of the stitch completed as before. The loops are cut at the end of each row and the pile trimmed if not quite even, although practice makes perfect very quickly. (Figs. IV and V.)

For the second and following rows the needle is inserted under the bar of the canvas immediately above the last completed row.

Length of Pile. The length of ¾ inch suggested above is suitable for canvas meshes up to 5 holes to the inch, but if finer canvas is used this length is correspondingly reduced.

The rug is, of course, begun with the full length of the canvas away from the worker, and it is advisable to work straight across the canvas from left to right, completing each row before beginning the next. Left-handed workers do the stitch in the opposite direction.

Colour is governed by personal choice but experience shows: (1) Rugs are floor coverings and as such must withstand hard wear and dirt; strong, rich colours do this better than pale shades. (2) One colour should always predominate. (3) Some of the colour used for the centre of the rug should always be introduced into the border. (4) The same depth of tone throughout the rug is advisable, but in any case the border should not be lighter than the centre. (5) Home dyeing of wool can be done with great ease with commercial dyes, and if the results are somewhat unexpected so probably will the rug gain in interest!

Design must also be a question of individuality, but a rectangular rug is preferable to odd shapes such as ovals and half-moons, which mean a great waste of canvas.

Geometrical patterns are more suitable and generally satisfactory than attempted reproductions of natural objects (except when using the finer canvases where more elaboration is possible), and rugs done entirely in well-proportioned stripes can be most effective. When a border is worked a good proportion for this is a third of the width, ie 90 stitches across would give 15 at both sides and ends as border.

There should be a certain relationship between the border and the centre of the rug. Where this occurs a more harmonious effect results than where there is complete lack of connection between the two.

When the borders are wide enough to allow it, it is advantageous to break them into 'stripes', ie to introduce a narrow 'stripe' such as a tooth edge, then to have the main border pattern and to repeat the narrow one before starting on the centre of the rug.

Local Recipes

BARA BRITH
(An original Welsh recipe)

1oz yeast
¾lb sugar (or syrup)
¾lb lard or butter
1lb raisins (stoned)
2 eggs
Milk

3lb flour
½ teaspoon pudding spice
1lb currants
4lb candied peel
1 teaspoon salt

Rub the fat in the flour, add salt, sugar, dried fruit, and spice and mix the dry ingredients fully. Form a well in the centre of the mixture, add the eggs, and the warmed milk and 1oz yeast. Mix well into a soft dough consistency. Put in a warm place, after covering – until it rises to double its original size, when the dough is turned onto a floured board and placed in a greased tin and baked in a moderately quick oven for 1 or 2 hours, depending on the size of the cake.

In order to preserve the characteristic flavour of the Bara Brith, on no account must the stoned raisins be omitted or substituted. The Bara Brith when cold is cut and buttered in exactly the same way as bread, and is delicious.

GRASMERE GINGERBREAD

6oz flour
½ teaspoon bicarbonate of soda
2½oz soft brown sugar
4½oz butter

½ heaped teaspoons ground ginger
⅛ teaspoon powdered cinnamon
Good pinch of ground mace

Sieve flour, ginger, cinnamon, bicarbonate of soda and mace together three times, the last time into a mixing bowl, rub in butter until the mixture looks like fine crumbs. Grease a flat tin (a swiss roll tin is the right size) and lightly press in the mixture by hand. Bake in a moderate oven 15 minutes. Take out and cut into oblong pieces without removing from tin. Replace in oven for 5 or 10 minutes. Remove from oven and leave in tin until cold.

Summer

Soon will the high Midsummer pomps come on,
Soon will the musk carnations break and swell,
Soon shall we have gold-dusted snapdragon,
Sweet-William with its homely cottage-smell,
And stocks in fragrant blow;
Roses that down the alleys shine afar,
And open, jasmine-muffled lattices,
And groups under the dreaming garden-trees,
And the full moon, and the white evening star.

M. Arnold

We are eternally optimistic. Every summer we are certain that the sun will shine brilliantly day after day and month after month so all plans are made on this assumption. When it rains we can only ignore it; plastic mackintoshes over cotton dresses, gum-boots instead of sandals, duckboards across the sea of mud and, much to our surprise, the Agricultural Show or the Garden Fete is a success after all – particularly enjoyable perhaps for all the 'helpers' who share that sense of companionship in disaster that most of us have not known since the air-raids of the War!

Faithful to this assumption I imagine us doing many of the things in this section. In the early part of the summer our gardens are at their best: azaleas, magnolias, rhododendrons, then lilies and roses. Many Women's Institute members will be filling their cars with huge sprays, magnificent blooms, leaves from globe artichokes or beetroot perhaps, large urns and tiny baskets. They set off for their County Flower Arrangement Competitions. Four and a half thousand people came to see our National Competition at Denman College.

As we pick the flowers we shall of course be surrounded by the 'murmuring of innumerable bees' and by August the bee-keepers among our members will be taking the honey from the hives.

In this perfect summer I picture a countrywoman sitting in the garden while a charming child sleeps in the pram beside her and she makes him a smock – probably, today, in nylon or some other synthetic material. Failing the perpetual demands of a growing child, a W.I. member may well be doing an exquisite piece of embroidery in readiness for a Handicraft Exhibition.

With this fine weather though there are many days when the country gardener/cook will be bent double under the strawberry nets, pricking her fingers on the gooseberry bushes or stripping for ever the currant bushes. But what a wonderful excuse it is to sit in the sun, slowly hulling or 'topping and tailing' the fruit. It is satisfying to see the store cupboard fill up with row upon row of translucent jellies and richly coloured jams.

When others may be at the Derby, 5,000 ladies, delegates from remote W.I.s all over the country, are travelling to London for the Annual Meeting in the Albert Hall. To Londoners this means chiefly the fascinating sight of the Prince Consort surrounded by hundreds of women picnicking on the grass, wrapt in the deepest discussions; but for the members themselves this means two days of most interesting debate, and debate that is remarkably well-informed. I am sure that no other 'body' that fills the great hall can provide such an immense variety of speakers: variety of accent, of attitude, of experience. Very often though it is the speaker who has seldom been further from home than her country town, who can best convince us that hers is the truly rural point of view that we are pledged to support.

Together, at home, this is the time of the pageant, of the painting expedition, of the Annual Outing. Contrary to many prognostications when television first demanded that we be mere spectators, W.I. members are keener than ever before to enjoy the trials of the creative artist. Painting and sketching courses are always over-subscribed at Denman College; many counties have already had their own exhibitions of members' work, and looking ahead to 1963 we intend to venture out and hold our own national exhibition in London.

Pageants continue, with the greatest fun for all those who take part. To them and to those who watch are thus passed on the local traditions and lore and history so easily lost in days of frequent moves and new towns.

The Annual Outing is simply an affair of the individual Institute. Members abandon their homes for a day and make off in a bus for a stately home, the potteries or the sea. Pure pleasure this and a wonderful chance to gossip with your friends.

From the Garden

BEE-KEEPING

Until the early part of this century the countryman often knew little more than a townsman about bee-keeping. He knew little about the denominations within the hive; each colony of bees with its queen bee, mother of all those in the hive; the limited number of male drones; and the workers, far the most numerous, often exceeding 50,000 to 60,000 during the summer months.

He had many uses however, for the honey and beeswax from the hives, both for food and for lighting and polishing, etc. The mysterious 'rites' of handling bees remained the province of the few who appeared to have some magical charm over them.

Today bee-keeping is no longer a secret cult but an important part of the agricultural and horticultural pattern of this country. Women, as well as men, are keen beekeepers and indeed women, if they are methodical and patient, are often outstandingly able.

During World War II bee-keeping in this country increased enormously, and whilst there has been some decline since, there is still the need for more bee-keepers. It is reliably estimated that, taking the country as a whole, some 10 to 12 million lbs of potential honey are lost annually because of a lack of beekeepers to gather it, so it is to be hoped that this harvest may in future be reaped.

Unlike the majority of fresh foods, honey will keep almost indefinitely if properly handled and stored.

We must not forget the great work of the honey-bee in the increased fertility of crops and fruit where hives are situated. There have been reports of 40 to 50 per cent increased yields in seeds and fruit under favourable conditions.

How to Start

Agricultural Shows, Farm Institutes, Field Days, etc, almost invariably have a bee-keeping section which is available to dispense reliable information on the subject of keeping bees.

There are, too, the manufacturers of bee-keeping appliances who are usually well versed in bee-keeping matters; and some run short courses. County associations hold summer schools of instruction and the educational authorities hold classes for would-be bee-keepers.

A beginner should join her local bee-keeping association for by doing so she will be able to get expert advice in time of need, a free insurance scheme against a third-party claim, should it arise, and against loss from disease. She can learn a great deal by attending the various meetings which take place during the season, especially for beginners. Subscriptions vary slightly but the average is about 10s 6d per annum.

The Cost

The initial cost of starting with a hive of bees may vary considerably; it depends upon how and when our intending bee-keeper obtains her first lot of bees. After this initial outlay the costs will be small. To buy new equipment and a nucleus of bees, ie four or five combs of bees with a queen, the cost would be approximately as follows:

A W.B.C. hive complete, veil for protecting the face,
  feeder for feeding the colony at certain times, smoker
  for subduing the bees before examining them, hive tool
  for easing up the cover of the hive and parting the
  combs, and a simple guide to bee-keeping   £ 9 10 0
                    Five-comb nucleus   £ 4 10 0
                              Total   £14 0 0

This is called 'A Beginner's Outfit'. If a National or single-walled type of hive is required instead, one should deduct about ten shillings from the amount quoted.

In addition there are likely to be a few accessories needed during a good season which will come to between £1 and £1 10s.

These are the essentials for maintaining one hive of bees from which it can be expected to gather a harvest, in a fair season, of from 25 to 30lb of honey, although double this quantity is quite likely.

When to Start

The best time to begin with bees is during May or early June for then the risk of losing a colony through inexperience is very much less than in autumn. At this time, too, the beginner has the opportunity to investigate the hive and learn to handle the bees and to admire their tireless industry.

Hive and accessories can be bought at any time during the year. It is often a good plan to collect together the hive in the winter or early spring, for then one can examine the parts carefully, compare each with the guide book and learn how to operate it.

Unlike other livestock, the honey-bee requires no rigid attention to feeding or cleaning, and provided certain fundamentals are grasped at the beginning is best left to attend to her own development. The bee-keeper can leave her colonies for long week-ends and take her summer holidays without having to find someone to look after them.

She can keep her bees in her garden, on the flat roof of a dwelling (so long as they are not placed so as to cause a nuisance to others), or several miles away from home in an orchard or out-apiary.

Honey-bees are not always on the alert to sting as some people imagine. It is surprising how small a number of stings a bee-keeper will get with the right type of colonies and the correct advice.

In Great Britain, bee-keeping produces an annual honey crop of about 6 to 8 million lb of honey, besides several tons of beeswax. It also provides a pollination service to fruit-growers, farmers, horticulturalists and gardeners, estimated at ten times the value of the honey collected.

MEAD AND METHEGLIN

Honey has been collected by man for centuries, not only as a source of sweetness but for making mead and metheglin. Mead is a fermented honey-water mixture, while metheglin is a mead flavoured with spices or herbs. These drinks are mentioned in ancient Norse chronicles and through the ages. They reached the height of their popularity at the time of Queen Elizabeth I who had an aromatic mead made solely for her own use. With the Restoration, and the greatly increased importation of French wines, meads fell into disfavour amongst the nobility.

It was still made in the depths of the countryside, but even here it had to compete with home-brewed ale or beer, a comparative newcomer introduced from Holland. Since the Second World War there has been a revival of interest in mead-making; these new adherents no longer use the ancient method of suspending the skep over a pit of burning sulphur and then fermenting the entire contents, dead bees and larvae included. Instead they have adopted the methods used in many modern fermentation industries. Another innovation has been the use of a suitable mead yeast, which is distributed at a nominal charge by some County Bee-keeping Officers; a number of Commercial Laboratories also sell this type of yeast. Directions for using this yeast are enclosed with each culture. A reasonable mead can be made with fresh baker's yeast, while brewer's yeast should only be used for heather-honey meads or metheglin: 1oz of either yeast is used for each gallon of honey-water.

Meads are made from only two simple components, honey and water. Great care is needed to produce a first-class mead. Mildly flavoured honey such as clover or lime are ideal, although heather honey may be used for full-flavoured, sweet meads, provided they are allowed to mature for several years before being consumed. Empire honey can also be used, but spoiled honey should be avoided. Clean rain-water or soft tap-water are preferable to water that is excessively hard.

The honey-water mixture can be prepared by one of three methods:

(a) Heat the water to boiling in an aluminium or enamelled pan and then remove from the source of heat. Add the honey and stir until dissolved; cool and add the mead yeast culture; *or*

(b) Warm the water to 120-140°F, stir in the honey until it is dissolved, allow to cool and add three Campden tablets★ per gallon to kill off any harmful yeasts and bacteria. Next day add the culture of mead yeast, *or*

(c) Heat the mixture of honey and water in an aluminium or enamelled pan until it dissolves and just bring to the boil. Cool it and filter through clean flannel or a jelly bag until it is clear. When cool add the culture of mead yeast.

It is not necessary or desirable to boil the honey-water for lengthy periods.

★Campden tablets: Where these are not obtainable from the chemist, the following may be substituted:
Dissolve 1¼oz potassium metabisulphite in 2 pints of water; 1 fl.oz of this solution should be used per gallon instead of 2 Campden tablets per gallon.

Dry, Still Mead

3lb mild-flavoured honey   1 gallon water
Mead yeast

Prepare the yeasted honey-water mixture by method (a), (b), or (c) above and pour into a clean jar or cask, keeping any surplus in a small bottle for topping up later on.

Stand the container in a warm room (60-70°F) and soon froth will begin to form as fermentation starts. Add more honey-water from the bottle to keep the container full; after a short while froth will cease to form since the gas bubbles eventually break on reaching the surface. Clean the outside of the jar or cask and insert an air-lock or a loosely fitting bung to keep air out and stop vinegar bacteria from growing.

The honey-water will continue to ferment for several months; sometimes it ceases prematurely, due to lack of nutrients in the honey, leaving the mead sweet. This can often be remedied by adding ½ salt-spoon of B.P. quality [British Pharmacopoeia] ammonium sulphate or phosphate and a 3 mgm. tablet of thiamine (sold under various trade names, e.g. Benerva) per gallon, and whisk well before returning the liquid to the container.

When fermentation finally ceases, and there is no hint of sweetness in the mead, remove the jar or cask to a cold room and keep it there for two or three weeks to allow most of the yeast to settle out. Siphon off the mead with a clean rubber tube without disturbing the yeast deposit. Pour the mead into a clear jar or cask until it is full. Insert a cork and carefully wax over the top with paraffin or beeswax.

Store for six months in the coldest room available to allow complete clarification. Again siphon off the mead, bottle, cork, wire and store the bottles on their sides in a cool room or cellar for at least six months to mature before drinking.

Dry, Sparkling Mead

Ferment the honey-water using the recipe and method given above. A thin twist of lemon peel added to the warm bulk of honey-water improves the flavour. When the mead has been stored sufficiently to clear, siphon off from any deposit and dissolve 2oz of sugar or honey in every gallon. Bottle, using champagne bottles, cork and wire down tightly. Plastic corks are more convenient to use in the home than bark corks; strong screw stopper bottles may be used if champagne bottles are not available.

Keep the bottles on their sides at 50–60°F for several months before sampling. The mead will be sparkling when there is a white yeast deposit in the bottle and the corks strain against the wires; if screw-stopper bottles are used, gas will escape when the stopper is loosened momentarily.

The bottles should be stood upright twenty-four hours before drinking to allow the deposit to fall to the bottom; chilling the mead also helps to prevent the yeast rising when the bottle is opened and improves the flavour.

Sweet, Still Mead (I)

6lb heather honey   1 gallon water
Mead yeast

Prepare as directed for dry, still mead but store at least two or three years in bottle before sampling: the mead will be sweet of course at time of storage. Meads made from heather honeys, being very strongly flavoured, need a much longer period to mature than those made from clover honey. For the same reason red wines need longer maturing than white wines. It is better to use method (b) for preparing the honey-water for this and the following recipe.

Sweet, Still Mead (II)

6lb heather honey   1 gallon water
Mead yeast

The sweetness of a mead prepared by method (I) above is uncontrollable and the resulting wine may be excessively sweet. In this formula the sweetness is controlled.

Ferment a mixture of 3lb of honey and 1 gallon of water as directed for Dry, Still Mead and, when dry, stir in 1lb of honey previously warmed to blood heat. Allow fermentation to continue and, when dry, repeat the process with a further 1lb honey. If the wine again ferments to dryness, repeat once more when very little further fermentation should occur.

Keep the jar or cask in a cold cellar for a month and siphon off the liquid without disturbing the yeast deposit, into a clean jar or cask. Fill completely, bung down lightly and store for one year, driving in the bung after the first two weeks and waxing over afterwards.

At the end of this storage period siphon off again, bottle, cork and wire and keep at least three years before sampling.

Metheglin (I)

1oz hops   1 gallon water
6lb honey   Mead yeast
½oz root ginger

Gently simmer the hops and bruised ginger in the water for thirty minutes, skimming if necessary, and adding more water to restore the original volume. Strain the hot liquid on to the honey, stir until dissolved and when cool add the yeast culture. Continue as directed for Sweet, Still Mead (I). The ginger may be omitted if not liked.

Metheglin (II)

2 sprigs each of marjoram, rosemary and sweet briar
¼oz each of cloves, mace and cinnamon
16lb mild-flavoured honey
Mead yeast   3 gallons water

Simmer the water and spices for fifteen minutes, strain on to the honey and stir until it has dissolved. When cool pour into a jug and add the herbs and mead yeast. Cover with a cloth and keep at 60°F for five days, mixing up the contents of the jug twice a day. Strain through muslin and pour into a jar or cask. Continue as directed for Sweet, Still Mead (I).

Metheglin (III)

16lb honey   3 gallons water
1 blade of mace   ½oz cinnamon
4 cloves   ¼oz root ginger
Mead yeast

Gently simmer the water and spices together for thirty minutes, then strain while still warm on to the honey. Stir the mixture vigorously and when cool add the yeast. Continue as directed for Sweet, Still Mead (I).

HONEY AND BEESWAX RECIPES

Honey Butterscotch

1lb fine sugar
6ozs. fresh butter

2 tablespoons golden syrup
2 dessertspoons honey vinegar

Put sugar, butter and golden syrup into saucepan; add a little water, stir slowly over slow heat, pour in honey vinegar when mixture begins to boil. When done, a little dropped into cold water will harden at once. Pour on to oiled tin when slightly cooled.

Honey Drop Biscuits

1 cup each of butter,
honey, chopped walnuts
and sugar

1 egg
1½ cups plain flour
2 teaspoons baking powder

Cream butter and sugar; add honey and beaten egg. Then add nuts, flour and powder. Drop from teaspoon on to a greased baking sheet. Bake in moderate oven 15 minutes.

Face Cream

1 dessertspoon honey
The well-beaten white of 1 egg
A few drops of almond oil

Beat until a fine smooth cream is obtained.

Queen Charlotte's Almond Paste for Chapped Hands

¼lb bitter almonds   4oz honey
¼oz gum benjamin   ¼oz oil of almonds

To be pounded and mixed up well together to the consistency of a soft paste.

Furniture Cream

2 oz beeswax   1 pint turpentine
2oz white wax   1 pint boiling water
2oz soft soap

Break up wax; put soft soap and wax into a large bowl and add 1 pint of turpentine. Leave for two days. Then pour on the boiling water. Leave it to get cold and then put into jars and seal.

IMPORTANT NOTE: Great care must be taken in melting down turpentine or beeswax, as both are highly inflammable. The method used in the above recipe is therefore strongly recommended.

FLOWER ARRANGING

In a time when standardisation is becoming prevalent, even in such personal things as clothes, it is a relief to turn to flower decoration, where, apart from a few practical basic rules, there is little chance of the wide variety of decorative material ever becoming stereotyped in its arrangement. The different styles produced in one class at any flower show are a good indication of individuality, showing that no two people ever see colours and shapes exactly the same. This should not be forgotten when criticising flower arrangements, whether the ultra-sophisticated or the homely bowl.

Containers

No longer can a hard and fast line be drawn between 'bowls' and 'vases', and it is now much safer to generalise with 'container'.

Glass. Must be clean and sparkling, and any arrangement in clear glass is a double one, the flowers above and the stems below. Slightly coloured glass is often easier to deal with, but many of the modern fireproof glass dishes and bowls are very suitable.

Silver, copper, brass, pewter can be complementary to any flower arrangement but like glass they should be clean and without fingerprints.

China and earthenware are practical, easily cleaned and can often serve two purposes, culinary and floral. Casseroles, pie-dishes, soup-plates, gravy-boats, cake-stands and jugs can all be used with success. Highly coloured and decorated ware is difficult to use without a garish and unnatural result, as flower colours can seldom be found to match.

Watertight tins can be made attractive if covered with paint or distemper, preferably in pastel shades. Square or rectangular tins in particular make very good wall vases, a hole being punched in the back above the water line.

Other suggestions. Shopping baskets, trug-baskets, baskets made especially for flowers can all be effective, while for large-scale work, use buckets, painted or covered with corrugated paper.

Holders

There is a wide choice of adequate flower holders available, to suit every pocket and every need.

Sand. Clean builders', or silver, sand can be used in most non-transparent containers, especially where the flowers are to stand in a draught or public place, when the weight of the sand will often prevent upsets.

Wire-netting. Galvanised 1-inch, 1½-inch or 2-inch mesh wire-netting which will not rust, will wedge into most containers, or can be anchored with sand or plasticine. Wire-netting should always be used in a double layer to support the stems in two places.

Glass holders, kept clean, have a good weight and are suitable for rather stiff flowers, such as daffodils or dahlias.

Wire-holders can be purchased cheaply, and those with suction pads at the bottom are more reliable than the weighted types.

Pin holders are reliable and easy to use for all but the very largest arrangements.

Cellulose material is available which can be cut to fit the container. It can be used about three times, and is suitable for arrangements that may have to be moved, as the flowers remain where they are placed. In shallow containers, white cellulose requires careful camouflage.

Potatoes with holes punched through are sometimes useful for small and difficult containers.

Awkward vases may often be made usable by cutting twigs or straws slightly shorter than the vase and putting them in a bundle to act as a support for flower stems.

Backgrounds

Arrangements should always fit into their backgrounds, and in spite of the modern trend towards line designs, most British homes are ideal for the mixed, rather generous arrangement.

Cutting and Treatment of Flowers

Bought flowers. Before arranging, all bought flowers should have their stems re-cut to allow free passage of water, as they may have been out of water for some time.

For either bought or home-grown flowers, a sloping cut is preferable, as the stem then stands on a point which does not prevent the water from entering normally.

Any badly drooping flowers should be cut and loosely tied up in newspaper, preferably round a stick, and then plunged up to their necks in water, after which they are easier to arrange. Some authorities suggest warm, or even hot, water as being preferable to cold, but usually two hours in cold water seems quite successful. Pennies, aspirins and sugar are also used to strengthen the stems, and keep the water pure. Most bought flowers are quite straightforward to handle, but sometimes in the winter, the rather tight greenish buds of anemones may be urged into opening by putting the stems into warm water and covering the whole bowl with a cloth, supported off the flowers. This provides a miniature hot-house which brings the flowers out in an hour or two.

Home-grown flowers. Where possible flowers should be cut either first thing in the morning or last thing at night as they do not last so well when picked in full sunshine. It is also better to pick them when they are dry as the petals may otherwise soon discolour and drop off.

Unless there is plenty of time and material available for frequent rearrangement, choose young flowers allowing space in the arrangement for them to open fully. Full blooms may be very effective for a short while, but tend to drop and make a mess. This is particularly so with roses. Daisy flowers of all kinds should have their tiny centre flowers still closed, and spiky things like lupins and delphiniums need picking when only a few bottom flowers have opened.

When picking from the garden, be careful to leave no horrid gaps in the borders. It is nearly always possible to choose from the back of the plants and shrubs, and to cut back to a tuft or leaf so that ugly snags do not show.

Hard stems should be slit or bruised to allow the water to penetrate more easily. Prickly stems are improved by running a knife down to take off the thorns which otherwise are difficult to deal with when arranging.

Many hardwood flowers, such as lilac, are often spoilt by badly drooping leaves after cutting. This is best dealt with by removing all the leaves from the flowering stem, and including a separate spray of leaves only.

Flowers with large hollow stems, such as lupins, delphiniums and cowparsley, can often be stiffened by filling the stems up with water, putting the thumb over the end and turning the flower the right way up, placing the bottom of the stem under the water in the container before removing the thumb. Atmospheric pressure will then hold the water up in the stems to keep them rigid. Another method, suitable particularly with tulips, is to wrap the bunch in a newspaper roll, and plunge it in up to the necks in water.

The poppy family will stand quite well when cut, if the ends of the stem are immediately dipped in boiling water or scorched in a flame. Even the heavy oriental poppy keeps quite well if treated like this.

The bottom leaves on flower stems should always be removed before arranging, as they soon rot and even smell. Normally it is more satisfactory to fill up the container frequently with clean water, rather than start the whole thing again. Most flowers last better on shorter stems, and it is amazing how long they will keep when they have been shortened as far as possible, provided that the petals do not actually touch the water.

The Arrangement

First of all, decide where the flowers are required, if possible what container is to be used, and what size and colour of flower would be most suitable. Then go and collect or buy accordingly. (With a garden it is often very tempting to gather, rather enthusiastically, a large collection of flowers and foliage and then not know where to put them.) Give the material any treatment it requires, select the container and flower holder and hope that no one will interrupt.

In this country the flower arranger usually graduates from the all-round mixed bowl (really one of the hardest of all) through the one-sided vase arrangement, to the line design. But do not become so set in any one type of arrangement (either with containers, design or material) that anyone in the district can pick out Mrs Jones's work at a glance. Experiment whenever possible and never hesitate to admit failure and start again. Even experts have heartbreaking experiences with flowers!

Whatever the type of arrangement intended, stand back from the container and measure roughly the outline of the finished design. Then insert two or three bold stems (or flowers) to fix that outline, remembering that an outline one and a half times the height and one and a half times the width of the container gives a good balance, unless a very stylised design is required.

Flowers in a very shallow container are usually taken up in height to one and a half times its width. Having fixed the outline fill in to the centre, taking care:

(a) That where the stems are effective in themselves they do not cross over each other;

(b) that no two stems in any arrangement are ever exactly the same length;

(c) to remember that uneven numbers of stems are more striking than even numbers.

Any heavy material, whether heavy in colour, size, shape or texture, should go to the centre and bottom of the arrangement and be comfortably balanced to the left and the right. Spiky and delicate material usually shows to better advantage to the outside of the design. Grouping of materials is often more satisfactory than the dotting system.

In any case, what is frequently forgotten these days is that a flower arrangement should provide colour, interest and, above all, peace. Many attempts at ultra-bizarre effects using peculiar balance and materials, fail to obtain the peace. The colour is a purely personal matter, and while some combinations of colour will give universal pleasure, never be put off by any outside criticism from something that appeals strongly. The interest lies in the choice of colour, shape and weight for any particular arrangement. No material should ever be chosen just because it is pretty, so look for things with a good colour, such as marigolds, a good shape such as ivy-leaves or bulrushes, a heavy-weight such as peonies or rhododendron leaves, or a light-weight such as grasses or gypsophila.

FLOWER RECIPES

Pot-Pourri

Put into a deep pan or basin, a layer of rose leaves and sprinkle them with bay salt – pounded, but not very small. Then another layer of rose leaves, and so on till you have used all your leaves. Cover them with a flat dish, to press them down and in about two days move the pan on to its side, and a quantity of water will run out. Take handfuls of rose leaves and after squeezing out the water that remains, pick them apart. Put a layer into a dry pan and sprinkle them with a little Pot-Pourri powder and continue these layers till all is used. The powder can be of orris powder, cedar-dust, mace, cloves, and cinnamon, with a few drops of otto of roses. Have the leaves turned once or twice a week with the hand, and add lavender and whole cloves and spices according to fancy.

OLD RECIPE BOOK, *c.* 1820

Lavender Pot-Pourri

½lb lavender flowers (free of stalk)	1oz common salt (well dried)
½oz dried thyme	¼oz ground cloves
½oz dried mint	¼oz ground caraway

Mix the whole well together. Far superior to 'just lavender'.

In the Kitchen

JAM-MAKING

To make good jam the colour and flavour should be characteristic of the fruit and a good set must be obtained, because if the set is too weak the jam will not keep and if too stiff, is uneconomical. The fruit should be evenly distributed. The jam should be stored in a cool, dark, dry place to retain the colour.

Equipment

Pan – large, shallow, aluminium or unchipped enamel
Spoons – 1 large wooden, 1 perforated stainless, 1 set graduated measuring spoons (British standard)
Scales

Knife – sharp for peeling
Lemon squeezer
Thermometer – sugar or preserving, to register at least 240°F
½ pint measure or jug
Jam jars – glass
String or stout rubber bands
Covers – vegetable parchment or strong transparent cellulose tissue
Discs – waxed tissue
Labels

Fruit

This should be dry, fresh, and firm ripe to give the best pectin and acid content, good flavour and setting quality. Fruit may be divided into three groups according to the amount of pectin contained:

(1) High pectin: Cooking apples, blackcurrants, acid cherries, damsons, gooseberries, plums, quince, and red currants

(2) Medium pectin: Apricots, early blackberries, greengages, loganberries, and raspberries.

(3) Low pectin: Strawberries, late blackberries, cherries, elderberries, marrow, medlars, pears, rhubarb.

Although quinces have a high pectin content they may need added acid to obtain a good setting jam; similarly acid cherries may only need half the quantity of acid given below.

Acid

The acid content brightens the colour, improves the flavour, prevents crystallisation of the sugar and is an important factor in obtaining a good set. If little or no acid is present in fruit, then some must be added. In the list above of fruits with poor setting properties, the following quantities of acid are needed:

To 4lb fruit:

2 tablespoons lemon juice, *or*

1 level teaspoon citric acid, *or*

1 level teaspoon tartaric acid, *or*

¼ pint red currant juice, *or*

¼ pint gooseberry juice

Pectin

Good setting properties depend on the pectin and acid content of the fruit. Pectin is a colourless jelly-like substance found in the walls of the fruit tissue and must be extracted to help the set.

Pectin Test. This is taken when the fruit is cooked and the skins are tender, and before adding the sugar.

Put three teaspoons methylated spirits into a glass tumbler, add 1 teaspoon of juice (no seeds or skins), shake gently, leave for 1 minute. If one large clot of jelly-like substance is formed, the set will be good; if there are a number of small clots the set will be weak and additional pectin will be required.

Home-made Pectin. Simmer either red currants, gooseberries, or unpeeled sliced apples in an equal volume of water, press the fruit with a wooden spoon to help break down the tissues. Cook for 20-25 minutes, strain through a flannel bag. Use the strained juice immediately or sterilise in small vacuum jars to 165°F for 20 minutes. Once the jar is opened the contents must be used quickly, as moulds may develop and the juice may lose its setting properties after about twenty-four hours. Use 2-4oz of liquid pectin to each pound of poor-setting fruit.

Water

The amount of water to be added depends upon the fruit, the season, and the pan. A little less water is necessary in a wet season, a little more in a dry season. Water is used to prevent the fruit from burning and to help in the extraction of the pectin and acid.

Sugar

Sugar is necessary as a preservative as well as to sweeten the jam. Granulated, lump or preserving sugars may be used. Too much sugar in jam will cause crystallisation; too little sugar, fermentation and moulds may occur. The fruit must be pulped and the skins soft before the sugar is added. If the sugar is warmed before using, it will dissolve more quickly, thus saving time in bringing the jam to boiling point and helping to keep it a good flavour and colour. Any undissolved sugar may caramelise and spoil the flavour and colour.

Setting Tests

The jam when set should have a 60 per cent added sugar content, ie 3 parts sugar to 5 parts jam.

Temperature. Heat a thermometer in water, dry and put into the jam. When 220°F is registered the jam is ready.

Flake. Dip a dry wooden spoon in the jam. Hold it over a plate away from the heat, turn the spoon over and over to cool the jam, then keep it stationary. When the drops run together forming a flake or curtain, the jam has been sufficiently cooked.

Weight. When the jam weighs 10lb for every 6lb of sugar used, setting point should have been reached. Before starting to make the jam, weigh the pan and wooden spoon and make a note of this. To find the weight of the finished jam, multiply the amount of sugar used by 10 and divide by 6, e.g. with 3lb sugar and 3lb fruit the sum is: 3 x 10 = 30 (divided by) 6 = 5lb jam, plus the weight of pan and spoon.

Cooking

The fruit and water are simmered together with the added acid when required and must never be allowed to boil; this is to soften the skins, extract the pectin and to drive off the excess liquid. When the stewed fruit has decreased by approximately one-third in volume, remove from the heat, take a pectin test, add liquid pectin if necessary, then add the warm sugar. Stir gently to help to dissolve it, and when not a grain remains, return the pan to the heat and quickly bring the mixture to boiling point. Continue to boil rapidly until setting point is reached (*see test for setting of jam*). The time for this boiling varies from 3-15 minutes, according to the fruit used.

Scum

Remove scum if necessary when boiling has finished. It is uneconomical and unnecessary to keep skimming the jam. If the inside of the pan is rubbed with a very little butter before use, this may help to prevent scum forming. Remove as many stones as possible. Jam for exhibition or sale should have not more than 5 stones to the lb.

Finishing

Filling. Allow the jam to cool slightly until a skin begins to form, then stir slightly before pouring into warm jars. Some fruits tend to rise more than others, in which case fill the jars one-third at a time until each is full to the brim. Put on the wax discs immediately, pressing gently from the centre outwards. As the jam cools it will shrink slightly, drawing down the disc tightly, which helps to prevent the growth of mould so long as there is no gap between the disc and the neck of the jar. Cover with a clean towel till cold, or cover immediately.

Covering and Labelling. Wipe the jars; cover lightly with a damp parchment top, damp side uppermost, or use strong cellulose tissues. Tie down tightly with thin string or a strong rubber band. Label with variety of fruit, day, month and year.

Storage. A dark, cool, airy place is the ideal storage.

Mixed Fruit Jams

When two or more fruits are used in jam-making, each fruit must be cooked separately until tender, then mixed and the procedure carried out in the normal way.

114

CHERRY JAM

To 1lb of fruit allow 1¼lb of sugar and ¼ pint of water. Boil sugar and water together for 10 minutes. Put in cherries and boil for 25 minutes. Leave until the next day and boil again for 10 minutes.

MULBERRY MARMALADE

Add 1lb crushed sugar to every 1lb of fruit. Place the mulberries in a preserving pan and cover with the warmed sugar. Simmer very slowly, stirring well, until the juice and sugar have thickened into a syrup. Boil fast for five or six minutes, skimming well. Pour into jars and cover.

RED CURRANT AND CHERRY JAM

Put 4lb of red currants into a pan without any water and stir them over a gentle flame until the juice comes out. Strain through a muslin without pressing the fruit so that the juice is clear. There should be about 2lb of juice.

For this amount stone 4lb of cherries and make a syrup with 6lb of sugar and 1½ pints of water; put the cherries into the syrup and let it boil gently until the syrup sets when a teaspoonful is put on to a cold plate. Now add the red currant juice, let the whole mixture boil again and the jam is ready to put into pots. These jams made of mixed fruits are very much liked in France and are often served with cream as a dessert.

RHUBARB AND ROSE-PETAL JAM

To each 1lb prepared rhubarb add the juice of one lemon and 1lb sugar. Cover the cut-up rhubarb with the sugar and lemon juice and leave to stand overnight.

Chop up 2 handfuls of scented rose-petals, red if possible, to each 1lb of fruit, and cook all together until set. This is a delicious jam with a lovely colour; 2oz of angelica, fresh or crystallised, can be used in place of rose-petals if preferred.

GOOSEBERRY AND ELDERFLOWER JELLY

Gooseberries	Sugar
Elderflowers	Water

Cover gooseberries with water and simmer for 2 hours. Strain as for jelly. To each pint of juice add 1lb of sugar. Allow warmed sugar to dissolve, add 12 heads of elderflower tied together in a bunch in a muslin bag, bring to boiling point and boil for 10 minutes. Finish. This jelly has a muscat flavour.

JAPONICA JELLY

Wipe the fruits, do not core or peel; cut into pieces, barely cover with water and simmer until soft and pulpy. Strain through jelly bag, measure, and to every pint allow 1lb warmed sugar. Dissolve sugar, bring to boiling point, test for set at approximately ten minutes. Finish.

QUINCE HONEY

5 large quinces	1 pint boiling water
5lb sugar	

Pare and grate quinces, dissolve sugar in water over heat, add quinces, and cook for 15-20 minutes. Pot and seal. When cold, should be the colour and consistency of honey.

In the Parlour

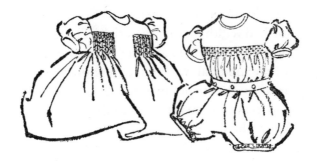

SMOCKING

Smocking, a traditional English craft of peasant origin, has been used for many centuries to decorate garments and arose from the need to control the fullness of the material when garments were cut on very simple straight lines. Today, although the original use has almost disappeared, the old stitches and designs with some modem variations provide a practical and attractive method of decoration for women's and children's clothing.

A wide variety of materials may be used for modern smocked garments, cottons, linens, silks, fine woollens, voiles and nylon. The materials used should have good draping qualities, be fine in texture and, with the exception of checks and stripes where the material can be included in the design, should form a background to the smocking, enhancing the design but not overpowering it. The threads used for the smocking stitches should match the material in thickness and texture, linen lace thread on linen, *coton à broder*, D.M.C. or sylko perle, on cotton materials, silk on silk; a twisted thread is preferable to a stranded one. Choice of colour for the thread is a matter of taste, but a matching colour, a contrast, or shades of the background give a better result than a variety of colours.

The amount of material required for smocking will depend upon the nature of the material, and may vary from three times the required finished width in thicker materials to four or even four and a half times the finished width in finer materials. The material should be cut on the straight of the thread and the gathering worked along the weft threads of the material, with the exception of stripes, when, for decorative purposes, the stripes may run across the tubings.

The whole success of smocking lies in the careful preparation of the tubings. When the top of the tubing is not set into a yoke or band but is left to form a frill, this should be kept narrow and the smocking design worked in close rows beneath.

In smocking the gathering threads may be worked in the following ways:

(a) With the aid of a transfer, for fine materials dots approximately ⅛ inch apart; ⅜ inch between rows; for thicker materials dots a little more widely spaced. Just the required amount of transfer should be ironed on to the wrong side of the material, allowing an extra ½ inch of material each side equal to four dots and 1 inch below the transfer to be gathered by the thread of the material. This ensures that no dots are shown when the gathering threads are removed.

Begin the gathering threads on the wrong side of the material with a knot and a small back stitch, using fine strong cotton and a fine needle, putting the needle in on a dot and out on the next dot, thus making the stitches and spaces even. A transfer with more widely spaced dots may be used and the gathering thread worked by putting the needle in on a dot and out midway between the dots, thereby using only half the number of transfer dots as in the previous method. This method may be used to advantage on fine materials.

(b) Dots may be marked with a ruler and pencil and worked as in (a).

(c) If the material is very fine, the transfer or squared paper may be tacked on to the wrong side of the material, the gathering threads worked through the transfer or paper and the material, the paper torn away afterwards leaving no dots.

(d) If checked or striped material is used, the gathering threads may be worked by the pattern of the material. The most effective result is obtained by ⅛-inch checks or stripes when the dark or light result of the gathering may form part of the smocking design.

After all the rows of gathering have been completed, the threads should be pulled up until the tubings are quite even and tight, then released a little allowing sufficient room in between the tubings for needle and thread to be inserted easily. The threads should be tied off in pairs and surplus threads cut off, with the exception of the top gathering thread which will need to be released for the setting-in process. It should be worked in the same colour as the material and need not be withdrawn.

Beginning the Smocking Stitch

To begin the smocking stitch, a knot may be used, but it is neater to start on the wrong side of the work on the back of the first tubing with a split back stitch and then two over-stitches.

The first row of smocking should be worked approximately ¾ inch from the top of the material, leaving ½ inch to be set into the yoke or band and a space between the yoke and the first row of smocking stitches.

Allow enough thread to complete the row of stitchery, as there should be no joins on the back of the work – except in certain modern patterns-and finish off on the wrong side on the last tubing, again with a split back stitch.

119

Smocking Stitches. In the old traditional smocks, there were usually three basic smocking stitches used on the tubings:

(1) Rope   (2) Basket   (3) Chevron

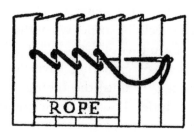

Rope stitch is similar to the embroidery stitch known as stem stitch, and is worked in a straight line across the tubings from left to right. The needle is inserted at right angles to the tubings, a small amount of material on the top of each tubing is picked up on the needle and the thread is held, either always below the needle or always above the needle. If two rows are worked closely together with the thread above the needle in the first row and below the needle in the second row (or vice versa), the finished result resembles a chain.

Basket stitch is worked in exactly the same way as rope stitch but the thread is held alternately above and below the needle for each consecutive stitch. When two rows are worked together a basket weave is formed.

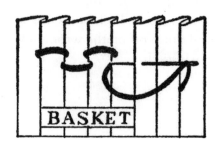

Chevron stitch worked again as rope stitch, but to form a chevron, of usually three or five steps. In each stitch working upwards the thread is held below the needle, and each working downwards the thread is held above the needle, working two stitches level at the top and the bottom. Two or three similar rows may be worked together, so forming a solid chevron, or rows may be worked to form a diamond.

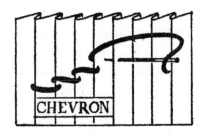

In working chevrons or diamonds, care must be taken to see that the pattern sits symmetrically into the tubings.

These three stitches may be used in varying combinations to form a variety of patterns, but in traditional smocking it was usual to start and finish with two rows of rope stitch to control the tubings. The needle is kept always at right angles to the tubings when working these traditional stitches.

A wide variety of stitches may be used on the tubings in modern smocking in varying combinations and patterns: rope, basket, chevron, vandyke, diamond stitch, honeycomb, surface honeycomb and feather stitch. French knots, satin stitch and detached chain are often introduced. With a little ingenuity it is quite simple for the worker to invent new patterns and fresh combinations of stitches. Some examples are in the diagram on page 123.

It is always advisable to work out the complete smocking design first on paper or on a specimen piece of material, counting the tubings to see that the pattern will fit symmetrically and to test the colour scheme, tension and material.

The secret of good smocking is:

(a) Well controlled tubings
(b) even tension
(c) elasticity
(d) attractive design and colouring to tone or contrast
    with the background material

When the smocking has been completed, the gathering threads (all except the top one) are removed, the tubings let out to the required width to fit into the yoke or band, marking the halves and quarters of both bands and tubings.

A double yoke is more serviceable for children's garments. Traditional smocked garments should be made up entirely by hand with flat seams, but for making up and finishing modern smocked garments, hand or machine work may be employed. The tubings in all cases should be set in by hand.

The making-up of the garment is just as important as the smocking, for both the smocking and the making-up contribute towards the standard of the finished article.

The true beauty of a smocked garment lies in its simplicity of design.

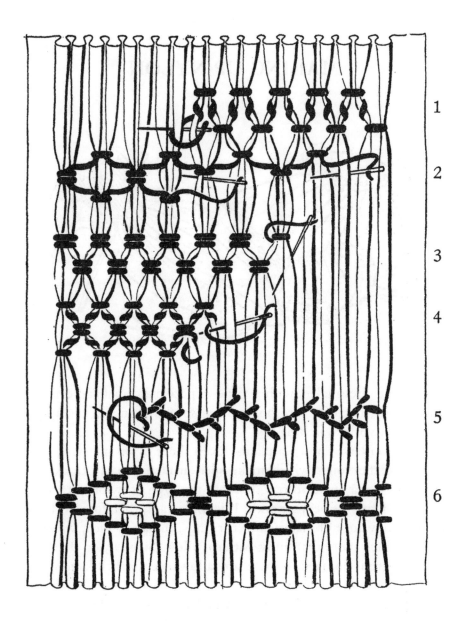

1 Vandyke 2 Diamond 3 Honeycomb 4 Surface Honeycomb
5 Feather Stitch 6 A varied arrangement of chevron

MAKING UP NYLON

Any home dressmaker with a little experience can handle nylon quite easily, but there are one or two special points of technique which are worth watching.

If you have chosen a plain-woven sheer nylon material, such as one of the voiles which make such attractive party frocks for children, it may tend to fray, because the type of nylon yarn used for these fabrics is very smooth. It is important, therefore, to leave a good allowance of material for turnings, at least ¾ inch, which is about ¼ inch more than most patterns allow. Since nylon does not shrink there is no need to make any allowance for shrinkage when cutting out.

Seams on nylon should never be left with raw edges, as these also will be likely to fray. Most good dressmakers prefer French or felled seams, but if plain seams must be used, the raw edges should either be turned in and stitched or finished by overcasting.

With some closely-woven nylon fabrics, such as taffetas or satins, it may be difficult to avoid puckering along machine-sewn seams, especially those in the warp direction, ie lengthwise. This puckering is a consequence of the elasticity of nylon; the yarns are displaced by the sewing needle but do not relax in their new position, as their natural tendency is to return to their former place. Seams on the bias of the fabric are less likely to pucker, so if possible the pattern should be adjusted to avoid long warp seams. Obviously, this is not always practical so the other important point to remember is to adjust your machine when this type of fabric is to be sewn. The tension of both the needle-thread and the bobbin-thread should be loosened; check that they are loose enough by running up trial seams on scraps of the material. Be careful not to stretch or pull the fabric as you guide it through the machine.

With all types of nylon fabric, use the finest and sharpest needle possible. If your machine has interchangeable parts, use those recommended for the finest materials. Nylon should be sewn with nylon thread, which makes fine but very strong seams which last as long as the fabric.

When pressing any nylon fabric there is only one important thing to remember: use a cool iron. Any of the usual pressing methods can be used: ironing dry, without a pressing cloth, ironing with a damp pressing cloth or ironing with a steam iron. With them all, however, the temperature of the iron should be low. If the iron has a temperature control it should be set at the lowest point.

There are now plenty of nylon trimmings in the shops, including a great variety of lace and ribbons and a number of attractive edgings. It is always worthwhile using nylon trimmings on nylon, so that the whole garment will wear and wash equally well.

With Our Friends

COSTUME – COLOUR AND CUT

The main reason for dressing a play in clothes of a period is to aid the action of the play and establish quickly by visual means the period, time of year and the kind of people that the author intends. If the designer has done the work well, a great deal can be known directly the actor appears on the stage, without a word being spoken. Every character has its own shape and set of colours. One knows at once if they are countrymen or townsmen, rich and elegant or poor and humble, or arrogant, stupid or wise; just as navy blue will suggest something to do with the sea, russet, reddish brown and green suggest the countryman; a loud pattern or blatant check, the sporting or flamboyant character; black or dark colours, the serious or sinister role. When five or six appear on the stage in black, a very serious or tragic episode is imminent.

Of course, it is not essential to keep rigidly to accurate period in stage design, but whatever licence is taken it should be from knowledge and not just accidental!

The cut of the garment which has so much to do with the fashionable shape is a slow evolution. No new fashion comes suddenly or before people are ready for it. One can see the 'new look' right through the ages appearing long before it is universally adopted. The main fashionable impulse was from the court; the advent of a foreign queen and her ladies, historical and social events, and often personalities too had their influence and caused the dropping or adding of some new phase of the dress of the day.

In the early days, workers, unless they were attached to the court circles, were just 'clothed' and not dressed. Of course, there was the mass of people who were never as extravagantly dressed as those at court, and often the countryman and his womenfolk were years behind the fashion but had a distinct yeoman type of dress. Even in the well-to-do classes elderly men were reluctant to change from the fashions of their youth.

Court clothes were not often seen by the country folks except when the people of fashion journeyed to the country on their visits to the great houses. London fashion houses did send round in the eighteenth century to the country towns small dolls showing the new materials and fashions. Later when magazines became more general, fashion spread somewhat quicker but country can never have had the finish and grand air of the people of the town, for to be well dressed was almost a profession.

The Effigy of the Wife of Sir R. Drury of Rougham, Suffolk

This is a typical dress of a lady of the end of the thirteenth and early fourteenth century. It is laced down the front and fits the figure closely to the hip-line when it falls into crossway folds. The side seams are very far towards the back and are curved. Note that both the centre back and front of seams of the skirt part are on the straight of the material, but are cut out on to the cross above from the waist upwards. The skirt is often long at the back and, being on the straight of the material, holds a beautiful straight train-line.

The neck is cut low and the sleeves are tightly fitted, being cut on the exact crossway, with a bulge left at the elbow for expansion. The head of the sleeve at the back is very rounded and comes well into the back of the gown, giving that narrow-backed medieval shape and a much lower bonnet-like head-dress draped in a black velvet hood becomes usual.

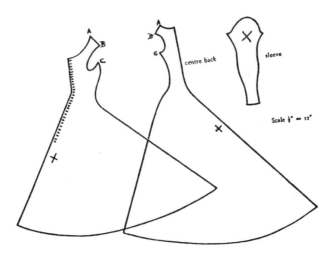

The Effigy of the Wife of Baron Camoys of Trotton, Sussex

This lady is wearing a sleeveless robe or surcoat over a tightly fitting robe or kirtle. This garment was in vogue from the early fourteenth to middle fifteenth century.

This lady wears a houppeland, a garment worn much as we would wear a coat. The shoulder seams and arm hole are cut almost on a level with the neck-line. so that when pulled downwards into place on the form the material is forced into several crossway folds across the chest. These folds or pleats are held in by a belt at the high waist-line. They are often padded out. This is the first indication of material artificially supported.

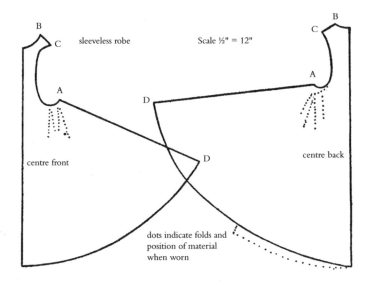

129

During the sixteenth century the gown (or pelisse) was divided down the centre front from the waist downwards and was still cut in one with the upper part. It was often a fur-lined garment as the name suggests. Some brasses of the sixteenth show this very clearly worn over an undergown.

It was during the beginning of this century that the bodice and skirt were cut separately. A tight and stiffened under-bodice was used to get the straight line in front: probably this was reinforced by husks. The sleeves fitted the upper arm to just above the elbow and then widened out and were turned back to form an immense cuff. The lower arm had an elaborate cuff which was tied together at the back of the arm by ribbons over the full sleeve of the shirt (or shift). The gable head-dress begins to appear and a velvet bonnet-like hood is worn over it. The diagram shows the skirt back, the bodice and sleeve.

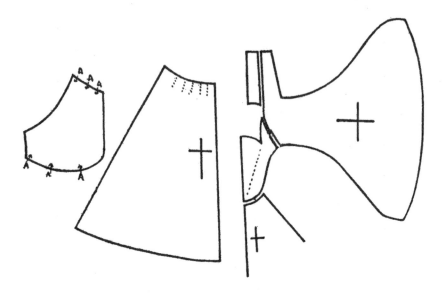

A Group of Elizabethans

The woman's dress is now often a bodice (doublet) and skirt, although the pelisse or gown was still worn as an over-robe by many.

The doublet has become long and pointed in the front and is either itself stiffened by whalebones or husks or is worn over a stiffened corset. The skirt is supported by a farthingale. The widest part of the sleeves is now at the top of the arm.

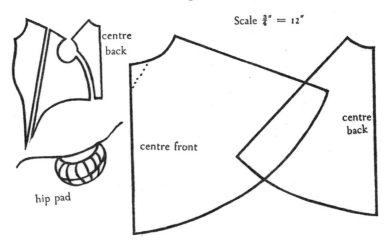

131

The ruff has grown from the small gathered heading of the shirt to be an important feature of dress. It becomes even larger during the reign of James I.

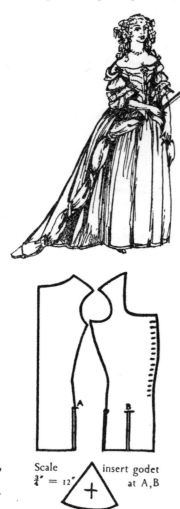

During the latter half of the seventeenth century the bodice becomes much longer and more stiffly boned, and takes the place of the corset.

A new seam comes into being owing to the greater length of body. This runs from the armhole to the point of the bodice in front, and across the shoulder-blade to the end of a point at the back.

The sides are cut into tabs over the hips. These tabs are worn under the skirt but the front and back points are worn outside. There are often loops on the tabs to which the skirt is tied to keep it in place.

During the end of the century the bunching of the skirt over the hips was most marked and was ousted later by the hooped petticoat and panniers.

Scale
$\frac{3}{4}'' = 12''$

insert godet at A,B

Towards the end of the eighteenth century the women's corsets became shorter in front, but the long line was accentuated at the back. Caracas and polonaises were worn over side loops. There were infinite varieties of fashion.

During and after the French Revolution and general unrest. the hoops disappeared and the dresses collapsed round the form, and by 1800 had almost reached their scantiest. The back of the dress had an extremely narrow look, the seams being placed to accentuate this. The back width of the skirt was gathered into the bodice and a very small roll was hung to keep the material from falling in to the figure. To the

front of the skirt is often attached the small front of the bodice, the opening being at both sides. A classic character was prevalent both in decoration of dress and hair style, no doubt stimulated by the excavations taking place at Pompeii. The material employed was soft and fine, cottons and muslins were most fashionable.

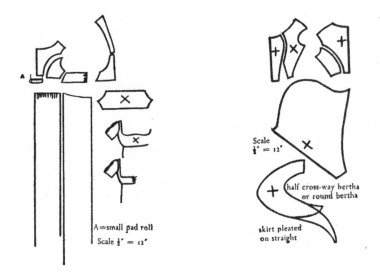

A = small pad roll
Scale ¼" = 12"

Scale ¼" = 12"

half cross-way bertha
or round bertha

skirt pleated
on straight

The straight silhouette gradually changes by first the skirt being trimmed at the hem and the bodice increasing in length. The sleeves swell out and everything possible is done to increase the width of the shoulders. The skirt is very full, usually on the straight of material and gathered into a small waist-line.

The beautiful printed cottons are giving way to lovely light silks which stood out with so much ease, although under-petticoats were many.

By the early 1850s the weight of these numerous petticoats had become intolerable and the crinoline was introduced. A whaleboned petticoat, it was at first a complete circle round the wearer, but the immense hoops worn towards the end of the decade gradually assumed a backward movement that became the bustle in the 1870s and 1880s.

In the 1870s the bust and the abdomen were emphasised by front draping. Dresses in two materials were popular and heads were neat and small.

The bustle disappeared towards the end of the decade when skirts became very tight, only to reappear in the 1880s, larger and more important.

Towards the end of the century the accent had gone to the top of the figure which was emphasised with leg-of-mutton sleeves, padded hair styles, large hats and feather boas.

The Edwardians retained this top-heavy look, adding high-boned collars and skirts with most of the fullness in the back and ending in a train. Hobble skirts and the fish silhouette were the final unpractical clothes of the last years before the 1914-18 War. As women took on active war work these fashions gave way to more practical clothes. By 1917 the skirts were beginning to rise, a trend which went on through the 1920s until the shapeless knee-length

1903

dresses of the end of the era were reached.

In the 1930s everything that could be, was cut on the cross, with the result that everything clung and nothing fitted. Skirts were longer and a fox fur slung over one shoulder was almost a uniform.

1917

The military years of the Second World War were emphasised by the enormous padded square shoulders and shorter skirts. With clothes rationing came a drab uniformity only relieved by the frivolous hats which were piled high with unrationed trimmings and veils.

Peace brought a great variety of fashion which is constantly changing and receiving new impetus from the many new fabrics being invented.

1935   1926   1942

PAINTING FOR PLEASURE

Practically anyone can paint some kind of picture. There are no rules or regulations about it, but it is best first of all to understand that a painter who paints for pleasure has a different approach from the professional artist – the amateur paints literally whatever pleases him or her in a way that gives her pleasure, and this must be the motive force behind all her efforts.

It is a tremendous help and encouragement to a complete novice to realise that there have been, and are today, and always will be, untrained painters who have produced accomplished and satisfactory works of art without great craftsmanship and even without a sense of proportion or perspective; just as the most skilful and highly trained craftsman can produce pictures without artistic merit of any kind.

Another source of comfort for some of us is to realise that it is never too late to begin. The lovely and sensitive works of Grandma Moses, the famous American artist, bear witness to this, as she only started to paint at the age of 75. Another help is that women are naturally creative, and in this sense are natural designers.

Those with skill in embroidery, patchwork, flower arrangements, house decoration, or even knowing how to dress well, will find that painting is merely applying the principles involved to another medium.

Perhaps our first impulse to make a picture comes from a deep response to the beauty of the natural world around us, or even to the things we see every day on the kitchen table or perhaps to the delight we feel in the movements of our children playing in the clear and sun-filled air by the seashore. Countless things may make us want to start, but if we have never painted before and know no one to help us we come up against the difficulties of knowing what medium to use and what materials to get.

Drawing with pencil or charcoal, pen and ink, pastels or water-colours are all media which can be used and are easily obtainable, but perhaps painting in oils is the most fun and the most rewarding. The equipment need not be at all expensive. In fact it is far better to begin with very little and build up what you want as you go along. You will soon find out what you need. Here are what are probably the minimum requirements

Something to paint on: Cheapest and perfectly good is cardboard (the top of a dress box will do), painted with size and for preference, though not necessary, then painted with flat white paint, both obtained from a decorator's shop; or hardboard which is excellent – obtained at an ironmongers who will cut it to the size you want. Daler boards or canvas mounted on stretchers.

Paints

Flake white	Raw umber
Ivory black	Viridian (green)
Cadmium yellow pale	Permanent green
Yellow ochre	Cobalt blue
Light red	Goya blue
Alizarin crimson	Cadmium red

These are a good selection and most can be obtained in 'Students' colours, cheaper than artists colours and just as good for the novice. Buy small tubes except for Flake White. You will need this for mixing with other colours. Get a large tube.

Oil and Turpentine, mixed (a small quantity). This is used to mix the paints with, but many artists use the paints as they are and this is a good method and much less messy.

Palette. A piece of glass or wood 16 inches x 12 inches will serve or one can be bought ready-made.

Palette Knife (essential).

Brushes. Flat hogs bristle in the shape called long filbert sizes 3 to 7. One of each will be enough to begin with. All these materials can be bought from an Artists Colourman and there is nearly always one in every town, however small. A small wide-necked jar with a tight lid filled with turpentine is very useful for rinsing brushes and can be used over and over again. Plenty of rag completes your requirements. A chair can be used as an easel. If you need an easel for painting outdoors, get a portable one with a canvas tilter. Everything else can be added in the light of experience.

Having got the materials and chosen a subject, the thing is to begin without thinking too much about it. Remember that essentially you are creating, not copying. Don't listen to uninformed criticism! The picture must be your own expression of what you have wanted to do. Even if the result is not all we have hoped (and if we are honest it certainly never will be), the absolute absorption in what we are doing – the complete release from the worries and difficulties of everyday life – and the heightened awareness of the colour and light which are all around us, are rewards enough. And there is always that 'next time' when we know we can do better.

Local Festivals

Religious ceremonies and secular celebrations make a widely varied calendar of local festivals for May, June, July and August.

The relics of a pagan festival occur in Devon at Kingsteignton on Whit Monday with the Ram Roasting Fair. This was long ago a sacrifice to the gods to give rain for the crops. A ram is paraded round the village: this is roasted later at the Gymkhana which is held on Oakford Lawn. After roasting, the meat is divided up and given as prizes to winning programme numbers.

Whitsuntide in Derbyshire is the date for well-dressing. At this ceremony the wells are blessed and thanks given for an unfailing supply of pure water. Life-size plaques, usually depicting scenes from the Bible, are entirely executed in flowers, berries, leaves and mosses, and then erected by the wells. A wooden frame is made and the flowers stuck into a bed of clay and moss.

Garlanding of quite a different sort occurs in Dorset. In the fishing village of Abbotsbury in Dorset garlands of wild and garden flowers are made by the children on May 13th each year and are brought round the village. At one time each boat wore a garland and once out to sea cast it overboard as an offering to the gods to grant a good fishing season.

At Castleton in the Peak (Derbyshire) on May 29th, Royal Oak Day, a procession of young girls dressed in white and garlanded with flowers dances its way through the main street. At the head of the procession a King and Queen ride on horseback. The king wears a garlanded head-dress in the shape of an acorn, and as they reach the Market Place the king's garland is hoisted to the top of the church tower where it stays until withered and dry. Finally, there is dancing round the maypole which is set up in the Market Square. To the certain knowledge of the inhabitants this ceremony has been unbroken for the last 300 years, but it is widely felt that it goes back much further, even to pagan times.

At Aston-on-Clun, Shropshire, on the Sunday following May 29th, a tree is dressed with flags; the custom of tree-dressing is very old but the festival held at the Arbor Tree at Aston-on-Clun is a modern one as the system of dressing is designed to symbolise the friendship of the Commonwealth and includes all the Dominions flags, new ones being added with each new Dominion that joins.

Trees again come into the annual Whit Monday Feast Day of the old Harting Club in Sussex. Early in the morning two club members, known as 'boughmen' go into the woods and cut beech boughs. These boughs are brought back into the village and used to decorate the door of the White Hart Inn – which is the headquarters of the club – the church gates and an especially large one is 'planted' in the village square. From 10 o'clock onwards members begin to gather outside the clubroom in readiness for the arrival of the band and for the Roll Call by the club secretary. The band forms up, behind them two stewards each carrying a six-foot stave, two others with red, white and blue flags, lastly the club members wearing red, white and blue rosettes and carrying freshly-peeled hazel sticks. To the strains of *Sussex by the Sea* the procession marches down the street, round the beech bough and to the church. After the church service the annual feast is held in the clubroom.

Other summer religious ceremonies are frequently concerned with rush strewing or rush bearing as at Tarvin in Cheshire, where parishioners in the Middle Ages cleared the church and brought new rushes to strew on the stone floor as protection against the coming winter cold. Today at Tarvin it is the churchyard that is tidied up and the rushes are used to decorate the church for a special afternoon service.

At Barrowden in Rutland the parish church is dedicated to St Peter and on the feast of his martyrdom (June 29th) the floor of the nave and aisles are covered as in old times with freshly cut rushes as part of the decorations.

At Grasmere in Westmorland again the rushbearing ceremony is different: it is celebrated on the Saturday nearest to St Oswald's Day (August 5th). Many of these rush 'Bearings' are traditional emblems which appear year after year – Moses in the Bulrushes, St Oswald's Hand with St Aidan's Prayer 'May this hand never perish', and the Serpent. Gathering of the rushes is commemorated by a handwoven linen sheet, trimmed with rushes, which is carried by six of the older girls at school. Almost every child in the village carries a bearing or basket with rushes, heather and flowers. The ceremony begins at 4.30pm when the bearings are brought to the churchyard well and each child receives a new penny. The bearers then process round the village, led by the clergy, choir, rushmaidens with their sheet, the banner of St Oswald and the Band playing what is known as *Jimmy Dawson's March*, an old tune handed down from the fiddler, Jimmy Dawson. After going round Churchtown, the children come – 'To the wide church door charged with these offerings that their fathers bore,' and a short service follows.

In other parts of the country new-mown hay or grass is brought to the church as on the Thursday after July 6th at Braunstone and Glenfield churches in Leicester and at Wingrave in Buckinghamshire on St Peter's Day. The church here was originally left a piece of land on which rushes grew so that the building would be sweet on its great day. The land was later sold and the money invested; the interest however is used for the upkeep of the church floor, while new-mown grass is spread once a year as a memorial to the original benefactor.

Of a different character is the altar service conducted at Stonehenge at dawn on June 21st, when a modern order of Druids holds a service round the Altar Stone. The service begins with the Druids in their white robes and scarlet hoods walking in procession round the circle of stones, saluting the sun as it rises.

Many summer festivals take the form of gay processions, one such is the Royal May Day Procession at Knutsford in Cheshire. On the first Saturday in the month the Queen and Maids of Honour (all local schoolchildren) and the bandsmen parade through the village to the heath where the Queen is crowned by a local boy. There follow displays of horn, sword and maypole dancing before everyone goes to the fair. The 'Royal' prefix was given after a visit to the village festival by the Prince and Princess of Wales, later King Edward VII and Queen Alexandra.

A procession that actually *is* danced is the Helston Furry Dance in Cornwall held each year on May 8th to celebrate the arrival of summer. The dance is preceded very early on the morning by the Hal-on-Tow when flowers and green boughs are brought into the town by the young folk to decorate the entrances through which the dancers will later pass. The first dance is a charming sight with scores of couples of children dressed in white following the recognised route.

At midday comes the most spectacular and exclusive dance when gentlemen wear morning dress with light gloves and silk hats and the ladies ankle-length summer frocks and picture hats; everyone wears lilies of the valley. The procession led by the town band goes through the streets, passing in through the front doorway and out by the back of certain houses, also going through some of the larger gardens.

Later in the day there is a general dance taking a somewhat similar route. The well-known song, *The Floral Dance*, is based on the traditional tune.

143

Padstow in Cornwall has a different and very old May Day tradition – the famous Padstow Horse.

As Midnight strikes the Morning song begins:

Unite all unite and let us all unite!
For summer is acome in today
And whither we are going, let us all unite,
For the merry morning of May!

This preliminary opening of the May Day soon ceases but is renewed with the dawn. The 'horse' is a fearsome creation made of black tarpaulin hanging on a large hoop – a tail plume, a tall cap and a frightening face-mask with 'snappers' to complete the outfit. The man inside is hidden save for his feet and must have an exhausting time prancing, dancing and making quick rushes at the crowd. In front of the 'horse' dances a man, usually in comic dress, who acts as 'teaser'. The May Song has a mournful strain, and one verse runs:

O where is St George? O where is he, O?
He's out in the long boat, all on the salt sea.

This causes Horse and Teaser to sink to the ground. Suddenly the singers reach a livelier verse, up leaps the Horse, the Teaser trips and the gay song continues through the streets.

Morris Dancers also sometimes have a 'horse', but more often a 'fool'. In Abingdon, Berkshire, they elect a 'Mayor'. For hundreds of years it has been the custom on June 19th for Morris Dancers to dance the length of Ock Street and for the people of that street to elect a Mayor for the day. This custom still continues and has been maintained largely by the descendants of one family named Hemmings for the past 250 years.

Dressed in white with top hats, coloured sashes and garlands, the dancers perform various jigs and reels to the accompaniment of a concertina. The dancing begins outside the inns along Ock Street: the first to be visited being the 'Ock Street Horns'. A fine pair of ox horns is carried on a staff in front of the dancers who can be seen in a perfect setting outside the Old County Hall or in the Courtyard of the Jacobean 'Crown and Thistle' where they conclude their programme.

Quite different are the 'Grovely men' who go from the village of Wishford in Wiltshire at dawn on May 29th, Oak Apple Day. They march up the streets with drums and bugles and a banner bearing the words 'Grovely, Grovely and all Grovely,' waking all householders and then going to the forest to cut oak boughs. These are set up before the doors of the houses. At noon there is a procession with the band followed by four women with faggots on their heads; next come the children, often in fancy dress, and finally the men with the oak boughs, all shouting 'Gravely, Gravely and all Gravely'. The ceremony ends with a feast near the Oak Apple Inn, followed by sports and games. The custom is kept up to preserve the ancient local right to gather wood.

One of the very few summer fairs is held each year at Honiton in Devonshire, starting on the Tuesday after July 19th. At 12 noon the Town Crier, dressed in a navy-blue coat and trousers and three-cornered hat trimmed with gold braid, comes out on to the street from the old Market House (now a tea shop) carrying a golden glove on the end of a long pole; the pole is garlanded with flowers. He rings his bell three times and shouts three times: 'The glove is up, the Fair has begun. No man shall be arrested until the glove is taken down. God save the Queen'.

The glove is then carried to the King's Arms Hotel, east end, where it is put on the balcony; from the windows about 14,000 hot pennies are thrown into a pool where the children have a fine time scrambling for them.

On Thursday at 12 noon the glove is taken to the White Lion Hotel at the other end of the town, the west end, and fixed again where it remains until the Friday, being removed at 12 o'clock and all is over for that particular year.

Of the summer contests, one of the more remarkable is the Bottle Kicking held each Whit Monday at Hallaton in Leicestershire. Men from Hallaton and the neighbouring village of Redbourne meet and after a service go round to the local inn and then to the rectory, where by tradition a hare pie awaits them, together with three 'bottles' of ale. These in fact are small brightly painted barrels tied with ribbon. Everyone with the pie and bottles then adjourns to a neighbouring ridge which separates the villages. The pie is cut and scrambled for and then the bottle kicking begins: the contest being to get the bottle by any means down their own side of the ridge and across the brook round the base of the ridge. The leader of the winning side has the honour of broaching the barrel, taking his drink perched on the Old Cross in the village street.

More sedate is the annual marbles championship going back to Elizabethan times, and held at Tinsley Green in Sussex on Good Friday. Teams compete at the circular rink, then the highest individual scorers play against one another to become for a year British Individual Marbles Champion.

A very gay ceremony is the trial for the Dunmow Flitch held each year on Whit Monday at Gt. Dunmow (or in a neighbouring market town) in Essex. The trial is said to go back to 1244. Before Judge and Counsel, duly robed, and with much traditional ritual and mock legal procedure, couples come forward from many parts of the country to swear that marriage for them holds no regrets and that they have never quarrelled. The giving of a flitch of bacon was first made in 1445 according to the records, but Chaucer knew of the trial a hundred years before. When bacon was hard to get in World War II, flitches were sent from the Commonwealth and the trials went on! It was not until the eighteenth century that the views of the wife as well as the husband were considered.

There are two July festivals deriving from medieval government, in the Isle of Man, Tynwald and in Jersey the Visite Royale.

Tynwald is an open-air parliament ceremony held at St Johns (the former capital of the island) on old Midsummer's Day (July 5th). The Lieutenant Governor, the members of the Legislative Council, the House of Keys, the Deemsters (Judges), the Bishop and Clergy and other Island dignitaries attend divine service in St John's Church. All wear a sprig of mug-wort, the plant of the Feast of John, to ward off evil influences. After the service a procession led by the Lieutenant Governor's Sword Bearer, carrying the twelfth-century Sword of State, walks to the hill composed, according to legend, of soil taken from each of the seventeen ancient parishes of Man. The 'hill' is only about twelve feet high and consists of four circular steps each three feet above the other, and about ten feet less in diameter than the one below, the bottom one being about 76 feet across. The Lieutenant Governor mounts to the top and sits facing east – a survival of Viking times and the worship of the Sun-God. The Legislative Council sits with him and on the second stage are the members of the House of Keys; the Coroners of the Sheadings (court officials) stand at the foot of the hill and the Coroner of Glenfaba opens the court by 'fencing' – warning the assembly not to fight or cause any disturbance. The laws which have been enacted during the year are then proclaimed, the First Deemster reading a summary in English and the official 'Llaihder' in Manx, when the Royal Assent is announced.

The Freeman of Man gives three cheers for the Queen and then the Court returns to the Church of St John, where a meeting of the Lieutenant Governor, the Council and the House of Keys transacts purely formal business.

The Visite Royale in Jersey is in fact a visit to one easterly and one westerly parish each year by the Royal Court including the Bailiff and the Jurats with the Connétable, the Road Inspectors and Les Voyeurs – twelve men resident in the parish.

The Court is constituted and after prayers have been said, books and accounts examined and the Voyeurs have taken the oath, a procession is formed. The Connétable leads the way, followed by the Vicomte with a measuring rod, and a Vingtenier with an axe and the Voyeurs whose duty it is to remark on trees and encroachments on the road. In this way landowners whose property borders on the roads have to keep their hedges trimmed and trees pruned, or suffer fines.

At the end of the walk the Crown provides dinners for the Court and the Voyeurs.

A modern festival seen each July by thousands in Jersey is the Battle of Flowers. Clubs and societies and whole parishes enter for the Annual Battle of Flowers, choosing, months beforehand, some subject or topical theme with which to transform a lorry or horse-drawn 'float' into a flower-clad picture of beauty.

The prepared structures are decorated feverishly during the twenty-four hours before the Parade, and then are driven out, with their complement of laughing girls and boys on to the wide Victoria Avenue to meet the delighted applause of the waiting crowds.

The judges have a hard task to award the coveted 'Prix d'Honneur'. The traditional 'Battle' however means a quick destruction of all this loveliness.

Alderney celebrates the approach of summer with no contest but Milk-a-Punch Sunday on the first Sunday in May. In the old days anyone might go round the farms and milk the cows and collect eggs to make the Rum Punch. They provided their own rum, but all the other ingredients were 'collected'. Today things are not quite so carefree, but most of the inns serve free Rum Punch to all their customers and many private parties are given. The punch is made with milk, rum, eggs and nutmeg, and is served in large bowls, ladled out with a soup ladle.

Local Skills

CORN DOLLIES

The making of corn dollies derives from old pagan ceremonies celebrated at one time in all parts of the world. The ceremonies were associated with the corn spirit which was supposed to live in the cornfield and die as the last sheaf was cut. To bring the spirit to life again a plaited straw ornament called a corn doll or kern baby was made from the last corn of the harvest. It was not necessarily made to look like a figure, but was respected as being the last resting-place of the corn spirit and was kept in the house until the next harvest to ensure the continuance of the crops.

Straw ornaments are also put on the top of ricks. At Little Waltham in Essex and Whalton in Northumberland, the last sheaf to be cut is dressed as a doll, her clothes being made of coloured paper, though head and hands are formed by the ears of corn. The doll goes to church for Harvest Festival, as in fact the pagan corn dolly has been turned into a Christian symbol of harvest. In Overbury, Worcestershire, corn is twisted into the shape of a pyramid with miniature 'dollies' at each corner and hung in the church porch. Members of a detachment of Gurkhas who visited Overbury were very interested in the 'dollies' as they said there was a similar tradition in Nepal.

Material and General Construction

Present-day farming methods demand a short, stiff straw, not altogether suitable for making Corn Dollies. The ideal is a long straw which is pliable down to the first joint, with sufficient cavity to enable joining one stalk with another.

Corn is a general term meaning wheat, barley, oats and rye. Corn Dollies can be made from any or all of these. The straw of oats or barley, though not of such pleasing colour as wheat, is more easily worked.

The corn should be gathered when just on the turn from green to yellow. As only the straw down to the first joint is used, it should be cut immediately above this joint.

The Dolly is best made at once. The old ones were nearly always made in the harvest field, but if it is impossible to use the straw at once, it should be soaked, until pliable, in rain-water in a butt or clean oil-drum. Care should be taken that the heads rest on wire-netting out of the water to ensure that they do not sprout. Having made the straw pliable, wrap it up in an old sack and leave it overnight.

Originally the Dolly was made from the corn of the last sheaf, but modern varieties of corn tend to become too stiff, and so the first corn is to be preferred.

Dollies can be tied with ordinary string, red or yellow ribbon, bass, or linen thread. Their shapes vary enormously. Some are made with a central core of corn, which is either partially or completely covered with a pattern made from the straw; while with others the pattern is achieved by weaving the individual stalks into a formal twisted cone. Others again consist of simple wheat plaits.

In Wales toys were made with the same patterns, using rushes instead of corn. Most European Corn Dollies are made by tying together single pieces of straw to form geometric shapes.

Joining

Avoid handling straw except at the point of work. Do not wait until straw is stiff and splits. Cut off any damaged portion and insert the thin end (with head removed) of a new straw of suitable size.

In fine work the twist holds the join in place, but in larger spirals the join is generally made immediately before a twist, and only the preceding and succeeding twists hold it in place. It is wise to distribute the joins throughout the work.

Seven Plait

Fig. 1. Tie together seven straws as near heads as possible and spread them out.

Fig. 2. Fold 'A' over 'F' and 'C', so that it lies in the space between 'C' and 'E'.

Fig. 3. Fold 'B' over 'G' and 'D', to lie in 'A's' original place. Fold 'C' over 'A' and 'E', to lie in 'B's' original place. This movement is repeated throughout. Each straw passes clockwise over two straws, thus 'D' passes over 'B' and 'F' into 'C's' original place and 'E' passes over 'C' and 'G' into 'D's' original place.

Fig. 4. Finished Plait

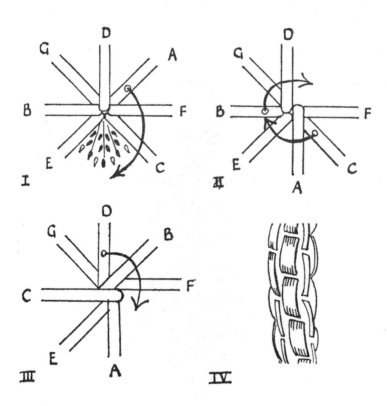

No two Corn Dollies are alike and in this lies their charm. In the older types, made quickly on the field, the corn stalks were often left unadorned and the whole effect is more individual and less finished than the elaborate ornamental examples made at leisure in the inn or barn.

Three Plait (Cat Foot)

It is important that the angles shown in the figures are maintained. The position of 'B' in Fig. 1 shows the line along which the plait must be built.

Fig. 2. Fold 'A' alongside 'B'.
Fig. 3. Fold 'B' over to take 'A's' original place.
Fig. 4. Fold 'C' alongside 'A'.
Fig. 5. Fold 'A' over to take 'C's' original place.

These four movements are repeated throughout.

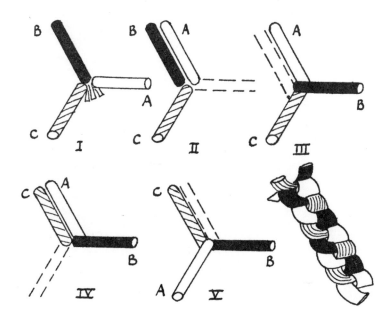

Two Plait

Fig. 1. Take two straws and place at right angles.

Fig. 2. Fold 'A' over 'B'.

Fig. 3. Give work a quarter-turn clockwise.

Fig. 4. Fold 'B' over 'A'.

These alternate movements are repeated throughout.

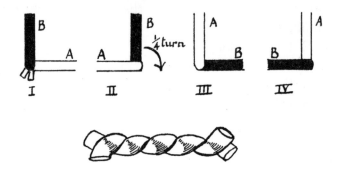

Local Recipes

DEVONSHIRE SPLITS

2lb flour	1½ teaspoons salt
1oz yeast	1 pint tepid milk or water
¼lb butter	2 teaspoons caster sugar

Put the yeast and sugar in a pudding basin and mix them for a minute. When they are liquid add the milk. Rub the butter into the flour, and make a hollow in the centre. Pour in the yeast and milk, and sprinkle the salt round the edge of the flour. Let it rise in a warm place for ten minutes.

When the top of the sponge is covered with bubbles stir in the flour and knead the dough on a floured board till smooth. Roll out the dough and cut it into small or medium-sized rounds. Place the splits on a greased tin, and let them 'prove' on the plate-rack till they have risen to twice their original size.

Bake in a quick oven for about 15 minutes. The splits are eaten with strawberry jam and clotted cream. Sufficient for sixteen splits, or more according to size.

CLOTTED CREAM

Use new milk and strain at once, as soon as milked, into shallow pans. Let it stand for 24 hours in winter and 12 hours in summer. Then put the pan on the stove, or better still, into a steamer containing water, and let it slowly heat until the cream begins to show a raised ring round the edge. When sufficiently cooked place in a cool dairy and leave for 12 or 24 hours. Great care must be taken in moving the pans, so that the cream is not broken, both in putting on the fire and taking off. When required skim off the cream in layers into a glass dish for the table, taking care to have a good 'crust' on the top. Clotted cream is best done over a stick fire.

Autumn

Season of mists and mellow fruitfulness!
Close bosom-friend of the maturing sun;
Conspiring with him how to load and bless
With fruit the vines that round the thatch-eaves run;
To bend with apples the moss'd cottage trees,
And fill all fruit with ripeness to the core;
To swell the gourd and plump the hazel shells
With a sweet kernel; to set budding more,
And still more, later flowers for the bees,
Until they think warm days will never cease,
For Summer has o'er-brimmed their clammy cells.

Who hath not seen thee oft amid thy store?
Sometimes whoever seeks abroad may find
Thee sitting careless on a granary floor,
Thy hair soft-lifted by the winnowing wind;
Or on a half-reap'd furrow sound asleep,
Drowsed with the fume of poppies, while thy hook
Spares the next swath and all its twinèd flowers;
And sometimes like a gleaner thou dost keep
Steady thy laden head across a brook;
Or by a cider-press, with patient look,
Thou watchest the last oozings hours by hours.

From 'To Autumn' by John Keats

August Bank Holiday seems to be the height of the summer, the beginning of the holidays; but a few weeks later autumn has begun. This is the busiest time of all the year for most Women's Institute members; so busy in fact that there is very seldom a meeting in August. A few, no doubt, are on holiday themselves; but most countrywomen whether as relations or friends, or as the farmer's wife with a few rooms to let or as a seaside landlady, are hard at work providing the holidays for all those who rush from the towns. Many farmers' wives are as preoccupied with the harvest as their husbands, helping in the fields or taking out substantial meals to

158

the men – Cornish pasties and farm-brewed West Country cider perhaps. Others, whether they are the wives of professional fruit-growers or simply housewives with a small garden and orchard, are busy in their kitchens, bottling or canning or pickling or watching the froth rise and spill from fermenting plums or blackberries–potent home-made wine for the next spring.

For those who are bargain-minded, this is the bargain season of the hedgerows and fields: elderberries, rosehips, blackberries, mushrooms and fungi, hazel nuts and sweet chestnuts, and by the end of the autumn, when the gales have blown all the leaves away, the willow, the poplar, the hazel sticks and the wild clematis for baskets.

As a result of all these riches, this is perhaps too, one of the busiest times of the year for the hundred and fifty W.I. markets. These market stalls which are set up in many parts of the country in country towns have an annual turnover of more than £220,000, of which more than £200,000 is returned to producers. Here is the countrywoman's opportunity to sell the surplus from an outstanding crop of Cox's Orange Pippins; the earliest, smallest Brussels Sprouts, the pot of raspberry jam or the home-made Swiss Roll to the more than willing city visitor. But as in all crafts, the W.I. members insist upon the professional finish – the properly graded fruit, the correctly bunched flowers. And no doubt the same standards must apply if you are not a W.I. member but sell your small surplus direct to your local fruiterer or flower shop.

The nights get colder and the skies more brilliant. It is the time of shooting stars; country people begin to think of the winter ahead. The fragile Roman hyacinths for Christmas should be in their bowls under the stairs. Hydrangeas and primulas are brought into the house, cyclamen and azaleas and cinerarias are potted in readiness for the winter.

As the evenings shorten we take up our needles again – to turn all that remains from a summer dressmaking session into a patchwork quilt or to decorate aprons with a flourish of Dorset Feather Stitchery. Institute activities begin again. A school perhaps is held in the county town for the theatrically-minded who spend two glorious days making up their friends as harridans or heroines or constructing a heavily bejewelled Norman belt or Tudor crown from a pile of old newspapers.

At this time of year many different County and Inter-County meetings are organised for members – sometimes in the form of schools for Handicrafts, for Drama or Music; sometimes as opportunities to hear about other countries and their women's organisations like our own; sometimes to help us understand atomic and other scientific developments; sometimes to go to our own Council Meetings as a delegate to discuss our own affairs. But from these occasions emerge perhaps the most remarkable achievements of all – thousands of countrywomen willingly and ably speaking in public at such meetings, taking back accounts to their own W.I.s and preparing talks for their County Panels of Speakers.

From the Garden into the Kitchen

THE MARKETING OF FRUIT AND VEGETABLES

Good grading and presentation will not turn bad produce into good, but lack of grading, combined with careless packing, will ruin even first-class produce.

FRUIT

All soft fruit should be sent in to market in clean punnets or chips. Where ½lb or 1lb punnets are used it is possible to get trays holding a dozen punnets. All fruit continues to ripen after it is picked and should, therefore be picked before fully mature.

Punnets or chips should be covered, but care should be taken to see that where transparent film is used, it is the correct moisture-proof variety with ventilation, otherwise moisture will form on the under-surface of the film, making it impossible to see the fruit and causing mould to grow. Grading should always be practised. Care should be taken in the harvesting and storage of apples and pears.

Apples

Separate hand-picked apples from windfalls. Keep varieties separate and do not market long-keeping varieties until they are ready. Apples should be clean and bright, reasonably free from skin blemishes and graded according to size. Send in packed either in chips or apple trays and pack carefully.

Blackcurrants

Currants should be firm, of reasonable size, not over-ripe, black in colour, free from leaves, dust and strings deficient of berries. When marketed on strings, should contain very few red or green currants. Market in punnets or chip baskets with cover.

Red and White Currants

As above, but always marketed on strings.

Cherries

Should be of good size, free from cracks. Should be picked with stalk. Black varieties coloured dark black or red. White varieties coloured yellow over whole surface with red tinge. Should be picked when firm and dry. Market in chips or punnets.

Gooseberries

Dessert varieties picked so as to be at correct ripeness when sold. All gooseberries in container should be reasonably uniform in size and of same variety. Market in chips or punnets.

Cooking varieties. All berries should be reasonably uniform in size, unripe and wholly green and hard, free from skin blemish and disease. Market in chips or baskets.

Grapes

Grapes should be mature, firm and free from mildew. They should be marketed in bundles of approximately ½lb or 1lb and should be carefully packed in order to preserve their bloom. Folded tissue paper should line the chips or punnets, and if more than one bunch is packed in container, each individual bunch should be wrapped in paper.

Loganberries

Pick when bright red in colour but not over-ripe. Do not pick with calyx. The berries should be reasonably uniform in size and should be marketed in punnets or chips.

Pears

Keep varieties separate. Market dessert pears ripe but not over-ripe. Should be free from blemish. No badly malformed fruit should be included. Market in chips.

Plums

Pick when mature but not over-ripe. Avoid fruit with cracks, wasp or bird damage. The fruit packed in each container should be uniform in colour and reasonably graded according to size.

Greengages should be marketed with stalks. Other varieties without. Send in chips or punnets.

Raspberries

Berries should be firm, not over-ripe and should be dry at time of picking and free from mildew and withered berries. The plug may be removed or not, as wished. Send in punnets or chips.

Strawberries

Should be picked firm with not less than two-thirds of the berry coloured. All fruit should be picked with calyx attached. Varieties should not be mixed and fruit should be reasonably graded according to size. Small strawberries can be marketed towards the end of the season as jam strawberries. Send in punnets or chips.

VEGETABLES

Artichokes

(June to September)
Globe. Cut with not more than 3-inch stem when leaves are good green, firm, compact and tender, before the flower bud has opened or turned purple. Should be sent packed in lined box or tray or punnet, graded according to size to help in easy pricing.

Artichokes

(October through Winter)
Jerusalem. Grow non-knobbly variety. Send in clean and dry, as even in size as possible, packed in punnets, boxes or baskets.

Asparagus

(Early May to mid-June)
Shoots should be reasonably straight and the buds reasonably closed. Grade into bundles according to thickness of shoot. Tie with two bands or ties, and trim stems even across bottom. Bundles should not contain more than 25 shoots and vary in size according to grade and season. Should be sent in to market packed in lined boxes or baskets with heads facing inwards.

Beans

(June to September)
Broad. Market young and tender before the eye of each bean has turned black. Pods should be straight as possible, free from disease and with at least five beans (Broad Windsor type four). Market in boxes or chips or half-bushel basket. Do not mix the long type and Broad Windsor type in same container.

Beans

(June to September)
French. Market when young and tender, pods as straight as possible. At beginning of season make into 1lb or ½lb bundles (two ties or bands), pack into chips or boxes.

Beans

Runner. Market young and tender, pods should be reasonably straight, green, free from stringiness and discoloration. Market in chips, half-bushel baskets or boxes.

Beetroot

(August onwards)
Store in dry sand, ashes or clamp. Should be marketed free from dirt, not flanged or split, red colour throughout, not woody. When young tie in bundles of 4 to 6. From store send in boxes or chips. Cooked beetroot sells best on W.I. markets. Wrap in greaseproof paper or cellophane.

Broccoli and Cauliflower

(October-April)
Should be cut when the curd is white or creamy white, firm and compact. Outside leaves should be trimmed back to just cover curd. Heads should be packed in boxes, crates or chips, curds facing inwards.

Brussels Sprouts

(September onwards)
Sprouts should be fresh, good green, reasonably uniform in size and shape and firm. Market in chips, baskets or sprout net.

Cabbage

(September onwards for Autumn; April onwards for Winter)
Heads should be firm and compact, outer leaves trimmed, free from
dirt and damage by insect and frost. Pack in crates or boxes, heads
to centre.

Carrots

(May onwards)
Early carrots should be reasonably uniform in size, tender, firm,
bright, reasonably smooth and regular in shape. Tops should be
uncut and fresh. Tie firmly in ½lb bundles and market in crates,
boxes, or chips. Tops to outside.

Main crop carrots sold unbunched with tops removed. Should
be reasonably uniform in size, firm, free from splits or fangs, clean.
If washed, must be marketed dry. Send in boxes, crates, or chips.

Celery

(October onwards)
Heads should be close, roots trimmed, hearts reasonably blanched
and clean, free from insect and frost damage. Pack in crates or boxes.
Better not to wash.

Celeriac

(September onwards)
Trim, send in free from dirt. Pack in boxes, crates, or chips.

Chicory

(November to May)
Tight, well-balanced heads, tips yellow – not less than 5 inches long,
free from sand, etc. No roots. Pack in layers in lined box or chip,
heads inwards. Usually sold by the pound.

Corn Salad

(December onwards)
Should be marketed crisp and free from soil. Pack into chips.

Cucumber

(July to October, earlier under glass)
Even colour, straight as possible, mature but not over-ripe. Pack in boxes or chips, lined.

Endive

(All Winter)
Heads reasonably uniform in size, hearts well developed and blanched, leaves green, reasonably compact, free from dirt, outer leaves trimmed. Packed in lined boxes, crates or chips, heads to centre.

Kales

(All Winter)
Tender, green, free from yellow discoloured leaves, should consist of young leaves and growing point of plant stem. Packed in boxes or chips.

Kohl Rabi

(July onwards)
Even-coloured, trimmed, free from dirt. Pack dry in boxes or baskets.

Leeks

(September onwards)
Stem blanched, firm, outer leaves green. Tops trimmed. Total length of leek should not be more than 15 inches, roots trimmed. Medium-sized leeks sell best. Market in bunches of either ½lb or 1lb. Tie firmly. Send packed in boxes or crates, heads to centre in layers.

Lettuce

(All year round)

Grade according to size and firmness of heart, must be clean, crisp and compact. Leave very short root beneath leaves and trim outer discoloured base leaves. Put rubber band or tie round Cos when necessary. Send in lined boxes, crates or baskets, packed hearts to middle.

Maize (Sweetcorn)

(July to September)

Cobs to be reasonably uniform in size. Leaves green, grain even milky, not too deep yellow. 1 inch of shank can be left at base. Pack in boxes, crates or chips.

Marrow

(July to October)

Sell best when small and tender, skin smooth and reasonably from thin, free from blemish, soil and bruising. Send in boxes or baskets.

Mustard and Cress

(All the year round)

Clean and fresh, reasonably free from seeds, stalks white, leaves green. Usually cut and marketed in small punnets, each kind separately, but can be sold mixed.

Onions

(Spring)

Fresh, tender, bulb small and white, leaves fresh green, free from discoloration. Tie in small bundles 6 to 12.

Onions

(September onwards)
Matured. Must be firm, bright and sound. Tops twisted off. Free from thick necks, loose skin, roots or dirt. Good size. Send in boxes, baskets, chips or string in rope.

Parsnip

Well shaped, not split or woody, reasonably free from dirt. Well trimmed. Pack in boxes, baskets or chips.

Pea

(June to October)
Pods fresh, well developed, firm and well filled. Do not send in 'flatties' at beginning of season and sell old peas for soup at end of season. Market in chips.

Pea Bean

(July to October)
Fresh and tender, well filled.

Sugar Pea

Fresh and tender, well filled. Pale yellow in colour, not shelled.

Potatoes

(May-July Earlies; July-September Seconds; September onwards Main)
Market free from soil. New potatoes are sometimes weighed up into 3lb or 7lb lots. No diseased pig or seed-sized potatoes should be included in main crop. Send in sacks. New in baskets or boxes.

Radish

(April to October and Winter radish)
Young, bright in colour, graded according to size. Tops fresh and green, bunched according to local custom. Pack in boxes, chips, or with other salad crops in mixed baskets.

Rhubarb

(March to April)
Forced. Avoid very thin stems. Grade reasonably according to size. Must be fresh and firm. If forced, leaf should be bright yellow (except Bristol type, when leaf may be green). Market in ½lb or 1lb bundles, tie firmly with two ties or bands.

(April to July)
Natural. Fresh, firm, not coarse, reasonably uniform in size, not more than 2-inch leaf. Tie firmly two ties in ½lb or 1lb bundles.

Salsify

(October)
Tender, free from dirt and roots. Marketed like parsnips.

Seakale

(January to May)
Fresh, firm, ivory in colour with pink or purple tinge to ends of stems, which should be thick and fleshy, root crown trimmed away to not more than 1 inch. Send in lined baskets, chips or boxes, heads to centre. Sell by 1lb.

Shallots

(August onwards)
Well shaped, matured, clean, firm and not peeled. Free from splits, sent in baskets or chips.

Spinach

Summer and Winter picked carefully, free from soil and brown leaves. Pack in chips. Spinach beet can be tied in bundles ¼lb or ½lb.

Tomatoes

(July to October)
Firm, well-coloured but not over-ripe fruit. Grade according to size and put different sizes in different containers. Send in lined chips. Sound, green tomatoes can be sold for chutney. Send in chips.

MAKING WINE AND CIDER AT HOME

Legal Position

Home-made wines and ciders may be made quite freely provided they are not sold. This applies both to private sales or to the giving of wines for subsequent sale for charity.

Anyone wishing to make wines or ciders for sale must comply with current regulations.

It should be realised that many home-made wines have a very high alcoholic content and should, therefore, be drunk in moderation. They should not, of course, be given to children any more than bought alcoholic beverages.

Principles of Wine-Making

Making wines at home is a fascinating hobby. There is the collection of the raw material, which often means a walk in the countryside; making the extract; watching the wine through its fermentation and the bottling with the help of the family. Finally comes the proud moment when all are introduced to the matured wine. Sometimes this is not the happy occasion that the itinerant wine-maker had pictured. It is the purpose of this article to outline methods whereby these misfortunes may be prevented. No one seriously expects to make anything like an expensive chateau-bottled vintage wine, but there is no reason why all the home-made products should not be clean in flavour and a pleasure to drink.

Only three things are required for making a wine: the right equipment, a properly prepared extract and a good yeast.

Equipment

When choosing equipment for wine-making it is essential to avoid anything made of iron, copper, zinc (galvanising), lead, antimony, resinous woods, or such plastics as bakelite and P.V.C. This still leaves glass, porcelain, lead-free enamel or glazed-ware, aluminium, stainless-steel, silver- or tin-plate, most woods and polythene.

Most of the implements are found in the kitchen – a chopping board, a sharp knife, simple juice squeezer, large saucepan or preserving pan, a bowl, jug or bucket, muslin, funnel, jars of 1-, 2- or 3-gallon capacity, air-locks, bottles and corks. A few chemicals will also be required and these are detailed later in this article.

Preparation of the Extract

The secret of a good wine lies in the preparation of the extract; a bad extract can never be turned into a good wine. Three points must always be observed; a clean dry raw material, removal of pectin, and destruction of spoilage yeasts and bacteria.

The raw material should be gathered on dry sunny days and it should be free of obvious mould growth; wet fruit, flowers, etc, will go mouldy very rapidly and give the final wine a musty taint.

Pectin is a complex molecule with a sticky nature that holds back juice in the fruit cells of the pulp and also leaves the final wines hazy by holding particles in suspension. It is broken down into more simple and soluble molecules partly by an enzyme from the fruit cells and partly by another secreted by some yeasts. Alternatively, one of several commercial pectin-destroying enzymes (known variously as Pectozyme, Pectinal, Pektinase, etc), containing both enzymes, may be used instead.

These enzymes are destroyed on heating so that it is best to make extracts using cold or only lukewarm water. Water at this temperature will not destroy spoilage organisms, whereas boiling, which would do so, also prevents the natural breakdown of pectin. Fortunately these organisms are sensitive to sulphur dioxide, making boiling unnecessary. Some special points should be observed in preparing extracts from certain raw materials. These are discussed below.

Fruits. Apart from the problems of pectin and bacteria, some fruits, such as blackcurrants, red currants, gooseberries, etc, are extremely acid. Either the excessive acidity must be diluted with a large volume of water or it may be partially neutralised with small quantities of an alkali, such as potassium carbonate, chalk or egg shell. The fruit should always be gathered ripe when it will contain its maximum sugar content and a minimum of starch.

Citrus Fruits. It is relatively easy to make extracts from citrus fruits, since the fruit cells are fragile and possess a strong pectin-destroying enzyme. The skins should be scrubbed thoroughly, grated or peeled thinly (leaving the bitter white pith behind) and the juice squeezed out from the halved fruit; the remaining ingredients are then added and the mixture put in a fermentation jar. Mandarins, tangerines and similar fruits have more subtle flavours than oranges; grapefruit should be used in moderation unless a bitter wine is liked; lemons are usually too acid to use on their own, but are valuable for increasing the acidity of a low acid juice.

Soft Fruits. Berries must be collected dry as they can go mouldy after only a few hours in a collecting basket. The fruit can be crushed in a large saucepan or preserving pan using a clean block of wood or the base of a strong bottle. Add the amount of water given in the recipe followed by the sulphur dioxide, which is added conveniently in the form of Campden tablets. Use ½ a tablet for very acid juices (blackcurrants, etc) and 2 tablets for medium acid juices (blackberries, raspberries) for every gallon of water. In case the fruit contains very little pectin-destroying enzyme, ¼ to ½oz of the commercial product may also be added for the same amount of water. Yeast the mixture twenty-four hours afterwards and leave two or three days if made from white fruits (e.g. gooseberries); six to eight days are required for red fruits to allow maximum extraction of the colour. Afterwards, pour the pulp and water through muslin and squeeze hard. If the extract came from very acid fruits, add ¼oz. of B.P. quality potassium carbonate or two clean crushed egg shells per gallon.

A more richly coloured juice, but with a less fresh flavour, can be made by heating the pulp in a double saucepan until the juice runs freely. A commercial pectin-destroying enzyme must always be added after this treatment.

Pome Fruits. It is difficult to extract juice from apples and pears without using a fruit press. Some suggestions are given in the section on '**Cider**' (See page 185).

Stone Fruits. The washed fruit is chopped coarsely with a knife and the requisite amount of boiling water poured on top. When cool, add the enzyme and yeast. Leave the mixture no more than forty-eight hours before squeezing through muslin; if left longer an undesirable and persistent flavour will be extracted from the stones.

Dried Fruits. Leave the fruit to soak for three hours, drain and chop coarsely or mince. Add the amount of cold water and sulphur dioxide given in the recipe, followed twenty-four hours later by a yeast culture. Forty-eight hours later strain the mixture through muslin.

Vegetables. Potatoes, parsnips and beetroots are the vegetables mainly used in wine-making, although there are recipes for swedes, turnips, etc (Rhubarb is usually grouped with fruits for the purposes of wine-making because of its high acidity.) If the following points are observed excellent wines can be prepared from these raw materials. Use old, well-scrubbed roots, cut into thin slices or small cubes and drop into a saucepan containing the necessary quantity of cold water. Leaving off the lid, bring the water to the boil and allow to simmer until a fork can just be pushed into the pieces. Remove from the heat and strain through muslin but do not squeeze the pulp. When the extract is cool, add the juice of a lemon, or ½oz citric acid, to each gallon, 3 Campden tablets and ¼oz of a commercial pectin-destroying enzyme. Pour the mixture into the fermenting jar and add the yeast culture.

Flowers and Herbs. Flowers must be steeped in cold water as their delicate fragrances will be destroyed if they are heated. Dissolve the sugar in the water, pour over the flower heads in a tall jug, and add any other ingredients, followed by the yeast. Cover with a thick cloth and leave for fourteen days, mixing the contents of the jug once or twice a day. Strain off through muslin, pour the extract into a fermentation jar and fit an air-lock. Occasionally herbs may need to be simmered for about twenty minutes, especially if they are dry or contain a lot of woody tissue. Strain through muslin before sugaring and yeasting.

Yeast Cultures

Yeasts are living single-celled plant-like organisms that multiply by budding. Just like any other living creatures, they must be kept alive by being supplied with nutrients, moisture, air, and kept at a reasonable temperature. Without these conditions yeast cultures cannot be kept alive for very long. Hence they should be used as soon as possible after purchase; dried yeasts, being in a state of suspended animation, will remain alive longer, but even so keep them in a cool, dry cupboard.

Several sorts of yeasts may be used for wine-making. The best type is a wine yeast; such yeasts have long been accustomed to growing in highly alcoholic solutions and have the added advantage of settling out readily at the end of the fermentation. These yeasts can be obtained from a number of suppliers, who usually give the necessary directions for activating the culture before use. In the absence of these directions it is necessary to boil for twenty minutes a mixture consisting of ¾ pint of water and 1oz each of sugar and raisins. Strain into a previously warmed pint bottle and plug with non-absorbent cotton-wool. When cool add the yeast culture and keep at 60°-70°F until the mixture starts to froth; it is then ready for addition to 1 to 3 gallons of juice. Should many gallons of juice require yeasting, add the activated culture to the first gallon; when this starts to ferment, add this to the remaining juice or extract.

Fermentation

Once the yeasted juice has been put in a fermentation jar, an air-lock (or a cork with a fine slit cut down the side) must be inserted. This device keeps a small back pressure of carbon dioxide above the fermenting juice, thus keeping out air and preventing the growth of any vinegar bacteria or film yeasts.

For a short time after the addition of the yeast culture, no obvious change appears to take place. In fact the yeast cells are absorbing air, a little sugar, nitrogenous matter, vitamins and mineral salts. The cells swell in size and each produces a small bud, which also enlarges until it is as big as the mother cell. At this stage the mother cell forms a second bud and shortly afterwards the first daughter cell does the same. In this way the number of cells increases rapidly until most of the available nutrients are absorbed. Mature buds split off at intervals: if all separate then the yeast will not deposit when fermentation is complete; the best type of wine yeast tends to remain in small clumps and to settle out readily.

After one or two days all the oxygen will have disappeared from the juice and the yeast lives anaerobically, that is, it ferments.

During fermentation the sugar is broken down to alcohol and carbon dioxide. At this stage gas bubbles appear at the surface and froth is also formed. The amount of froth produced depends on the quantity of pectin in the juice. As soon as the pectin is broken down by the pectin-destroying enzymes, froth is no longer formed and the bubbles break on reaching the surface.

Yeast growth (and fermentation) continue until the number of living yeast cells reaches a maximum. If the original juice was rich in nutrients (ie from fruit grown on heavily manured land), the number of new cells formed thereafter equal the number of old cells that die, consequently the number of living yeasts remains fairly constant. Should the juice have been low in nutrients, insufficient new cells are formed and the total number of living cells decreases steadily for the remainder of the fermentation.

In extreme cases, the yeast may die out before the fermentation is complete, leaving the wine low in alcohol and unnaturally sweet. This can be remedied by the addition of the following nutrients to each gallon of wine: one level saltspoon of B.P. quality ammonium sulphate or diammonium hydrogen phosphate and one milligramme of Vitamin Bl. This vitamin is also known as aneurine or thiamin; it is sold as tablets of several milligramme weights under a variety of trade names such as Benerva, etc. All the yeasts may have died out if the fermentation has stopped for a long time; if fermentation does not start within ten days after adding the nutrients, then a fresh yeast culture must also be added. The wine will now continue to ferment steadily until all the sugar has been consumed, when it is said to be dry.

Different Types of Wine

At this stage one must decide what type of wine is required – dry, sweet, still or sparkling. Dry wines, whether still or sparkling, are drunk with meals to increase the appetite. Sweet wines are better drunk with a dessert or on social occasions; sweet, sparkling wines are also suitable at these times, but, being more difficult to prepare, should only be attempted after some experience of winemaking has been gained. The necessary methods are given below:

Dry, Still Wines. The first fermented wine is taken into a cold room and left for two or three weeks to allow most of the yeast to settle out. The wine is carefully siphoned off with a rubber tube into a clean jar, leaving the yeast deposit behind in the original jar. The second jar must be full, if necessary top up with a little water, sealed with a cork and waxed over. The jar of wine is kept in the coolest room in the house for six months, then siphoned off into bottles. Seal the bottles with screw stoppers or corks as appropriate for the bottle. Soak bark corks for one hour in lukewarm water before use; the new plastic stoppers need only be moistened. Store the bottles on their sides for a few more months before drinking the wines. The wines may be drunk, of course, soon after bottling, but the flavour of a sound wine improves with storage.

Dry, Sparkling Wines. Instead of storing the jar of dry wine for six months, wait only until it clears; then siphon into strong champagne bottles, adding a small cube of sugar to each bottle. Cork and wire down tightly, store the bottles on their sides in a warm cupboard until a line of yeast deposit can be seen inside the bottles. Transfer to the coolest room and leave two or three months. Two days before the wine is required, put the bottle upright to allow the yeast to settle to the bottom of the bottle. If the wine can also be chilled for two hours in a refrigerator before serving, it will enhance its flavour and sparkle.

Sweet, Still Wines. It is necessary to stabilise a sweet wine by increasing its alcohol content until the yeasts are killed, there is then no danger of the wine re-fermenting once it has been bottled. Many years ago brandy was added for this purpose, but with the present price of spirits this is no longer possible. Instead the alcohol content is increased by progressive fermentation. Dissolve ¾lb of sugar in each gallon of first-fermented wine but do not siphon it from off the yeast deposit. Replace the air-lock and keep the jar warm. Fermentation will slowly recommence and gas bubbles will be produced for a time. When these cease, taste the wine, and if it does not taste sweet then all the added sugar has been consumed, or, if it has some sweetness, all the yeast cells have died. If dry, add another ½lb sugar per gallon and again allow the wine to ferment; eventually the wine will cease fermenting because of the high alcohol content, and remain sweet. The wine can be sweetened further to taste, if necessary, siphoned into a storage jar, an air-lock inserted and the jar put in a cool room. If the aeration introduced during siphoning does not encourage further fermentation after three weeks, replace the air-lock with a cork and wax over. Store, siphon and bottle as given for dry, still wines.

Sweet, Sparkling Wines. When the first fermented wine has clarified in the storage jar, sweeten ½ pint with ¾oz of sugar, put into a 1-pint champagne bottle, cork and wire down securely. Keep this bottle on its side in an airing cupboard and examine at weekly intervals. Should the wine form a thick yeast-line in the bottle and the cork strain against the wire, then the bulk of the stored wine is too young to be treated. Wait another month and repeat the test; this testing is repeated until only a thin yeast-line is formed after three to four weeks with a reasonable but not violent gas pressure in the bottle. The bulk of the wine can now be siphoned, sweetened at the rate of ¾lb sugar per gallon, bottled, corked and wired securely. Store the bottles on their sides in a cool room for several months after which the wine is ready for drinking. Two days before it is required stand a bottle upright and chill two hours before serving.

Final Notes

In this chapter and the recipes that follow, the instructions have been based on a unit of one gallon. While this is suitable for beginners, experienced wine-makers will know that it is better to ferment 3- or even 4½-gallon batches. The percentage loss on siphoning is reduced and there is much less chance of undesirable oxidation changes taking place.

Wines can be improved even further if several are blended together after fermentation. Thus a mixture of elderberry, damson and blackberry, when mature, is better than the individual wines. Similarly a dandelion, elderflower and cowslip mixture makes a delightful white wine. Blending gives ample scope for experiment and is one of the pleasures of wine-making.

If the raw material has been extracted and fermented as outlined, the wines will never be vinegary or obstinately hazy.

★★★★★

TYPICAL RECIPES

Two recipes are given in full while only the quantities and special directions for starting the wine are given for the remainder. Reference should be made to the relevant sections of *Principles of Wine-making* for the necessary details.

Blackberry Wine

Ripe blackberries	White sugar
Campden tablets	Yeast

Blackberries are a most versatile raw material for winemaking; it is possible to prepare from them dry, rosé or red dinner wines or a full-bodied dessert wine. A few sloes added to the blackberries give an even more fully-flavoured wine.

Collect ripe fruit on a dry day and remove most of the stems and leaves. Put in an aluminium preserving pan, crush with the flat end of a bottle and just cover the mash with boiling water. For a rosé-type of wine add an equal volume of boiling water. Mix in two crushed Campden tablets and ½oz Pectozyme (obtainable from Messrs Norman Evans & Rais Limited, Unity Mills, Woodley, Stockport, Cheshire), for each fourteen pounds of fruit. Next day add a wine yeast culture or baker's yeast. Leave three days covered with a cloth, mixing the contents of the pan twice a day. Pour through a coarse cloth and squeeze out the liquid from the pulp: dissolve 3lb sugar in each gallon of combined extract. Fill a jar (or jars) with the sweetened liquid and leave in a room at 55°–65°F. Froth may be produced for a few days; when it ceases, clean the outside of the jar and insert an air-lock or loosely fitting bung. Gas bubbles will continue to be evolved until all the sugar has been consumed. At this stage, further processing will depend on the type of wine required.

For a dry wine the jar must be moved to a cold room and left for 14 days. The wine is then siphoned into a fresh jar (without carrying over the yeast deposit) which is completely filled and sealed and left until the wine is clear. The wine is again siphoned from any deposit and run into bottles which are corked, wired and stored on their sides for a few months before drinking the wine. Dry sparkling wines can be made by adding a lump of sugar to each bottle before corking.

Sweet wines can be made by dissolving another ¾lb sugar in each gallon of dry, unsiphoned wine and allowing fermentation to continue. Siphon off this wine, sweeten to taste, store under an air-lock and if no further fermentation occurs, re-siphon, sweeten to taste, store and bottle as for dry still wines. If fermentation sets in after this last sweetening, allow it to continue under an air-lock, re-sweeten, store, siphon and bottle.

Dandelion Wine

Dandelion heads	1 gallon water
4½lb white sugar	3 Campden tablets
Yeast	

With a pair of scissors cut off the petals from *freshly picked* dandelion heads, leaving behind the bitter green 'button' on top of the stalks. Collect about a quart measure of pressed-down petals and add 1 gallon of cold water in which the sugar and Campden tablets have been previously dissolved; next day add a wine yeast or fresh baker's yeast. Fill a jar with the liquid, and leave for two days, mixing up the contents two or three times a day. Strain through muslin, squeeze the residue dry and fill a jar with the liquid. Fit an air-lock, or loosely fitting bung, and keep at 55°-65°F until gas bubbles no longer form. Leave in a cool room for four weeks, siphon off the wine from the yeast deposit, sweeten to taste (usually ¾lb per gallon is sufficient), return to the cleaned jar and refit the air-lock. *If* the wine does not re-ferment after three months it is safe to siphon it off once more. Bottle, cork, wire down and store the bottles on their sides for at least another month before drinking the wine.

Damson Wine

3lb damsons	1 gallon water
3lb white sugar	2 Campden tablets
¼oz Pectozyme (optional)	Yeast

Select ripe sound fruit, remove the stalks, wash and drain. Place in a bowl and bruise well with a wooden spoon. Add the boiling water and when cool, the Campden tablets and Pectozyme; 24 hours later add the yeast. Leave six days, stirring at least once a day, then strain through muslin. Dissolve the sugar in the juice, put in a fermentation jar with an air-lock. Proceed according to the directions given for the type of wine required. The bottled wine will repay storing for at least two years.

Elderberry Wine

3lb elderberries	1 gallon water
3lb white sugar	2 Campden tablets
2 oranges	Yeast

Remove the berries from the stalks with a fork before weighing, then bruise in a bowl. Add the orange juice and grated rind and pour on the cold water in which the Campden tablets have been dissolved. Next day add the yeast and leave four to six days, stirring at least once each day. Strain through muslin, dissolve the sugar in the juice and proceed as directed for Blackberry wine.

Alternatively 1lb damsons and 3lb elderberries can be used instead; this is said to resemble Burgundy when prepared as a dry wine.

Parsnip Wine

2½lb parsnips	3 Campden tablets
3lb white sugar	⅓oz tartaric or citric acid
4oz Pectozyme	Yeast
1 gallon water	

Use well-frosted parsnips, scrub them thoroughly, cut out any scabs but do not peel the roots. Slice thinly or cut into small cubes and boil in the water until a fork can just be pushed into the sections, *never* allow the sections to go mushy. Leave the lid off the saucepan during boiling and replace any water lost during cooking. Strain the hot liquid through muslin, but do *not* squeeze the residue; add the sugar and acid to the hot liquid and stir until they have dissolved. When cool, add the Campden tablets and the Pectozyme and run into the fermentation jar. Twenty-four hours later add the yeast, insert an air-lock and keep warm. This wine is best prepared as a dry wine, either still or sparkling, according to preference.

If parsnip wine is made following these directions exactly, the result will be a brilliantly clear, vinous-flavoured, white dinner wine. It should have no trace of a parsnip or earthy flavour.

Raisin Wine

2lb muscatel raisins
2½lb white sugar
¼oz ammonium sulphate
  (B.P. quality)

1 gallon water
2 Campden tablets
3 mandarins or tangerines
Yeast

Just cover the raisins with cold water and allow to soak for three hours; pour off and discard this water. Chop the raisins coarsely and put in a tall jug with the thinly sliced mandarins or tangerines. Pour on top of the mixture a syrup made by dissolving the sugar, Campden tablets and ammonium sulphate in the gallon of water. Stir well and twenty-four hours later add the yeast. Leave for a week covered with a thick cloth, giving the contents an occasional stir. Strain through muslin, squeezing out any liquid retained in the pulp; put the combined liquids into a fermentation jar and insert an air-lock. Continue according to the directions previously given. This wine is most successful when prepared as a sweet, still wine.

Rosehip Wine

4 pints rosehips
3lb white sugar

1 gallon water
2 Campden tablets

Gather the rosehips after the first frost. Wash, drain and crush with a mallet. Dissolve the sugar and Campden tablets in the water and pour over the crushed rosehips that have previously been pushed into a jar. Next day add the yeast, insert an air-lock or loosely fitting cork and leave in a warm room until gas is no longer formed. When fermentation ceases, strain the liquid through muslin followed by organdie, put in a clean jar. Leave in a cool room and continue as detailed for Dandelion wine.

Sloe Wine

3lb sloes	1 gallon water
White sugar	Yeast

Put the washed and drained fruit, free from stalks, into a jug and pour on the boiling water. Mash the fruit well and, when cool, strain through muslin and dissolve 4lb sugar to each gallon of juice. Add the yeast and continue as for a sweet, still wine.

If ½ to 1 pint of brandy is added to the stabilised sweet wine before the final storage period, it will make a most attractive dessert wine.

CIDER

Ciders have a lower alcohol content than wines and thus are most useful for quenching the thirst; further, they do not need to be stored as long as wines.

Cider can be made from dessert apples or from the true cider apples of the West Country, each imparting its characteristic flavour to the beverage. Worcester Pearmain, Cox's Orange Pippin, the Russets and similar medium acid varieties may be used of the dessert sorts. If cider apples are available, choose such varieties as Kingston Black, Crimson King, Langworthy, or a blend of Sweet Alford or Sweet Coppin with a small quantity of cooking or crab apples. A few quince added to the mixture will impart a most delightful flavour. Never use cooking apples on their own, they are too acid.

The principal difficulty in preparing cider in the home is the extraction of juice from the fruit. Small fruit presses now on the market are suitable for pressing out apples, previously smashed with a mallet or piece of wood. Fresh juice may also be purchased quite reasonably in season if there is a cider-factory in the neighbourhood. In the absence of these short cuts the following recipe gives a useful but slightly laborious alternative.

Cottage Cider

Dessert or cider apples	Water
Campden tablets	White sugar
Pectozyme	Yeast

Wash, weigh and grate or mince the apples; do NOT use a grater or mincer made of zinc-plated (galvanised) metal. Put the pulp in a jug and, for every 14lb weight, add ½ gallon water, 2 Campden tablets and ½oz Pectozyme. Next day add the yeast culture and stir the mixture once or twice daily for a week. Run the contents of the jug through a thick cloth or two clean, heavy-gauge, nylon stockings one inside the other. Allow to drain overnight, squeeze out any remaining liquid and then discard the pulp. Dissolve ¾lb sugar in each gallon of extract and run into a fermentation jar; fit an air-lock and keep in a warm room until gas bubbles are no longer formed. Remove the jar to a cold room and when most of the yeast has settled out, siphon off the cider and run through organdie into a clean jar. Make sure this jar is full, if necessary topping up with water, cork and wax over. Keep in a cold room until the cider is quite clear. Siphon off again, leaving the yeast deposit behind; bottle, cork and wire as usual.

Many people prefer sparkling cider which can be prepared by adding one lump of sugar to each bottle (champagne type for preference) before filling. Alternatively, the cider can be sweetened with ¼lb sugar per gallon and bottled in strong screw-stopper bottles. Keep the bottles upright in a warm cupboard and loosen a stopper occasionally. The cider is ready for drinking when gas pressure develops in the bottles.

Cider should never be left in a half-filled cask, jar or bottle for more than a week, otherwise it will go vinegary. Cider, unlike wine, does not have sufficient alcohol to protect it against the ravages of this disorder.

PICKLES AND CHUTNEYS

A pickle is made of fruit or vegetable suitably prepared and then preserved by the addition of sweetened or unsweetened spiced vinegar. Pickles may be clear, sweet, mixed or crisp according to the type and method of preparation.

A chutney is a preserve made of fruits such as apples, gooseberries, plums, ripe or green tomatoes, to which are added onions, garlic, raisins, dates, salt, sugar and spices according to taste and variety. Vinegar is added and with the salt and spices acts as the preserving agent.

Equipment

To avoid a metallic flavour when making any preserve containing vinegar, pans and utensils must be made of enamel, monel metal or stainless steel.

Finishing, Labelling and Storing

Wash, dry and warm jars and bottles before filling. Pickles and chutneys need not less than three months to mature, and in order to avoid evaporation and shrinkage during this time careful covering is essential. A ceresin or plastic disc (vinegar resistant) under the metal top is a necessity. For home use the ceresin disc may be covered with white cotton or linen, tied down firmly, trimmed, and completely covered with paraffin wax, thereby making it airtight and preventing evaporation of the contents; alternatively, synthetic skin may be used. All preserves should be clearly and neatly labelled with kind, variety, day, month and year of making before storing in a cool, dark, dry place.

Ingredients

Salt. This draws the water and carbohydrates from the vegetables and at the same time causes a slight toughness and darkening of colour. It also prevents many bacteria from growing. Rock or cooking salt must be used, not table salt.

Vinegars. These may be brewed (ie wine, cider or malt) or non-brewed. Malt vinegar is often preferred as it gives a better flavour to pickles. Colourless vinegars are distilled and give a good appearance sometimes at the expense of flavour. Vinegar for pickling should have an acetic acid content of at least 5 per cent.

★Spiced Vinegar. The best flavoured spiced vinegar is made by putting the spices in muslin and leaving them to soak in the vinegar for one or two months, shaking the bottle often.

Quickly spiced vinegar is made by putting the vinegar and spices into a basin covered with a plate and standing in a saucepan of cold water. The water is heated slowly to boiling point, then removed from the heat and left to stand for at least two hours, when the vinegar is strained and ready for use.

The following quantity of spices tied in a muslin bag may

be used to each quart of vinegar: ¼oz cinnamon bark, ¼oz whole clove, ¼oz whole mace, ¼oz whole allspice, and a few peppercorns.

Tarragon, Mint and other Herb Vinegars. Rinse a wide-necked jar with vinegar, half fill with fresh leaves of the herb – the best flavour is obtained if the leaves are used before the flowering takes place – fill the jar with plain vinegar and cork tightly. It will take at least two weeks to get a well-flavoured vinegar. Mint sauce made with mint vinegar has a strong, typical flavour.

* The use of these vinegars in making chutneys and sauces gives a more varied flavour to the product.

PICKLES

Preparation. Prepare fresh vegetables, cutting to a uniform size. The pieces should be small enough to eat without further cutting, thus packing is easier and the vinegar penetrates evenly.

Brining. ½lb of rock or cooking salt to 4 pints of water. Dissolve the salt in the water, add the prepared vegetables, which must be submerged by covering with an upturned plate, and leave for 12 to 48 hours. Rinse the vegetables in cold water and drain thoroughly. This is important. Pack the vegetables in the jars up to the shoulder, cover with cold, spiced vinegar. Make sure that the vinegar fills the neck of the jar; there will be some evaporation in storage, but flavour and colour should be retained if the vegetables remain fully covered.

Dry salting is used in some cases, see recipe for pickled cabbage.

PICKLE RECIPES

Red Cabbage

Use a firm, well-coloured cabbage, cut into shreds, put layers of cabbage and salt alternately in a basin, finishing with a layer of salt. Leave twenty-four hours. Drain, rinse, pack loosely into jars, and cover with cold spiced vinegar. Finish. Cabbage is ready for use after one week.

Cauliflower

Fresh, unblemished cauliflowers are broken into small sprigs. Cover with brine. Leave twenty-four hours. Drain, rinse, pack, cover with cold spiced vinegar. Finish.

Onions or Shallots

Small, even-sized onions or shallots should be used for exhibition work. 'Silverskin' is one of the best onions to use. Put in brine for 12 hours, peel, replace in fresh brine, stand 24 to 36 hours. Rinse and drain. Pack and cover with cold spiced vinegar. It will take three months for the spiced vinegar to penetrate to the centre of the onion.

Mixed Pickle

Cauliflower, onions, small cucumbers, and french beans are a good mixture. Cut the vegetables into suitable pieces, soak in brine for 48 hours. Wash and drain, pack, cover with cold spiced vinegar. Finish.

*Beetroot

Wash, peel, cut into ¼-inch slices or cubes. Put 1 teacup of water, ½ teaspoon salt in a pan with a tight-fitting lid. When the water is boiling put in the prepared beetroot, bring quickly to boiling point, and cook for 10 to 15 minutes. Drain, and when cold pack into jars, and cover with spiced vinegar. Finish. This pickle is ready for eating within a week.

*Piccalilli

Suitable mixed vegetables are diced cucumber, marrow, beans, green tomatoes, small onions and sprigs of cauliflower.

3lb mixed vegetables	¾oz plain flour
¾oz dry mustard	4½oz sugar
½lb salt	¼oz turmeric
¾ teaspoon ground ginger	1½ pints white vinegar
4 pints water	

Make a brine of the salt and water, put in the vegetables, stand 24 hours. Drain and simmer for 20 minutes in the sugar, spices and 1¼ pints vinegar. Drain, pack the vegetables into hot jars. Blend the flour and turmeric with the remaining vinegar, add to the hot sauce and boil for 1 minute. Pour over the vegetables.

* Pickled beetroot and Piccalilli are neither crisp nor clear pickles so are not suitable for competitive work unless there are special classes.

Sweet Pickles

Sugar is added to the vinegar and spices, and this makes the pickle more palatable to those who dislike the acidity of vinegar.

Sweet Pickled Gooseberries, Damsons, Morello Cherries, Small Plums

4lb fruit	½oz allspice
2lb brown sugar	¼oz cinnamon
1 pint vinegar	Rind of ½ lemon
½oz cloves	

(The cloves, spice, cinnamon and lemon should be tied in a muslin bag.)

Pack the fruit into pickle jars and put in a warm oven. The low heat is continued until the fruit just begins to crack. The vinegar and the bag of spices must be simmered for ¾ hour. Remove pan from heat, add sugar, allow to dissolve, return to heat, bring to boiling point and boil rapidly for 5 minutes till thick. Pour over the fruit. Finish.

Sweet Pickled Apples, Quinces, Pears, Peaches, Apricots

4lb fruit	5 drops lemon juice
2lb sugar	1 pint spiced vinegar

Prepare fruit and cut into ¼-inch slices. Dissolve the sugar in the spiced vinegar, add the lemon juice and fruit. Simmer until the fruit is tender. Strain, returning the liquid to the pan. Pack the fruit in hot jars, keep hot. Meanwhile boil the liquid until it forms a thick vinegar syrup and then pour over the fruit. Finish.

CHUTNEYS

Personal tastes vary in chutney more than in any other preserve. A subtle blending of spices makes for a good-flavoured chutney. Fresh and dried fruits, onions and/or garlic, salt, sugar, spices, and bottled vinegar are used in chutneys which must be smooth and mellow. The ingredients should be chopped or minced. Cook the onion and garlic separately in a little boiling water, keeping the lid on the pan; they take a long time to soften, and will spoil the smoothness of texture if cooked with the other ingredients. A better chutney results if the vinegar is added in two parts. The chutney is of correct consistency when a spoon drawn through the mixture leaves a clear path and no trace of liquid.

Chutney Recipes

Apple

6lb apples, peeled, cored and minced
2lb onions, peeled and minced
2½lb brown sugar
½ pint water
2 pints vinegar
1½oz ground ginger
½oz ground cinnamon
¼ teaspoon cayenne pepper
1½oz rock or cooking salt

Cook the onions and apples separately, using ¼ pint water in each case. When tender, put in a pan with the spices and half the vinegar (1 pint). Simmer until all are tender and well mixed, add the sugar, the rest of the vinegar and simmer until the correct consistency is obtained. Finish.

Green Tomato

1lb apples, minced
3lb green tomatoes
½lb sultanas
½lb demerara sugar
½lb onions, minced
¾ pint vinegar
2 teaspoons ground ginger
½ level teaspoon cayenne pepper
1 level teaspoon dry mustard
½oz salt

Skin and slice the tomatoes, cook the onions separately, when tender put them to cook with the other ingredients in ½ pint vinegar. When the apples are pulped, add the rest of the vinegar and cook until the correct consistency is obtained. Finish.

Plum

2lb stoned plums	2 level teaspoons ground ginger
1lb apples	2 level teaspoons ground allspice
1lb onions	2 level teaspoons cayenne pepper,
1lb raisins	clove, ground nutmeg and mustard
6oz demerara sugar	1 pint vinegar

Method as above.

Ripe Tomato

6lb tomatoes	1 level teaspoon paprika
½lb onions	¾oz rock or cooking salt
¾lb granulated sugar	1 pinch cayenne pepper
1 pint spiced white vinegar	

Mince the onions and cook with the lid on the pan. Skin and slice the tomatoes, tie the skins in a muslin bag, and add both slices and bagged skins to the onions when tender. Add the spices, salt and ½ pint vinegar. Simmer until thick, then remove the muslin bag, add the sugar and the rest of the vinegar. Cook until thick. Bottle at once. White sugar and vinegar will give the best colour.

Tomato and Apple

4lb apples (windfall), peeled and minced
4lb tomatoes, skinned and chopped
¾lb onions or shallots, minced
½lb raisins, minced
2 level teaspoons paprika
4oz rock or cooking salt
1½lb granulated sugar
1½ pints spiced vinegar

Cook the onion, add the apples; when tender add the tomatoes, raisins, paprika, salt, and 1 pint spiced vinegar. Continue simmering until thick, then add the rest of the spiced vinegar and the sugar, cook until the correct consistency is reached. Finish.

EDIBLE AND INEDIBLE FUNGI

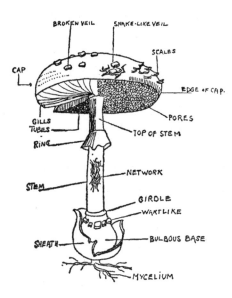

During the latter part of August throughout September and on until there are frosts, the woods produce a glorious collection of fungi in almost every colour and shape. The uninitiated walker will more often than not kick them over out of sheer curiosity, without giving them another thought. That is the worst thing that could be done.

Many trees depend greatly on the growth of fungi; they live together and without them, the forestry experts say, our woods would suffer.

When gathering fungi, one should always carry a knife and carefully cut near the end of the stem, so that soil adhering to its base will not fall on the caps.

Everybody knows the field mushroom which grows in grassland, usually during damp warm nights and has so much more taste than the one we buy. Other fungi, many of which we call toadstools, are often more secretive; they do not welcome the sun but prefer the shady woods. They appear suddenly where the trunk of a tree is rotting and the ordinary plant is no longer drawing new life from the earth. Their span of life is short and they are soon gone.

The beauty of the vast number of species is amazing. Under the definition of fungi are also moulds which play so great a part in the life of man and the working of nature. Penicillin produced by green mould (penicillium) has saved many lives in recent years and other moulds are used in the manufacture of substances of medicinal and commercial use. Moulds also bring about the ripening of certain cheeses. Yeasts are also fungi: all fermented drinks are due to their activities.

Some fungi are destructive; the parasitic fungi which cause illness and disease in humans and animals; others which cause enormous loss to crops and plants; wood-rotting fungi and many more. This article is to help you recognise on sight some of the larger fungi, most of them suitable for human consumption and a few which are not. Their food value is that of fresh vegetables.

Fungi do not contain chlorophyl (the green substance by which plants manufacture the sugar and starch they need), they have to obtain all their organic food needs ready-made. When they get this from dead plants they are called saprophytic and, when they 'live' on live plants or animals, they are called parasitic. Sometimes two different fungi live together to their advantage.

The reproduction of fungi is not by seed, but by spores which are not visible to the naked eye. Sometimes dusty black powder stains the hands when gathering fully grown fungi; those are the spores. A spore differs from a seed, in that it does not contain an embryo, but has usually one cell only.

The fruit-body of mushrooms and toadstools consists of two parts: the 'stem' and the 'cap'. The spores are formed in the latter and when they fall to the ground and come into contact with the decaying leaves, they begin to grow immediately, if the humidity is right, into a fine thread, known as 'spawn' to mushroom growers. Spawn differs from the roots of plants in consisting of threads which grow in all directions. Spawn may live under the protection of leaves during the winter, but the fully grown fleshy fungus is on the whole short-lived. Some species live only for a few hours, though others, of the leathery kind which grow on wood, may last years. Some spawn masses together and has a protective, hard covering to help survival for a long time. 'Ergot', the fungi that grows on grain and is very dangerous when eaten in milled flour, is of this kind.

The next development in growth is the small thickening which appears in the spawn. It develops into larger oval shapes but as yet shows no resemblance in form to the mushroom we know. Some are enclosed in a membrane or 'veil' which expands as the fungus grows, developing the 'cap' and the 'stem'. As the veil bursts, the 'valva', on the base of the stem, as well as the 'ring' nearer the cap, remains, also often some white scales on top of the cap. This is most noticeable in the bright-red *Amanita muscaria*, or *Fly Agaric* (poisonous). Underneath the cap are the 'gills,' but some fungi have small crowded 'tubes' opening by 'pores' instead. The gills produce the spores literally in millions, but obviously only some can reproduce.

In a short article it is impossible to describe all the fungi in order to identify them, but many have characteristic odours. One may touch a mushroom with the tongue to taste it, but one should never swallow. If the taste is acrid or bitter, it is not edible. The old supposed test of peeling easily for being edible does not hold. There are, however, quite a number of easily recognisable edible fungi and the gathering should be limited to these only. For this purpose a flat-bottomed basket is ideal, as the larger fungi are fleshy and fragile; they should be laid in a single layer, then a sheet of paper on which the next layer can be placed.

It is useful to note the place where a particular fungus grows and to revisit it after a few days, as it will yield another harvest.

It is important not to disturb the thread-like roots with careless walking because trampling compacts the soil and the mycelial threads are deprived of air.

A simple rule would be not to collect any of the fungi that have the remains of the characteristic two veils which leave a very distinctive valva at the base of the stem.

The cap comes off easily and the gills are white. These poisonous fungi include *Amanita muscaria*, *Amanita phalloides*, *Amanita pantherina* and *Amanita citrina*; the *Amanita phalloides*, or death-cap, has a delayed action of up to some twelve hours, by which time it is too late to administer antidotes. An exception in the Amanita family is the *Amanita rubercens* which is edible.

[Publisher's Note: Do not eat any mushrooms unless you are 100% sure that they are non-poisonous. Cross-reference carefully.]

Amanita Muscaria – Fly Agaric
Poisonous

This is a very well-known fungus and needs no introduction. It has a bright scarlet or sometimes orange flat cap with small adhering patches of torn veil and is to be found both under birches as well as pines. It feels moist and sticky to touch, the edge of the cap is delicately toothed, the gills are thin and free, always white, the flesh is soft. The stem is white, tapers upwards from a club-like base which has fragments of the volva attached in wart-like rings. The ring is like a skin hanging down, sometimes bordered with yellow. This fungus was, in former days, used to kill flies by crushing some of the flesh with milk. It has intoxicating qualities in small quantities; when eaten in larger quantities it may cause severe illness.

Amanita phalloides – Death Cap **Deadly Poisonous**

It is very necessary to get to know this fungus well. It is found in all woods, but especially under oak trees, mostly in the autumn. The cap usually of a yellowish-green colour, olive, brownish and even white, smooth and shining, is at first rounded and enclosed in the universal veil. The flesh is white with a tinge of yellow or green on the outside of the gill. Small adhering patches, left by the broken veil on the cap, have often disappeared. The gills are white and crowded; the stem is white, sometimes with a tinge of green tapering upwards from the knotty base and sheathed by a loose, whitish or yellowish valva and the ring is hanging down. This fungus is responsible for a great many deaths on record.

Amanita pantherina – Panther Cap
Poisonous

This fungus is rather like the scarlet *Amanita muscaria*, only the cap is dull brown or greenish-brown, with toothed markings at the edge of the cap. The valva consists of two or three bracelet-like girdles, ring hanging down. White gills, white flesh.

Amanita citrina (A. mappa) – False Deathcap **Poisonous**

Found in coniferous woods and also under beech from late summer till autumn; the cap is lemon-yellow or white, shining and smooth, with pale ochre-tinged loose patches of the torn universal veil. White gills with yellowish edge; the stem is pale white or yellow tinged, tapering upwards from a bulbous base, the volva finishes with a straight edge. From the stem hangs the ring, it has faint downstroke markings. Flesh white, sometimes yellowish under the skin. Has a definite smell of raw potato.

Lepiota procera – Parasol Mushroom **Edible**
Found both in deciduous and coniferous
woods, also on the grassy edges of copses
in late summer and autumn. The shape of
the young parasol mushroom is that of a
drumstick but later the cap expands and
becomes flat and retains a little dome in the
middle of the cap. It is covered with thick,
brown scales. The gills are whitish and broad,
the stem is covered with a brown coating
which cracks as it expands with growing and
gives the appearance of a snake. Ring: thick,
movable. Very good for soups.

Lacterius deliciosus – Saffron Milk Cap **Edible**
Found under pines from summer to autumn.
The cap and gills are orange or carrot-red,
often toothed at edge; the flesh is pinkish-
orange. When broken, it oozes with orange
milk which turns green when exposed to the
air. Good for grilling.

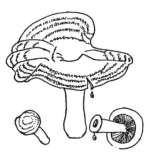

Cantharellus cibarius – Chanterelle **Edible**
Found both in deciduous and coniferous
woods, summer and autumn. The colour is
egg-yolk yellow; the cap funnel-shaped, and
the gills are replaced by thick folds, branched
and forming a network running down the
stem. Long, slow cooking is required – very
good with scrambled eggs.

Boletus edulis – Cep **Edible**

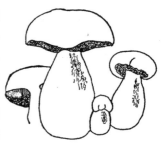

Found in deciduous woods in summer and autumn. This is a large fungus. The cap is brown and rounded like a 'penny-bun'. Under the cap are long narrow tubes with small pores; first whitish and when older greenish-yellow. The stem is cylindrical but often short and swollen; it is pale with a fine network of white raised lines on the upper part. The flesh is white and does not turn bluish when broken. The cap is suitable for frying in olive oil with seasonings and also for drying. The very poisonous species (not to be confused with *Boletus edulis*) is *Boletus satanas* which has a cream-coloured cap and reddish-mauve stem, the tubes are also reddish-mauve and the flesh turns bluish when broken.

Boletus scaber – Rough-stemmed Boletus **Edible**

Found under birches in autumn. The cap is greyish or dull brown and sticky when moist. The stem is rough with blackish or brownish, dotted markings; it is rather long, whitish in colour becoming greenish at the base. The tubes are white or buff; the flesh is white, sometimes with a trace of pink.

Boletus versipellis – Redcap **Edible**

Similar to the above but has a tawny, orange cap and is found also under birch trees; the markings on stem are blackish. Good for frying and drying.

201

Boletus elegans – Larch–Boletus **Edible**

Found under larches in summer and autumn, medium in size; colour gold to deep yellow, cap slimy and will peel easily; there is a white veil under the cap. After the veil bursts, the ring thickening stays. Good for frying but not for drying.

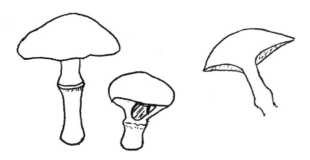

When dried, fungi are very useful in soups, stews and sauces. This is done in the following way: cut both stem and cap in thin, long fingers and either lay on paper in the sun to dry or string up fingers on cotton and hang in the sun to dry. Kept in a bag in a dry place, they will still taste good after two years.

The peasants in Austria almost live on edible fungi during the autumn and cook them in this way: fry finely chopped onion in butter to a light-brown colour, add cutup fungi. ('Cep' is very good for this.) Then add 1 tablespoon of water, some salt and pepper, caraway seed if liked, and finally 2 tablespoons of chopped parsley. One can add cream instead of water and serve the mushrooms with a poached egg on top. If any are left, they can be served with lemon and oil as *hors d'oeuvre*. They can be marinaded, are excellent in *béchamel* sauce over boiled beef, in omelets and soufflés.

About the House

GROWING PLANTS INDOORS

From time immemorial, plants have been grown in pots for house decoration, and since the introduction of glass many households (in congested towns or in countries with long, hard winters) grow flowering plants, foliage plants and herbs in pots and boxes in their windows. The increasing tendency to give pot plants as presents has meant a wide distribution of many kinds. Too often, however, when the donor pays a visit some weeks later, the erstwhile glory has departed to the compost heap and the feeble apology, 'I don't know what I did wrong with it, it just died', is poor thanks for the time, trouble and money taken to produce a worthwhile gift. The majority of plants are suitable for autumn and winter growing though it is always wiser, if a plant is given to you, to enquire if there are any special seasonal characteristics.

General Maintenance

Pots. Many ornamental and elaborate plant pots are available today, but for efficiency over a long period the standard earthenware flowerpot is outstanding, being porous to allow the roots to breathe,

203

and easy to keep clean, inside and out, cleanliness being essential to healthy growth. Unfortunately, these pots (even if clean) are seldom an asset to a room, while the bottom hole for drainage often results in marks on polished surfaces, but if the pot is placed in another decorative container and the space between the two packed with damp peat or sphagnum moss, the roots are kept at an even temperature and there is no risk of drying out.

Temperature. It is not easy or safe to lay down hard-and-fast rules on heating, but generally speaking most plants are happier in a cooler constant temperature than they are in a room which gets very hot in the day and then cold at night. On bright, sunny days plants can stand higher temperatures than on dull days, when too much heat may result in pale, leggy growth. It should be remembered that the window-shelf at night in the winter can get very cold indeed, so the plants should be moved into the room away from the glass; also that if the rooms get very hot, more water will be needed on the foliage, in the peat or moss, or in evaporating bowls, in order to provide the humid atmosphere in which pot plants flourish.

Light. Most pot plants (especially in the winter) can do with all the light available, so the pots are best stood near the window (moved at night for warmth), and turned at least every other day to keep the plant straight. With climbing foliage plants this is not so necessary. It is always easy to tell if a plant is getting sufficient light, as lack of light produces pale, spindly plants with weak-growing points, instead of dark-green firm shoots.

Watering. So many people are frightened of seeing plants wilt that far more damage is done by drowning than by drought. The water, preferably rain-water, for indoor pot plants should stand in the room for several hours before using to take off the chill. Cold water straight from the tap may be fatal. Arguments as to the best methods of watering can become quite violent, the main ideas being (a) standing the pot constantly in a shallow saucer of water, (b) plunging the whole pot in a bucket of water every week, or (c) giving a little water on the top every day. A safe combination of these three methods that seems to work quite well entails: (1) ALWAYS plunging a newly-acquired pot plant in a bucket of water (room-warmed to take off the chill) so that it starts in its new home at least well watered, (2) if by any ill-chance the plant is allowed to dry out, or if there is a heavy display of flowers, plunge again until the bubbles disappear, (3) if the room is constantly hot, stand in a saucer of water to ensure a steady flow of moisture to the roots and humidity to the air. When a real knowledge of the plant's requirements has been gained, top watering daily or less often may be found to be very satisfactory, especially combined with a damp peat or sphagnum moss wrapping.

N.B. – Be careful not to get the crown of cyclamen corms wet.

Ventilation, Gas and Oil Fires. Unfortunately, most plants are fatally injured by even a minute quantity of gas in the air, and if most of the house is lit and heated by gas it is better to grow only gas-resistant foliage plants (see list of unsuitable plants on page 210). Oil fumes can also be harmful, but in both cases mild fresh air, NOT a draught (fatal), can help to keep the plants healthy.

Washing. All plants breathe through their leaves which must therefore be kept clean. Firm, glossy leaves and stems benefit from an occasional gentle sponging, while leaves with furry surfaces can often be cleaned with gentle blowing from a bicycle pump or vacuum cleaner. During spells of mild, damp weather, pot plants like a thorough wetting from gentle rain. This is probably the best method of all for cleaning.

(N.B.-Not for African Violets.)

Feeding. Any plant growing in a pot has its roots very restricted; they soon come to the end of the nutrient materials in the soil, and careful feeding is then necessary. Too much feeding will result in rank, lush-green growth and few flowers; too little will probably produce many tiny flowers (or none at all) followed by the death of the plant. There are many proprietary fertilisers on the market today; most are very good and give clear instructions for use. A good home-made food can be made from keeping a strong sack of manure in a water butt and using the manure water diluted once a fortnight or more often if the plant shows signs of starvation, but do not overdose.

Repotting. Most flowering pot plants when bought will not need repotting until their flowering period is over, and the hard-hearted will then say that it is best to scrap them, buying again next year. Many people, however, get much satisfaction from pointing out the profusely flowering cyclamen or azalea that they have had for years and years. For this success a good knowledge of repotting is necessary. First be sure that the plant really does need repotting; to do this, put one hand flat across the surface of the pot, with the plant stem between the fingers, turn upside-down and strike the rim of the pot sharply on a firm surface until the whole plant falls out.

If the plant has shown signs of starvation but there is still some soil in among the roots, shake it all out carefully, wash and dry the pot thoroughly and repot in the same pot. If there is only a jumbled mass of roots in the pot, then repot into a slightly larger size. It is a mistake to make a move from a small pot to a much larger one, which is more difficult to handle and rather swamping for the plant, whose roots cannot for a long time reach the air they need coming in through the porous sides of the pot.

Make sure the pots are really clean and uncracked and that the crocks for drainage are also clean (sterilising in boiling water is a good thing). Put one large crock convex side up over the hole in the bottom, cover with small crocks and then smaller ones. Turn out the plant to be repotted carefully and work out the crocks clinging in among the roots. Shake out old soil and repot, working the new soil down among the roots, keeping the level of the soil approximately the same as before and firming carefully. Water in and replace in the same temperature as before.

The real enthusiast is advised to buy a small quantity of John Innes Potting Compost with the John Innes Base Fertiliser already mixed in. It is not expensive and well worthwhile, being sterilised and free from pests and diseases. Otherwise, a good home mixture might be made up from three parts good garden or preferably turf loam, two parts peat or clean leaf mould, and one part good sharp sand. A little charcoal mixed in helps to keep the soil sweet. But the John Innes Composts are safer and cheaper in the long run, except for lime-haters like azaleas, when the compost should be made up without the chalk.

When ready for potting, the compost should be moist enough to hold its shape when squeezed in the hand, without water seeping out. The plant to be repotted should also be normally moist to lessen the risk of a bad check to the roots.

SPECIAL POINTS ABOUT POPULAR PLANTS

Flowering Plants

Azalea (indica). Hates gas. Needs plenty of water. Can be kept on by looking after it once it stops flowering, planting it in the pot in a shady place when the frosts are over. Shaking out and repotting it early in September.

Begonias. Winter-flowering types. Easily propagated year after year by cuttings, can be used as bedding plants in the open during the summer. Gay, but need keeping nipped back for tidiness. Very susceptible to draughts.

Cinerarias. Need plenty of water. Very subject to green fly and white fly if kept in hot, dry rooms or in draughts. Spray with proprietary insecticide. Frequent syringing with tepid water above and below the leaves will help check pests. Throw away after flowering.

Cyclamen. Do not allow top of corm to get wet. Always pull off, not cut off, decaying leaves and dead flowers. Keep leaves sponged. Feed during flowering period. Can be kept on by gentle watering in cool conditions until safe to plant out in a shady, damp corner of the garden (in or out of pot). Take up and repot in early September. Bring on slowly in cool, shady conditions. Feed sensibly.

Geraniums. Easily propagated by cuttings year after year. Like plenty of sun but not too much water. Very easy and accommodating plants for flowers, foliage and fragrance.

Heather. Very tricky. Easily ruined by cold journey from shop to house. Keep well watered in a humid atmosphere out of draughts. Throw away when flowering is finished.

Hydrangeas. Usually in too small pots requiring a great deal of water and feeding during the flowering period. If blue when bought, will probably keep blue for that flowering. Can then be planted out in a sheltered spot in the garden as a permanent shrub. To keep blue in the garden, feed with aluminium sulphate, half a teaspoon watered in every two weeks. Easily propagated by cuttings in warmth.

Impatiens (Balsams). Easily propagated by cuttings in soil or water only. Need plenty of water and light and careful trimming to keep tidy. Flower continuously. Can be used as bedding plants in the summer.

Primulas. If carefully grown and fed may be divided into new plants at the end of the flowering season, particularly *P. obconica.* But *P. sinensis* and *P. malacoides* are really better bought new each year, or raised from seed. Need plenty of water, and plenty of light (not direct hot sunlight). *P. obconica* can give a rash to sensitive skins.

Solanums. Can easily be raised from seed. Dry off a ripe 'orange' and sow the seeds thinly. Grow in cool, moist conditions. When fruiting need little root moisture, but regular spraying of leaves with tepid water to keep down aphids and white fly.

Ferns

Stand up to bad conditions. Need dividing and repotting once a year.

Adiantum cuniatum (maidenhair fern) can be very untidy; should be kept in small pots for neatness. Does not like draughts.

Asplenium bulbiferum has long, rather untidy, palegreen fronds bearing little plantlets, which may be taken off and potted up as separate new plants.

Asparagus medeolioides (smilax). Very robust. Good trailer. (Not a true fern.)

Asparagus sprengeri. Very robust with long trailing, pale-green foliage. (Not a true fern.)

Asparagus plumosum. Very robust with dainty bright-green trailing foliage. Useful with cut flowers. (Not a true fern.)

Pteris sp. Usually found mixed with bulbs in Christmas bowls. Strong, upright pale-green fronds. Good grower.

Common Foliage Plants

Coleus. Brightly coloured, variegated leaves. Needs bright light, feeding and plenty of water. Can be raised easily from cuttings. Nip the tips off occasionally to get compact plants.

Begonia rex. Does best in shady, damp conditions when it bears large bright leaves. Pinch back to shape.

Less Common Foliage Plants

All easily grown. More or less resistant to gas.

Aspidistra (cast-iron plant). If well grown can be most effective.

Cacti want very porous, slightly chalky soil and as bright light as possible in the winter months.

Ficus Elastica. Strong, upright heavy-leaved plant.

Hedera (Ivies). Try Hedera Helix Montgomery or H. H. Holly. Will grow well indoors, either trained up supports or as trailers.

Scindapsus Aureus. Very strong trailer; dainty dark-green foliage.

Tradescantia flumenensis. Prolific trailer; green, white and pink leaves.

Not Gas-Resistant

Chlorophytum. Variegated, grass-like. Small white flowers. Strong grower.

Fatshedera Lizei. Strong, upright growth.

Ficus pumila. Good, dainty trailer or climber.

Grevillea Robusta. Shade-lover requiring plenty of water. Strong growing, upright plant with dainty foliage.

Philodendron Scandens. Cool, damp, rich soil. Spray frequently.

Sansevieria Trifasciata (mother-in-law's tongue). Interesting green and yellow contorted spear-like leaves rising straight from the soil. Keep dryish but sponge the leaves.

Less Well-Known Plants

Saint paulia (South African Violet). Small purple flowers rising from furry grey-green leaves. Cannot stand gas. Do not allow flowers or foliage to get wet but always water from below. Will strike fairly quickly from leaf cuttings.

Fuchsias. Can be grown in very wide range of beautiful colours and sizes. Easily raised from cuttings struck in warmth each year, and can be used for bedding out in the summer. Need plenty of water, good soil and frequent spraying. Watch for white fly.

Genista (Cytisus fragrans). Very sweet-smelling bright-yellow flowers on dainty, bright-green foliage. Raised from soft wood cuttings in sand in heat. Do not need much watering but benefit from frequent overhead sprayings.

Spiraeas. Rather fussy, need plenty of water and frequent feeding especially as they come into flower. Do best in cool conditions.

Calceolarias. Raised from seed each year and thrown away after flowering. Need cool, damp conditions. Suffer badly from aphids and require frequent spraying with tepid water.

For really brilliant ephemeral colour, do not forget that annuals may be sown and will flower extremely well in pots, particularly if kept in cool conditions and not too wet in not very rich soil. But above all, remember that far too many home plants are killed by kindness; a little basic knowledge and common sense produce much better results.

INDOOR BULBS

On the whole indoor bulb growing is fairly easy and it is very satisfactory to be able to say 'Oh, yes! I grew them myself,' when someone admires your Christmas flowers. All the same there is an art in getting the blooms out at the right time and success depends largely on two things – the choice of bulb and early planting.

First of all: if you are going to spend time on indoor bulbs, you will get much better results by giving 2*s.* for 2 bulbs, rather than giving the same 2*s.* for 6 bulbs advertised as a 'bargain.' Buy the biggest bulbs you can get from a reliable and well-known firm. Many bulbs sold nowadays for indoor growing have been specially treated to bring them into flower earlier and only the big bulbs respond evenly to this treatment, the smaller ones tending to produce blooms one at a time instead of all together.

Secondly: Remember in time about bulb planting, not just before Christmas but way back in July. Mark it in the calendar and order the bulbs in July for planting in August and early September. Don't wait until the popular shops have forcing bulbs for sale but order them from a good firm well in advance.

(1) Choose the pots, bowls and boxes and clean them thoroughly, washing and drying them if necessary. Put an inch-thick layer of clean crocks or clean stones at the bottom of each container.

(2) If there are no facilities for mixing up a compost, use the fibre obtainable at most garden shops. Bulbs growing in this usually exhaust themselves in flowering and if planted outside afterwards take several years to recover.

(3) If a compost can be made up, use a 3:2:1 mixture, of 3 parts loam (a good soil), 2 parts peat or well-rotted leaf-mould, and 1 part sand. Mix well.

(4) Damp the fibre or compost until a ball of it squeezed lightly in the hand does not drip water.

(5) Put at least an inch-thick layer of compost or fibre over the drainage stones.

(6) Place the bulbs on the compost or fibre; it does not hurt them to touch each other.

(7) Pack round the bulbs with fibre or compost, firming well. Drench each container in water, and drain.

(8) Where possible put the pots out in the garden in a cool shady spot and cover all over with 3 inches of peat, sand or old ashes. Except in very dry weather no watering should be needed.

(9) If no outside spot is available, put the pots into the coldest, darkest, cupboard in the house and check every 14 days to see if more water is required. The pots should be damp but not dripping.

(10) Leave for at least 8 weeks, by which time really good root growth should have been made; without these good roots, the later results are very disappointing.

(11) After the eight weeks, the pots may be brought into daylight and mild heat. If several pots of the same variety are grown, a succession of blooms may be obtained by bringing in the pots at fortnightly intervals.

(12) If moss is available, a little over the surface of each pot is pleasing; small clean pebbles can also be used.

(13) The taller bulbs may need support; choose thin inconspicuous but strong sticks (old knitting needles are good) and if they will not stand in the compost or fibre, push each stick actually down into the bulbs themselves. Tie with inconspicuous

thread, either using one stick per bulb or running the thread right round the outside of the group.

(14) Keep the pots damp but not wet and NEVER bring into a really warm room or the flowers will be sickly and poor.

(15) After flowering, the bulbs may be planted outside in the garden but they may take a year or two to recover.

Variations on Above Procedure

(1) Bulbs can be grown touching each other in wooden boxes; the method is the same until the blooms are nearly ready to come out. Then each bulb is lifted carefully, disturbing the roots as little as possible and planted into the flowering pots. In this way bulbs at the same stage of development can be put in the same pot and all the flowers come out at once. Small–growing greenhouse or wild ferns can be planted in with the bulbs to give added interest. Pots filled in this way will want more watering than those planted up from the beginning. This replanting is particularly suitable for the dwarf tulips, crocus and hyacinths, but is not recommended for narcissi and daffodils.

(2) Specially designed glass jars are available on the market for growing bulbs, particularly hyacinths in water alone. This method often produces good results and it is interesting to watch the root growth through the glass. BUT keep the jar in the dark until a good start has been made by the roots.

(3) Water culture in pots using clean stones for the supporting mixture is satisfactory, but both (2) and (3) more or less wreck the bulbs for any further use.

(4) Bulbs and corms may be lifted straight from the garden, just prior to blooming and planted up and brought indoors in pots. The flowers do not usually last very long, but this method works quite well with snowdrops and aconites, neither of which like forcing at all.

New varieties of bulbs for indoor flowering are constantly appearing on the market, but on the whole, however, the older varieties that have withstood the efforts of enthusiasts over the years are the most reliable. Only a few are given below but any grower's catalogue makes exciting reading, even if you can't afford all the ones you tick.

Hyacinths: The roman hyacinths are small, sweet-smelling and produce many spikes on each bulb. They can be obtained in pinks, blues and white.

Of the large types, L'Innocence is a good white; Yellowhammer is still the best of the yellows; La Victoire is a heavy red and King of the Blues a good dark colour. Hyacinths prefer an August planting for Christmas.

Daffodils and Narcissi: The old Paper White and Soleil D'Or narcissi are very reliable varieties, but the Pheasant Eye need a very cool slow growing.

Of the daffodils, the huge King Alfred and the dainty Golden Spur take a good deal of beating. Plant in August if possible.

Tulips: Again August planting is preferable. The Due van Thol, dwarf double and dwarf singles do best for private indoor growing as the tall varieties respond badly to the fluctuating temperatures of most homes.

Freesias: One of the loveliest of indoor flowers; they need at least 3½ months from planting to flowering in very cool conditions and they appreciate a teaspoon of general fertiliser per pot once a fortnight as the buds form.

Scillas, Chionodoxa, Grape Hyacinths and the little Iris Tingitana will all grow indoors quite satisfactorily, given the long slow-growing period.

Of the more exotic indoor bulbs, those with glasshouse or conservatory facilities can try lachenalias, lilies of the valley, ixias, nerines, and hippeastrums, all of which want more specialised treatment, and probably personal on-the-spot advice from an expert.

But for the ordinary housewife, there are few things about the house which need so little attention as indoor bulbs and very few things which can give as much pleasure to the nose and to the eye.

In the Parlour

PATCHWORK

Hexagons, Diamonds and Shells

Patchwork has been the means, for many centuries, whereby country people have made use of every scrap of material worth saving from the left-overs of dressmaking and house-furnishing, and the discipline of this economy is still essential to good patchwork. Although it is sometimes necessary to supplement the left-overs with an additional half-yard or so of bought material, there is a subtle but noticeable difference between the work of true economy and that in which material has been bought for the purpose of making it into patchwork.

The tradition of patchwork as a country craft is known to be at least two hundred and fifty years old. The variety of shape and colour offers unlimited possibilities for pattern-making and if used in this way patchwork can be looked upon as a form of relaxation and not an economical penance.

Materials

Material of almost any kind may be used; its choice is governed by its quality, and its suitability for the article to be made. That it is of good quality, whatever the kind, is of the highest importance. Those which lend themselves most readily to the work and processes are linens and cottons such as calico (bleached or unbleached), sateen, twill, casement, cretonne, chintz, gingham, marcella and pique. Generally speaking it is inadvisable to mix different kinds of materials, but some linen and cotton of equal weight and texture are found to wear well together. Woollen fabrics are generally used alone; silk, satin and velvet may be used with discretion in the same piece of work, but all must be of superlative quality. It should be remembered that velvet is virtually unwashable and that when cutting the patches they should be given a wider hem than usual, owing to the tendency of velvet to 'creep' when handled. Rayon has not yet proved very satisfactory, it does not lend itself to the various processes, and it frays; as a general rule it is advisable not to use material which frays easily. Drip-dry cottons are difficult to fold neatly; materials containing man-made fibres, such as nylon, are in too experimental a stage to recommend.

Bleached or unbleached calico, cotton or sateen are serviceable for most linings.

Templates

The templates, or patterns, used for cutting out should be metal, and these are worth the initial outlay in money as they are practically indestructible. Hard plastic makes a good substitute and some workers like perspex. Templates can be cut at home in copper, brass, tin or zinc; most of the geometrical shapes are simple to draw but they take time to make and it is often more satisfactory to buy them.

It has become customary to use templates in pairs – one as a guide for cutting materials and another smaller one for papers (see HEXAGON A and B; DIAMOND A and B; SHELL A and B). The value of a template for use with material is twofold – the exact amount of material required for a patch can be gauged and greater accuracy assured in cutting for pattern.

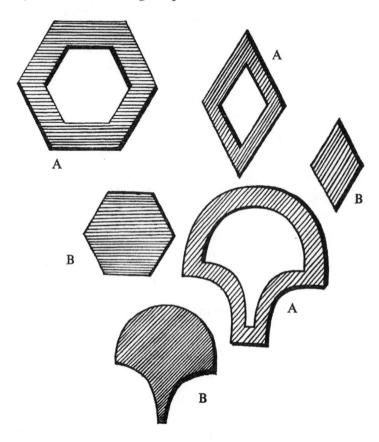

Needles, Threads and Scissors

A fine needle and thread are advised for use with most dress materials and light-weight furnishing fabrics; numbers 9 or 10 needles, threaded with 90 or 100 cotton give good results for seaming and hemming; a fine cotton is also recommended for tacking. Sewing cotton in the finer grades is only available at present in black and white; sewing silk should be used for joining silk and satin dress materials but it will be found that furnishing fabrics of all kinds — and also all cotton velvets — require to be sewn with a cotton thread. Sylko is essentially a machine thread and is labelled so, and it should not be used for hand-sewing on patchwork.

Scissors require to be kept very sharp. A separate pair should be kept for cutting paper, as this destroys a keen edge. Short-bladed scissors (such as nail-scissors) should be avoided — materials and paper need to be cut cleanly at the edges — not nibbled.

Paper

The good shape of each patch is dependent on the quality of paper over which it is made. Letters are a useful source of supply, and annual reports of company directors are recommended. Card is not advised except for shell patches as it makes the work clumsy to sew and heavy to hold. Papers are removed when the work is completed by drawing out the tacking threads and lifting the paper from each patch. If this process is done with care and good quality paper used, it is possible to re-use each paper several times.

General Planning

The materials available are the deciding factor in all patchwork design and it is premature to make any definite plan for the work before collecting enough material of the right kind and colours. Materials may decide the size and shape of the patch to be used; thick fabrics are not satisfactory for small or sharply pointed shapes; striped materials often are more effective on square and diamond shapes, and so on. The proportion of colour to the background is important, and in many cases a white background will give the best result.

In shell patchwork the curving shape of the patches should be emphasised and this effect is best achieved by colour contrast — dark patches lying on light colours — plain patches lying on patterned ones.

Important detail can be added by making full use of the printed or woven patterns of the materials. This can best be done by the use of the 'A' templates when cutting out. The finished result of each patch can be foreseen by laying the template on the material before cutting so that the required area shows through the 'window' of the template. Grouping and balance of colour can therefore be carefully worked out.

Making Hexagon Patches

The hexagon, the square and the octagon shapes are the simplest to prepare. A hexagon in course of preparation is given to illustrate the method used, but any straight-sided geometrical shape, in which the angles are 90° (a right-angle) or more, is made in the same way.

A pair of templates is advised, but if this is not possible it is essential that a rigid template is used for paper-cutting. In the diagrams, HEXAGON A illustrates the template required for cutting the material and HEXAGON B that for paper-cutting. The papers must be cut accurately and carefully, direct from the template HEXAGON B and never more than two at a time; the patches may be cut along pencilled lines drawn on the wrong side of the material.

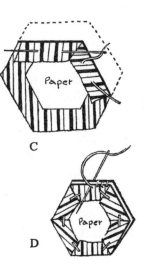

To prepare a patch, one paper should be placed on the wrong side of a material patch, the hem turned over the paper and the turning tacked down, as in diagram HEXAGON C.

The papers may be pinned to the patches for tacking as this helps to keep them in position, but it is not advised with glazed cotton or fine silks.

Joining the Patches. The patches are joined by seaming the edges together on the wrong side (HEXAGON D). The stitches should be even and the tension firm. The patches should fit neatly at the corners as the lasting quality of the workmanship depends on it, and careless fitting can spoil a good design. The sewing thread should be begun without a knot; it is better to sew in the end of thread at the beginning, and to sew back three or four stitches when finishing off.

Making Diamond Patches

In order to produce a trim and neatly finished patch, it is better to make a mitred fold at the sharply angled corners, as shown in the stages of preparing a diamond patch.

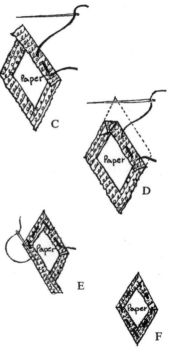

The first stage DIAMOND C is similar to that for preparing a hexagon, and notice should be taken that the direction of the first tacking is towards the pointed end.

The second stage DIAMOND D shows the corner being mitred by folding down the hem at the point so that the fold lies parallel to the edge of the paper but does not overlap it. The process is repeated for the other half of the patch DIAMOND E.

Joining the Patches. Diamond patches are joined by seaming but particular care is needed with the fitting of the pointed ends if the patches are joined to make a star pattern. It is advisable to work from the 'shoulder' towards the points when seaming.

Making Shell Patches

Shell patchwork requires a more advanced technique than for most other geometrical shapes. It is necessary that especial care is exercised in cutting out the materials to see that the warp of the material is in line with the point of the shell, so that the 'pull' of the finished work runs in one direction. A pair of templates is an advantage (see SHELL A and B).

Using template SHELL B, a number of thin card shapes should be cut; the template should be placed on the card and a thin pencil line drawn around the outline, from which the pattern is carefully cut.

Using template SHELL A, a number of patches should be cut out in material. A pencil line may also be used as a guide for cutting out, but it should be drawn on the wrong side of the material.

A card pattern is then pinned to the right side of each patch exactly in the centre (SHELL C) with the pins put in diagonally, as shown.When using glazed or delicate materials, one pin is put in at the point of the patch.

With the card pinned in position, the work is turned with the material uppermost (SHELL D) and using the card pattern as a guide only, a hem is turned down on to the wrong side, following carefully the shape of the pattern. (Note that the hem on convex side only is turned down and tacked.) The

C

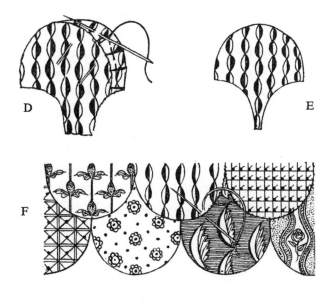

D   E

F

fullness of the hem should be taken up neatly by pleating in folds and not by gathering. The patch should not be sewn on to the card.

The pins and card are removed when the tacking is completed (SHELL E) and more patches made, until there are enough to complete at least two rows across the intended piece of work; the same card pattern can be used until it is too worn to retain its shape.

The prepared patches are joined in straight rows; each succeeding row overlapping the one before (SHELL F).

Joining the Patches. The joining is done by hemming on the right side of the work (SHELL F). The tops of the curves must be kept strictly in line, as also the points of the patches, one below the other.

Lining And Finishing

Bedspreads, curtains and cushions need to have the edges straightened or 'squared off' before they can be finished, and this is done by turning in the uneven edges of the last row of patches and tacking them in this position. All patchwork needs backing, and such things as pincushions, tea cosies and quilts have a padding or interlining as well as a lining. The accepted tradition allows for material to be bought for lining large pieces of work, but part-worn sheets, even if mended, will be found satisfactory. It is not necessary for the lining to be in one piece, and large squares or other shapes can be joined to make a satisfactory lining for a curtain or bedspread.

The lining and patchwork top should always be joined together at other points than at the edges, and sometimes the most satisfactory method is to put the work into a quilting frame and quilt the two sides together. This is not always possible, and if the work is carefully tacked first, the joining can be done by tying or knotting, by which the sides are tied together at intervals with a linen or strong cotton thread. The edges of the work are most satisfactorily joined with a piping cord or binding, as both these methods give added strength to the finish.

HEDGEROW BASKETRY

This craft is an adaptation of the technique used in willow basketry. It has two great attractions for the worker: she can gather her own materials and by using them finds she has most beautiful natural colourings, unknown to any other form of basketry.

Among the common terms used are: *randing* – weaving with one cane; *pairing* – weaving with two canes; and *waling* – weaving with three canes.

Materials. These are gathered from leaf-fall to spring, and it is advisable to gather for each basket individually. Willows are the most useful, as they are pliable and of many colours: red, golden and green. Sallow is apt to be coarse and difficult to bend. Garden dogwood, poplar and willow are the best for stakes. Wild dogwood, snowberry, privet, hazel and wild rose are good for siding. Lime has a lasting fragrance. Old man's beard, blackberry, and honeysuckle, stripped, are good where long lengths are needed as in upsetting, middle and top wales. Gather from the north side of a hedge, as here the plant uses its strength in making long growths to find the sunlight; on the south side the strength is used for flowering and seeding. Materials can be dried and stored in a cool shed, then soaked for several days before use, but it is preferable to use shortly after gathering to have the full pleasure of their colouring.

Tools. Sharp penknife, secateurs, bodkin, picking-knife or side-cut pliers for finishing off.

Methods for round basket in yellow willow and wild clematis:

Gather 50 rods of willow as long and thin as possible. Twelve lengths clematis, stripped. Sort out sizes and lay all ready before beginning.

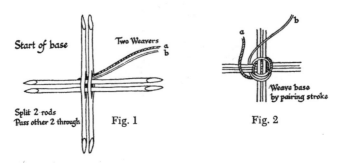

Fig. 1

Fig. 2

Start as Fig. 1. Pair out to 6-inch diameter with clematis. Stake up with 16 rods in willow.

Upsett with 3-rod wale 4 rows, clematis. Sideup with 'straight weave' in willow, using as many weavers as uprights, working from right to left, Fig. 3.

Ordinary randing may be used, e.g. each rod, beginning with the shortest, worked out and each succeeding rod introduced behind next stake to the right, but the first method gives a much better finish.

Weave out to tips or if randing, work to depth of 3 inches. Tap work well every few rows to allow for considerable shrinkage. Work two rows of 3-rod wale in clematis. See that work is even before finishing off with three rows of waling in clematis. Use a simple trac, as in Fig. 4, or 3-rod one-behind border. Cut all ends off neatly with picking-knife or side-cuts. Finish with twisted rod handle or for a light flower basket thrust double rods either side, tie these across basket desired height, pass through border and make firm by a 'cross-stitch' round handle and border.

Other combinations of material:

Garden dogwood (narrow), bands of snowberry or blackberry;

green or red willow, wild dogwood, honeysuckle; wild rose or poplar, blackberry or ivy.

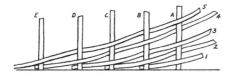

Fig. 3. Straight weave or French rand

Fig. 4. Simple trac border

In succession, behind one, in front of two, away. May be varied according to depth of border required and length of willow, e.g. in front of two, behind one, in front of two away, gives deep and strong border.

Slightly more complicated border, done in two stages:

1st stage: 1 behind 2, 2 behind 3, 3 behind 4.

2nd stage: 1 in front of 3 and 4 behind 5, then 4 behind 5 also (Fig. 5).

Fig. 5. Three-rod, one behind border

After 3 strokes of this second stage the worker will find she has 3 prs. turned down. Continue by taking the longer right-hand rod of the left-hand pair, in front of 2, round one and the next upright stake down beside it. Continue this rhythm throughout, remembering each stake goes behind the next upright to the right which is in front of 2 and finishes down on the last row of weaving and to the front.

225

With Our Friends

STAGE PROPERTIES AND MAKE-UP

Stage Properties

Under the general heading of Stage Properties can be listed a great variety of objects from small pieces of furniture to stage jewellery. In fact any portable object which is necessary to the action of the play or to its 'dressing' can be termed a stage-property. 'Personal' properties are those which the actress looks after herself and which form part of her costume or character.

The design and making of all these properties is a necessary part of the preparations for a production. It is an interesting and often exciting job, for the properties must look convincing and pleasant in size, shape and colour and must be soundly constructed so that they do not fall apart or leave smears of sticky paint on the fingers. Much ingenuity is exercised in finding just the right kind of raw material for each object and in choosing the most suitable method for making it.

The property list for the play should be worked out very early in production so that the people who will use the properties know what they have to handle and the working party can begin to construct them in plenty of time.

Many properties are made from such materials as newspaper and paste, old felt hats and scenic size, rope and chicken-wire, odd pieces of hard-board and wooden dowling and so on. Papier maché which is built up by layers of torn pieces of newspaper and paste is the basis of the newspaper technique.

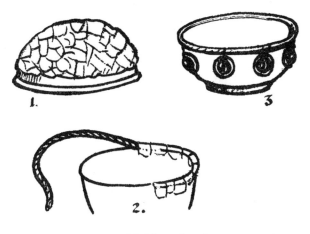

Making a bowl

For example, a piece of jewellery such as the clasp for a cloak or an ornament for a chain of office can be built up in paper over a simple model made in plasticine. The model is covered with a layer of wet tissue paper and then four more layers of dry newspaper torn up and pasted one over the other. Any good white paste is suitable but do not use gum or glue. The paper covering is left to dry thoroughly for three days and then, with the aid of a knife to lift the edge all round, the paper shell is lifted off the plasticine. The ornament is now trimmed with scissors and the edge is made firm by the addition of a picture cord laid round it. This is held in place by means of small pieces of tissue paper and plenty of paste. It is important to give a final coating of paste over the tissue paper.

Further decoration can be added in this way by pasted-down cords or 'jewels' made by pasting strips of tissue paper and rolling them up to form round or square stones. These are also held in position by the use of tissue paper and paste and perhaps a piece of picture cord placed round as a setting. Bowls of fruit and articles of food can be faked by this method and all manner of other small

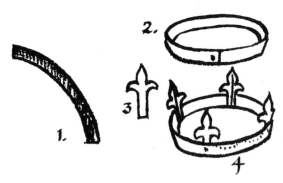

objects. The final painting is done with poster colour. Stones set in jewellery are painted a bright colour and given highlights by means of small pieces of coloured foil or toffee paper in a matching colour glued on to catch the light. A crown, coronet or tiara is made by pasting pieces of newspaper over a foundation made of thin cardboard or stencil paper. This foundation is made by cutting a curved circlet (*see diagram above*) and joining the ends together. The circlet itself may be tapered towards the back if a tiara is required or shaped in any way thought desirable. Ornaments such as strawberry leaves and spikes are cut in the same material as the foundation and held in place by means of paper clips. Four layers of newspaper should be sufficient covering (inside and out) and additional decoration can be applied in the form of cords and tissue paper as before.

When the head-dress is completely dry it is painted with a background colour in poster paint (brown for a gold object and grey for a silver one) before the metallic paint is used. Metallic powders mixed with a little white varnish or with strong liquid size will be found to be more satisfactory than gold and silver enamels.

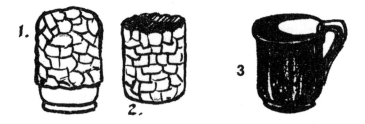

Jugs and Tankards

Old felt hats are often used to make ornamental belts, neck-chains, collars, etc. The sections are cut out, stitched on to a cord or linen strip and stiffened with glue size. Any felt object which is shaped while saturated in size will hold its shape when dry. For this size solution use one tablespoonful of concentrated size to a cup of boiling water. Make sure that it is completely dissolved and use it warm. Properties made in this way are very light in weight and quite unbreakable.

Chicken wire is useful for shaping rather larger objects which can then be covered by layers of torn brown paper and paste.

Bowls, jugs, tankards and properties of this kind are made by finding a suitable model (a jam jar, for example, makes a very good model for a tankard) and covering the surface with grease so that the papier mache does not stick to it permanently and building up four or five layers of torn-up newspaper and paste. Always begin by using one layer of wet tissue paper before the newspaper as this helps the papier maché shape to come cleanly off the model when dry.

The final stage in all these pieces of construction is important. Any surface decoration should be big and bold and the painting should be such that it will 'read' well from a distance. Fine detail is unnecessary but a good size and shape, sound construction and telling colour are all essential.

Make-Up

Why is make-up used on the stage? A simple answer to the question is that it is necessary to replace colour drained away from a face by the use of stage lighting. This means that the amount of make-up used is governed by the strength and colour of the lighting. It is also determined, to some extent, by the size of the auditorium and the distance between the majority of the actors and the audience.

Make-up is used too, of course, to help the actress to create her character, ie to look older or younger, to look evil or like someone quite unlike herself. A 'straight' make-up, on the other hand, should emphasise her good points and give colour and life to her face when it is seen under light.

A make-up should never be thought of as something superimposed upon a face – a kind of 'Magic' – but should be put on with the costume. The wig, hair style or hat is always of great importance, for the make-up is only part of the whole conception of the character which is expressed in movement, action, voice and dress.

The first essential is a good foundation, well and evenly applied extending over the neck to avoid a mask-like effect. The foundation can be in the form of a liquid base such as that worn for everyday make-up or can be in the form of a paste or a blend of grease paint. For those with naturally oily skins the latter is apt to be too greasy and the make-up may begin to run in streaks.

Rinsing the face with very cold water before applying the foundation will help in every case. Lip colour depends upon the character but in general the mouth is assisted by broadening or thinning the lips and by drawing a clearly defined edge to them. An orange stick coated with the colour will be found useful for drawing fine lines.

Colour in the cheeks (again the amount depends upon the age and type of character) can be applied by adding dry rouge or by grease paint. It is a mistake to think that Carmine is the only colour for the cheeks. A most satisfactory 'glow' can be achieved by using a Leichner grease paint stick No. 9, which is a rather brown, sunburnt colour.

The position of the cheek colour depends upon the bone structure of the individual face. It should be placed high on the cheek-bones and blended away round to the sides in an upward direction. Don't forget that the make-up must look as well when the face is in profile as when it is seen full face. Cheek colour when placed too low is most unbecoming and when it is placed close to the nose it tends to narrow the face.

A rather long and prominent chin can be softened by the use of a little of the cheek colour on the tip blending away under the chin.

Eye make-up, particularly in a small hall or for open-air performances, should be limited to eye shadow on the upper lids (green, blue or grey, according to age and type of character) and a firm line drawn with a dark-grey or dark-brown 'liner' just above the eyelashes of the upper lid and extending outwards for perhaps a quarter of an inch. The pointed end of an orange stick coated in the colour is a firmer implement with which to draw lines than the grease paint liner itself which is blunt and has a tendency to smudge.

Shadows under the eyes give an illusion of age or illness so that, unless this is the intention, shadows here should be avoided. The colour used for hollowing the eyes can vary but do experiment with a little grease paint, stick No. 9, blended for purplish shadows with a grey or blue liner colour.

Hollowing of the cheeks to give an impression of age is also done successfully with the same mixture of colour but it is easy to make the face look dirty. A shadow painted on to a very smooth rounded cheek is never convincing. With this type of face a more successful method to follow for creating a picture of age would be to use a paler, more waxen foundation colour and to concentrate upon hollowing the eyes and temple and whitening the eyebrows.

When all the colour has been applied, the make-up should be fixed by powdering with plenty of blending powder. A very soft powder puff is an advantage and so also is a soft baby brush for brushing away any surplus powder round the eyes and nose. The eyebrows should be defined after the powdering but do not use too heavy a colour or make them too emphatic. The lips may need a little retouching too, after the powdering. Always make up in a good light – for stage purposes it should approximate as nearly as possible to the lighting under which you will be acting. If possible use a second mirror to check the profile make-up as you go along.

It is much more satisfactory to learn to do your own make-up than to rely upon someone to do it for you. For one thing you know your own face and bone structure far better than anyone else and for another thing you understand exactly what kind of character you hope to create on the stage.

Reproductions of good portraits can be studied very profitably particularly when you are playing in a period other than your own. A great deal of information is gained from this study with regard to head-dresses, hair styles and the 'period face' in general.

A basic stock of make-up for most purposes would consist of the following

A. Foundation:
(i) A liquid foundation such as one would use for everyday make-up or a cheaper version of it made up by a chemist, *or*
(ii) A tube make-up by Leichner, 'Spot lite Klear,' which is sold in various tints to suit individual complexions, *or*
(iii) A mixture of grease-paint sticks blended on the face to produce the right colour. The most useful sticks would be Leichner No. 2 (for very fair skins), No. 5 and No. 9.

B. Grease-paint Sticks:
The three already listed above (No. 9 being used for cheek colour and shading) with the addition of Carmine II for lips.

C. Grease-paint 'Liners':
Dark grey, dark brown, blue, mid-green, and white.

D. Blending Powder: Rose colour for most women; 'brownish' for men.

E. A soft swansdown puff; a small, very soft brush; orange sticks; liquifying cream for removing make-up; soft tissues or cotton-wool.

SPEAKING IN PUBLIC

'Will you come and speak, please?' How many thousands of people must be asked that question each year, so that sooner or later it seems everyone is asked. Surprise is quickly followed by alarm when you hear the question for the first time and your suggestions for alternative speakers are rejected! They want you and no one else. Every later invitation is accompanied for most of us by the same emotions and 'before-speaking nerves' are universal – even the most experienced speakers show their qualms to some degree as anyone who has been to a dinner or watched one on television will have noticed: the tenseness, however slightly apparent, will have gone once the speech is over, and in its place will be relaxation.

This nervousness is no bad thing in itself as it shows that the speaker has a respect for the audience and is therefore setting herself or himself a high standard. But while the 'butterflies' may never die they can be accompanied by a certain confidence which comes from practice and knowledge of the subject.

It is important from the start to know what subject you are expected to talk about and from what aspect; there is nothing more exasperating to speaker and audience alike than to find that the one has gone to a lot of trouble preparing a talk on a subject that the other did not want to know anything about!

Having discovered the general aspect on which the talk is to be based, consider the time allowed and, on a basis of speaking at approximately one hundred and twenty words to the minute, the length of your speech. There may be time for a general survey and considerable detail; or the details may have to be curtailed, or the survey abbreviated but illustrated with vivid examples. It is better to balance the talk and not overcrowd it, so that the audience does not get exhausted and more information can be given at the end if questions are allowed. If at question-time an unanswerable question is asked, or one to which you do not know the answer, do not hesitate to say so, and either tell the questioner where you think they can find the answer, or offer to do it and send it to the Chairman.

Never try and bluff your way out!

The approach of the speaker is also different whether she speaks as an expert in her own subject or as someone retailing her experiences and thoughts which may have a parallel in the audience, for example a couturier lecturing on running a fashion house and a traveller to Tibet talking about the life there. In the first case he or she can be didactic, in the second he would be unwise to claim to know all the answers, for there will surely be a member of the audience with some specialist knowledge possibly as great or greater than his own! All general facts should of course be checked and public libraries, government departments, specialist associations and embassies are all helpful, but some require a little time before they can produce information.

Once the information is at hand and the length known, there comes the job of preparing the talk in detail – the most important part being to establish the sequence of thought. This sequence or thread should be sufficiently strong to be obvious to the audience so that afterwards they will remember not only single points of your talk, but also retain a general grasp of the subject. The sequence – how in fact you propose to tackle the subject – can be mentioned briefly at the opening, then a return can be made to the first main point or heading in your notes.

Most people have their own methods of compiling notes. There are two dangers to beware of – if they are in too great detail there is a tendency to read them, and if they are too brief they may become incomprehensible. Some speakers, anyway at first, prefer to write out the whole talk. Alternatively a very simple method is to have a series of main headings on the left-hand side of the page and an indented paragraph of amplification on the right. Sub-headings can be indented half-way across. Elaborations and anecdotes to illustrate the point and lighten the speech come in the right-hand column. The best material for notes is either a loose-leaf notebook or numbered postcards written on one side only. Both are easy to handle and will keep for future use; they can also be added to if necessary.

It has been said that the construction of a talk or lecture should be sufficiently clear for anyone taking notes to be able virtually to reproduce the lecturer's own notes. While few audiences take notes if the presentation is clear, the talk as a whole will be remembered.

Concluding is always difficult. Sometimes it is a good idea to sum up the main points briefly; but if the speech is a short one it is quite unnecessary. At other times it is better to return very briefly to one key point that you want the audience to take away.

Use the simplest language – not because you under-rate the audience, but because it is the best – and give definitions of technical terms, abbreviations and abstract phrases. Speak to the back row of the audience with your normal voice, but use your lips a little more than in normal speech. Modulate your voice to avoid monotony and according to the size of the room, and reduce your speed a little for large halls and audiences. Keep an eye on the clock to make sure of not over-running; it is also an idea to have in your notes one or two optional headings or sub-headings, to be inserted or omitted entirely according to time and the mood of the audience.

Everybody has some mannerisms and provided they do not distract the audience they will probably be appreciated. Fidgeting, however, must be avoided and the constant repetition of one word can also be exasperating: it is wise also to avoid standing immediately in front of a window or strong light.

Finally, if you can establish within the first few minutes an atmosphere of mutual interest between speaker and audience in the subject, the talk will 'get over.'

Local Festivals

The old autumn festivals are not kept up with the same enthusiasm as those of other seasons, except in a few cases such as the Horn Dance performed each year at Abbots Bromley in Staffordshire. Then, on Wakes Monday (the first Monday after September 4th) early in the morning the Six Horns are taken from the parish church, and after a blessing are carried to the market-place, where the first dance takes place. The horns are from reindeer, three light-coloured and three dark; the largest weighs 25½ pounds and measures 39 inches from tip to tip. The smallest horn weighs 16½ pounds and is 31 inches across. The dancers wear costumes of green knee breeches patterned with brown oak leaves and acorns; three men wear crimson coats and three pale-green; all wear green stockings and green caps. With the dancers is Maid Marion, a man dressed as a woman in yellow skirt, blue tunic and cap with flowing veil; a Jester with bladder and stick; a Hobby Horse; a boy with a bow and arrow; a boy with a triangle, and an accordion player. The twelve leave the marketplace to visit neighbouring farms and the 'big house', where they have lunch. After more visits they return to the village where a grand dance takes place, the antlered dancers weaving and charging one another many times before finally making their way back to the church, where the horns are again hung up. Tradition has it that the dance is 800 years old, but no one knows how it began; tradition also has it that the horns may not go into another county.

The Oyster Feast at Colchester in Essex, which is held in September, also dates back to medieval times. The Mayor goes down to Pyefleet Creek and makes the season's first dredge, after which a proclamation is read granting to Colchester the fisheries of the River Colne, which it has had 'from time beyond which memory runneth not to the contrary.' A feast follows at which oysters are served and also traditional gingerbread.

The autumn fairs are now but shadows of the medieval gatherings when merchants came from far and near to trade and sell their merchandise. Traces of the old Cheese Fair of Frome, Somerset, may still be found in the cheese exhibits at the Frome Agricultural Society Show, held on the last Wednesday in September, but there are no geese at the Nottingham Goose Fair held during the first week in October on the Forest Recreation Ground. Nevertheless, despite its frequently being a sea of mud, thousands come from the city and surrounding districts to enjoy themselves at the fair.

Enjoyment is also had by the ale-tasters at the fair at Market Drayton, Shropshire, each October. There is still a Michaelmas Fair at St. Ives, Huntingdonshire, which lasts three days, beginning on the second Monday in October.

The Stratford-upon-Avon Mop Fair in October flourishes still, and children still save up their pennies. For this one day, many of the streets of Stratford-upon-Avon are filled with roundabouts, coconut shies, and the usual sideshows, together with the succulent smell of a roasting pig. The Mayor opens the 'Mop' from a traffic island in one of the streets, at 11am, and is then offered the freedom of the mop by an official of the Showmen's Guild of Great Britain. For this day public houses remain open, and extra trains and buses are put on to bring the numerous Midlanders to this traditional 'Mop' at Stratford-upon-Avon.

Pack Monday, or St. Michael's Fair, at Sherborne in Dorset, is also keenly celebrated. The day is always the first Monday after October 10th, on which day – so they say – the workmen on

Sherborne Abbey packed up their tools as it was finished in A.D. 1490. One ceremony which takes place in the town in connection with the fair is 'Teddy Roe's Band.' Who Teddy Roe was nobody knows. As midnight strikes, the last bell is a signal for bedlam to break loose. A concourse of boys, men, girls and women of all ages armed with every conceivable means of making a noise, gather at the top of the town, move off and go through certain streets.

At the head of the band is a leader carrying a pole with a large illuminated triangle marked 'Teddy Roe's Band.' At houses where there is illness or death, the lights go out and there is silence before and after that house. It is said to be a very quiet ceremony now compared with the 'good old days.' Then, anybody who had upset the townsfolk, was well and truly serenaded with a vengeance. The band playing finishes on the Parade, with dancing until 2am to a jazz band.

Pack Monday was originally a famous hiring fair: the Pack Men also came with their pack horses and packs. It was given a charter by King Charles I.

One of the few local religious ceremonies to fall at this time of year is the Painswick (Gloucestershire) Clipping Service. This takes place in the churchyard but, though the exact origin of the 'clipping' or embracing is not known, it would not appear to have any sinister tradition. It is principally a children's festival and is held on the Sunday after September 19th. All the children of the parish, the little girls crowned with flowers, and the boys with buttonholes, process right round the churchyard led by a band and the church choir, singing hymns of which *The Church's One Foundation* is always one. Then the children link hands right round the church, and after a short service they sing an ancient hymn, *Daily, Daily, sing the Praises*. At the refrain they dance forward and back with their hands raised, thus 'clipping' the church. After a sermon, some of the little girls make a collection in flower-decked baskets and the ceremony ends with buns for all at the school.

At Painswick, and also in September, footballers used to be given a meal at the 'Bunch of Grapes' in which 'Puppy Dog Pie' was included. This was in fact a pie of steak and kidney or rabbit, in which was hidden a china dog. Today some families are believed still to make the pies, or sometimes apple pies with china dogs hidden in them on Feast Sunday in September.

Hallow'een, the eve of All Saints Day, 31st October, is an autumn festival that is celebrated in many different parts of the country with many turnip-lantern processions, mimes and traditional dances. 'Punkie Night', however, seems native to Somerset. On the third Thursday in October the children of Long Sutton gather on the village green carrying their punkies, which are mostly made from hollowed-out mangolds. Some have faces cleverly cut out, others are painted and many have beards or moustaches attached. Inside are placed lighted candles. Sometimes a child will use a hollowed-out marrow and cut it to illustrate a ship, but this is rare. The children are marshalled into classes according to their ages which are from 5 to 11 years and prizes are given for the first and second best in the three classes, with an extra prize for the funniest according to the judge's decision. Judging over, the children troop down to the Institute room (an uncanny picture they make with their punkies bobbing in the dark), where a splendid tea is provided, the prizes are distributed and the party ends in games and much noise and excitement.

Local Skills

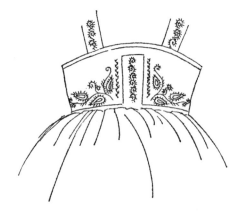

DORSET FEATHER STITCHERY

This easy work is a revival, by Dorset's Women's Institutes, of some
old stitches in modern form.

Here is embroidery that a moderate needlewoman finds she
can do. This does not mean, of course, that it can be done carelessly.
Care and accuracy are part of its beauty, but the basic stitches are
commonplace and known to everyone, and it is as easy for left- as
for right-handed people.

Only four stitches are needed for the work: (1) Buttonhole
(also called Blanket) stitch, (2) Feather stitch, (3) Chain stitch and
(4) Lazy Daisy (Fly stitch).

With the skilful use of good designs, colour and surface
overwhipping, embroidery of originality and beauty can be achieved.

The hand soon gets accustomed to the work, the stitches
become rhythmic and almost automatic, as soothing to do as knitting
is for knitters. A delightful relaxation at the end of a tiring day.

Experience has shown that a trial and error sampler should
be worked first and this applies to skilled and unskilled workers
equally.

The first piece of work after the sampler should be something small and not too elaborate – a table mat, or apron, for instance. Let the first piece of work be simple. Do not rush off and buy a large and expensive piece of material and iron on an elaborate transfer; or in due course this may find its way into the melancholy drawer of unfinished masterpieces.

When this work was first started in 1950 it was agreed to call it 'Feather Stitchery' – variations with feather stitches.

Then it evolved into something more elaborate, though simple and amusing to do. Basic stitches were surface overwhipped in various ways and some central European ideas were introduced. Small ric-rac braids were embroidered into the work, strips of contrasting material were appliqued on, worked in reverse colours, and home-made lace, so popular on European aprons, was sometimes added. This type of work we called 'Dorset Feather Stitchery'.

In evolving this work, Dorset has drawn on traditions from many sources, notably a book of designs taken from nineteenth-century smocks collected by Alice Armes and published some thirty years ago by the Dryad Press under the title 'English Smock'. A beautiful Balkan apron has also contributed many ideas. One clever design from a Welsh smock and another from a Staffordshire gardener's have proved particularly effective after a little modification.

The Welsh design incorporates some of the most ancient shapes and symbols in the world, known in a dozen different lands under a dozen different names. The Womb or Seed of Life in Greece, the Peacock's Eye of Persia and India, and here in England called the Pine Cone. This is combined with a charming flowing scroll pattern so frequently found on primitive pottery.

Not all designs are suitable for Feather stitches. What looks well on paper does not necessarily work out well when embroidered, but artists and experts who delight to evolve their own designs have here a great opportunity. They will discover that lines and curves must be near enough to give the impression of rich heavy embroidery, but also separated enough to take the stitch and enable a glancing eye to recognise what the design means.

241

This new craft began on a small scale. Eighty W.I. Handicraft members volunteered to learn this work and make things for an exhibition and the result was very exciting.

After experimenting with these old-fashioned stitches Loan Boxes were made for the County. Boxes of embroidery were also made to send about the world as gifts in the hope that other women in other countries would enjoy doing this needlework as much as we did.

Materials

This needlework lends itself especially well to dark backgrounds worked with light-coloured threads. The materials should be firm and even, but not too heavy, and coarse loose weaves should be avoided. Dupion, strawcloth, poult taffeta, and of course dress linen are excellent and so are a number of the new fabrics which are now being manufactured. Felt is also admirable for things that do not have to be washed and is a very pleasant medium to work upon.

Embroidery Threads

Round twisted rayon threads like Cronit, sold on spools which can be hanked and home-dyed can well be used. They are a little difficult to work at first for they need a frequent counter-twist of the needle to prevent unravelling or knotting, but this soon becomes automatic.

Feather stitches use thread up at an incredible rate so unusually long needlefuls seem necessary.

As well as rayon threads, many other varieties can be used together with lovely effect provided they are about the same weight and suited to the material, and much interest is added to the work if threads are varied, sometimes bright and sometimes dull surfaced.

Twisted threads for the foundation stitches are really much the most effective as they give each separate stitch distinction. Stranded cottons are excellent for surface overwhipping.

Choice of Colours

If you have chosen a coloured material for your work (and this is strongly recommended) it would be wise to try using only two colours for the embroidery. For instance, white for the foundation stitches and a strong contrasting colour like vivid blue, red, yellow, or black for the surface overwhipping; concentrating on the perfection and regularity of your stitches.

Here is another simple and beautiful colour scheme for a cushion made in gros grain or poult taffeta of some pale tone like grey or primrose yellow. Suppose you have chosen grey, work it entirely in varying tones from white up to medium grey. These self-coloured tones are lovely and restful to live with.

The Needle

Perhaps the most important thing of all is the needle. You *must* have the right-sized one to enjoy this work. A packet of assorted Chenille needles is recommended; Chenille No. 22 or size 3 Crewel needle will take most threads comfortably.

If you wish to do a trial and error sampler, trace this Welsh design on to an eight-inch by six-inch piece of material and work it with the following stitches. Beginning and ending with four tiny back stitches and no knots.

Line 1. Work in Buttonhole (also called Blanket stitch).

Line 2. Single Feather Stitch.

Line 3. Double Feather Stitch.

Line 4. Two rows of Buttonhole and a Satin stitch eye.

Line 5. Scrolls in alternate left- and right-handed buttonhole stitch.

Line 6 and 7. Loose Chain Stitch.

Line 8. Buttonhole stitch for the small scrolls.

This description is of course very brief and only an indication of what should be done. After careful and accurate embroidering, it can be surface overwhipped in half a dozen different ways with a contrasting coloured thread.

Local Recipes

THE CORNISH PASTY

The Cornish Pasty is, and has been from time immemorial, the staple dish of the county, and in giving various recipes for making it, it may be noted that the method does not vary, but the name of the pasty varies according to the filling.

Pastry. Any good pastry may be used but it should not be too flaky, nor too rich. A very useful pastry is 1lb flour, ½lb lard and suet, ½ tablespoon salt, mix with water.

When the pastry is made, roll out about ¼-inch thick, and cut into rounds with a plate the size desired.

Lay the rounds on the pastry board with half of the round over the rolling-pin and put in the fillings, damp the edges lightly and fold over into a semi-circle. Shape the pastry nicely and 'crimp' the extreme edges where it is joined between the finger and thumb. Cut a slit in the centre of the pasty. Lay on a baking sheet and bake in a quick oven so that it keeps its shape.

Meat and Potato Pasty. Always use fresh steak, potatoes cut small, salt and pepper, flavoured with onion.

Egg Pasty. Bacon cut into dice, parsley and one or two eggs, according to the size of the pasty required.

Apple Pasty. Peel apples, slice thinly, and lightly sprinkle with brown sugar. In summer-time blackberries are usually mixed with the apple.

BAKEWELL PUDDING

Puff pastry (light).

Filling

3oz. butter (creamed)	2oz chopped almonds
3oz sugar	Grated rind and juice of one
3oz bread crumbs	lemon
A little grated nutmeg	3 well-beaten eggs

Line a flat dish with puff pastry, then put a layer of raspberry or strawberry jam, lay the filling on top of the jam and bake for 20 minutes. When cool sprinkle with caster sugar.

Winter

A wrinkled crabbed man they picture thee,
Old Winter, with a rugged beard as grey
As the long moss upon the apple-tree;
Blue-lipt, an ice-drop at thy sharp blue nose,
Close muffled up, and on thy dreary way
Plodding alone through sleet and drifting snows.
They should have drawn thee by the high-heapt hearth,
Old Winter, seated in the great armed chair,
Watching the children at their Christmas mirth;
Or circled by them as thy lips declare
Some merry jest, or tale of murder dire,
Or troubled spirit that disturbs the night,
Pausing at times to rouse the mouldering fire,
Or taste the old October brown and bright.

Winter, by Robert Southey

Nothing but chrysanthemums and I feel winter has come; shaggy, sombre blooms in mauves and browns and ochre decorate the table of the retiring President for the Annual Meeting of the local W.I. But the meeting itself is anything but sombre; all the excitement of a local election when every candidate (for Committee or for Office) is known intimately to every voter; the words of congratulation, of criticism or advice from the visiting V.C.O. (Voluntary County Organiser) and a new year has begun in that Women's Institute.

There is now the job to be learnt and the mysteries of 'amendments,' 'standing orders,' and 'nem. con.' uncovered.

Outside in the country it is the time for shooting, for crouching before dawn to watch the sun rise with the duck and the great migratory geese, for standing silent in a bare, darkening wood waiting for the pigeon to circle overhead or, in a field, ready to kill the hare or the woodcock that breaks from the covert. For the fortunate there is the resulting mound of spoil to be transformed into Hare Paté or Pigeon Casserole.

It's not very long though before she finds herself in a gathering momentum of Christmas plans. First, a list is written which envisages plenty of time and great economy. Presents will be made for everyone; gloves for many – some leather, some fur, some knitted; teddy bears or rag dolls for the children; home-made fudge and toffee for friends. Some of us perhaps get no further than this well-intentioned list transformed a week before Christmas into that nightmarish squash and scramble in the local shops. But many of these things are finished peacefully at home by the fireside, or, if they are ladies of the W.I., in weekly classes with expert instruction.

Soon though it is time to think of the holiday itself; relations descend in hoards from urban isolation for a 'quiet Christmas and New Year in the country'; but for weeks beforehand the country housewife has been busy preparing all the traditional foods: plum puddings, plum cakes, mince pies, brandy butter, and no doubt the 'extras' too that complete the sense of festive well-being – a superbly iced cake or a great box of candied fruits perhaps. Whether or not the birds have left the berries on the trees, there is the search to find the holly, the mistletoe, the evergreens and the bare branches; these must be tucked precariously behind the highest picture, or turned into a kissing bough, or, if they are twigs, dipped into lime and hung with baubles. With tact and good fortune some at any rate of this may be done on Christmas Eve by more or less willing guests.

It is also the time for children's parties; for riotous games and – the hope of all mothers – an interval of comparative rest when Punch and Judy take over.

For the pleasure of singing together, many Institute choirs may well make use of the delightful cantata *Folk Songs of the Four Seasons*, specially written for our great Music Festival of 1950 by Ralph Vaughan Williams and which contains within it so many of the traditional folk songs from all parts of the country.

This is not only a time for family reunion though; in many counties it is also the time for Institute re-union and many members meet to share the joy that this Festival recalls – a satisfactory English compromise for a non-sectarian movement – Carol Rallies in county halls.

From the Garden

CHRISTMAS DECORATIONS

The decoration of our homes at Christmas time is traditional and has not changed materially since Victorian times, when evergreens were lavishly used. The Christmas Tree was first seen in this country about 1820 and Prince Albert introduced the custom at Windsor in 1841, since when it has steadily increased in favour until almost every home boasts a lighted tree.

Evergreens are a symbol of continuing life, and for our decorations we use holly, mistletoe, box, bay, laurel, fir, rosemary and ivy. The work of collecting them begins fairly early in December. They are then treated in different ways to make them more attractive. They can be painted white, red, silver or gold and while the paint is still tacky sprinkled with glitter or powdered glass. Branches or twigs treated in this way, look most effective when used with dark-green leaves, each being complementary to the other. When holly, bay and laurel is used in its natural state, rub the leaves with olive oil to make them glisten. When the evergreens have been painted for any particular colour scheme it is quite easy to make them up into the various shapes and designs. Christmas Decorations fall into three categories, for: (a) outside the door, (b) hanging, (c) table or mantelpiece.

Outside the Door

Wreaths of holly are made on wire or wooden-hoop foundations. The hoop is usually covered first with red or silver paper, and the holly twigs bound on neatly with fine silver wire. A large red cellophane or ribbon bow is tied to the bottom of the wreath, then it is attached to the door-knocker with similar ribbon.

Another kind of front door decoration is made on a wooden coat-hanger. Here fir and holly are bound on with wire. Begin at the ends of the hanger and work towards the centre to hide the stems. Group fir or cedar cones at the centre and tie a large gay bow just below the cones.

Hanging

The most spectacular hanging decoration is the Kissing Ring or Kissing Bough. The framework used to be made of osier or iron but is more easily made today from wire or wooden hoops. Five circles or hoops are decorated all the way round with a small-leafed evergreen such as box or rosemary. The twigs must be bound on very evenly and neatly with fine wire. Four of the completed hoops are then tied together at top and bottom to form a globe and the fifth fastened around the centre forming the equator. Seven red apples, oranges, or silver balls are then attached to the top with ribbon, and hung half-way down the centre of the globe, while a large bunch of mistletoe hangs from the bottom. The Kissing Bough must hang high enough from the ground for a couple to stand and kiss beneath it. The diameter of the hoops is about 18 inches to 2 feet and the

foundation can be used year after year with the evergreen, fruit and mistletoe renewed each Christmas.

Holly balls to hang in a window are easily made on a raw potato. The slight moisture in the potato keeps the holly quite fresh until Twelfth Night. Select a potato 3 inches or so in diameter, and a piece of pliable wire about 8 inches long. Push the wire right through the potato and join the two ends by twisting them together thus forming a loop by which to hang the ball. Stick into the potato selected pieces of holly about 4 to 6 inches long (the stems of which have been pointed) to form a complete ball of holly. Tie a gay ribbon bow at the base and a loop of the same ribbon at the top.

Garlands of mixed evergreens are most attractive for large rooms or the village hall. They provide a dignified decoration and are made on fine rope or twine. Selected twigs of holly, fir, ivy or cupressus are bound round the rope as evenly as possible with clusters of berries, cones or ribbon bows at intervals. They can be looped around the walls or across the room from each corner and held together in the centre with a large bunch of mistletoe.

Table or Mantelpiece

A very simple table decoration can be made by selecting large rosy apples, making a hole in the top of each, large enough to hold a candle securely. Form a frill of holly leaves at the base of each candle by pushing the stems of the leaves, one at a time into the apples.

A small birch log, hollowed out in the centre for a wad of moss, is a good medium for a mantelpiece decoration. Candles are arranged in a group to one end of the moss, and holly, ivy and cones placed as attractively as possible around and to the side of the candles. The holly and ivy stems can be wedged into the moss and the cones wired into position.

Children's parties are incomplete without a decorated Christmas Tree. Most people are content to put it in a bucket, tub or pot. If small, it can be wedged in with earth or moss, but a large tree needs to be cemented into its base. The container is covered with coloured paper, or camouflaged with paint and the tree decorated with candles, silver and coloured balls and tinsel. At the very top will be the Star of David. Exciting-looking parcels, tied with gay paper and ribbon are crowded round the base.

Each year sees an increasing number of small lighted Christmas trees in the windows of our homes. This is a charming practice, giving much pleasure to all who pass particularly in villages where there is no street lighting.

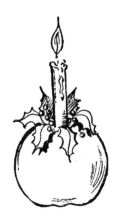

253

In the Kitchen

CAKE ICING AND DECORATIONS

Cake icing and decoration is a fascinating subject giving scope for artistic skill and originality. It can be carried out successfully by anyone prepared to give the necessary care and precision to the work, especially in the preliminary stages. In this article it is only possible to deal with cakes iced and decorated with Royal Icing, suitable for Christmas, birthdays, weddings, etc.

The first essential is a good foundation, therefore a good recipe for the cake must be used, and the cake-tin carefully and neatly lined.

The top and sides of the cake should be coated with almond paste, then with two coats of royal icing. If the cake is to be used soon one coat only may suffice, but oil from the almond paste will come through if the cake is kept, and if the sides are not coated with almond paste two coats of icing are essential as the first coating will show crumbs from the cake mixed with it.

Great care must be taken in putting on the almond paste to get a good shape, with a flat top and straight sides.

Almond Paste

½lb ground almonds   1 teaspoon lemon juice
¼lb icing sugar   ¼ teaspoon each of vanilla,
¼lb caster sugar   almond and ratafia essences
1½ eggs or 1 egg and 1 yolk

Sieve icing sugar. Put sugars and egg in bowl and mix thoroughly. Then whisk over hot (not boiling) water until thick and creamy. Remove from heat. Stir in ground almonds and flavourings. Turn on to sugared board, and knead slightly to a smooth paste. Wrap in wax paper, and a polythene bag, if not used at once. (This paste will keep for months in a cool dry place.)

To coat cake. Brush top of cake with apricot jam. If necessary build up edge of top with roll of paste pressed out round top, to make it level. Roll must not overlap sides. Roll out piece for top. Put cake upside down on to paste. Press well. Trim sides if necessary.

Roll out strip for sides to length and width required. Trim edges exactly to width. Brush strip with jam. Put cake on strip with top edge exactly to edge of paste, and roll on. Put cake upside down on to sugared board, and roll round with a straight sided jam jar. Place right side up on cake board. Stick cake on to board with a little royal icing.

Note. The diameter of the board should be at least four inches greater than diameter of the cake (if round). If possible, leave a day or two for the almond paste to harden before icing, but the cake may be iced quite satisfactorily at once if necessary.

Royal Icing

½lb icing sugar   ½ level teaspoon blued sugar
1 white of egg   (to keep icing of uniform whiteness)
1 teaspoon lemon juice

The above quantities should be sufficient to coat a cake of 7 inches diameter, height 2½ to 3 inches, but approximate quantities only can be given as eggs vary in size, and sugar in the amount of moisture it absorbs.

To make royal icing. Sieve sugar with blued sugar twice. Put white of egg and lemon juice into bowl, and add sugar gradually, beating all the time. Beat well while icing is soft (about 10 minutes), and add sugar until required consistency is reached. For first coating and forcing, the icing should stand up in points when spoon is pulled up.

Note. To prevent icing from becoming too hard, 1 teaspoon glycerine may be added to each lb. sugar.

Blued Sugar. 1 teaspoon lime blue (powder) to 1½lb icing sugar. Sieve together 3 times. Store in a tin. To use: 1 level teaspoon to each 1lb sugar.

Royal Icing first coat. Cover top with icing, pressing out air bubbles. Draw stainless-steel palette knife across top of cake until smooth. (Blade of knife should not be less than diameter of cake.) Spread icing round sides, and draw smoothly round with knife or plastic scraper. Trim edge.

At this stage, the essential point is to obtain a good shape. A poor shape, and rough projecting bits of icing will spoil the final result.

Leave to dry for some hours.

Second coat. Make a soft icing (or add white of egg to that already made). Icing should *just* find its own level when jerked.

To get rid of bubbles knock bowl of icing gently on the table, then gently stir out bubbles as they rise. Repeat several times, letting icing stand 10 minutes before use.

Note. The icing when made must always be kept covered with a damp cloth. If kept for any length of time a piece of wax paper should be placed on the icing, and the bowl covered with a damp, not wet, cloth. A polythene cover under the damp cloth is useful.

When icing is ready spread on top as before, pressing out any remaining bubbles. Then draw palette knife gently over once. If not quite even and smooth, gently knock cake board on the table, and the soft icing should run quite smoothly

Stiffen remaining icing with a little sugar, apply to sides as before, and smooth with plastic scraper or knife. Trim edge. Leave in a warm place to dry.

Decoration. Over-decoration should be avoided. A cake of good shape, and well iced, will not need heavy decoration to cover blemishes. An attractive border forced round the top and bottom edges with a simple design on the top is usually all that is required. The design should, when possible, be suitable to the occasion for which the cake is made, e.g. a cradle for a Christening cake, name and date with appropriate flowers for a birthday, holly and mistletoe for Christmas, and so on.

Icing for Forcing

The icing should be stiff enough to stand up well, and to keep its outline when forced, but must be easy to force. Large pipes need stiffer icing than small ones, and icing for flower petals must be stiffer than for borders and trellis work.

Equipment needed

1. *Forcing bags*. Best made of strong grease-proof paper. Nylon and plastic bags may also be used.

To make a paper bag: Use double thickness of paper. Cut sheet of greaseproof paper into 6 squares. Fold square in half to make triangle. Mark centre of base of triangle (B). Bring each point of base to apex of triangle, forming a cone. Fold over points at top of cone.

The essential point is that the pipe must fit exactly into the paper bag when the end has been cut off, leaving no space between bag and pipe. Half an inch of the pipe should project from the end of the bag. Overlap ends of paper for a narrow pipe.

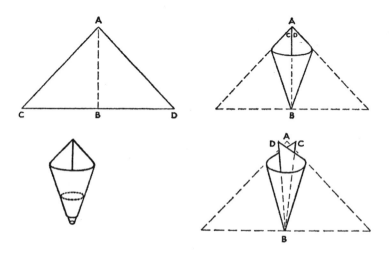

2. *Forcing Pipes.* A large number of different pipes are not needed. A great variety of decorations and quite elaborate work can be produced with the following:

> Several sizes of writing pipes, Nos. 0, 1, 2, 3
> Several sizes of petal pipes
> Several sizes of star pipes
> Ribbon pipe for basket work and bows.
> Shell pipe and Leaf pipe (not essential)

The writing pipe can be used for many purposes as well as lettering, such as: dots and outlines, trellis work, basket work, flowers, run-in work.

Trellis may be forced directly on to the cake, or if a raised dome shape is required, on to a 'net nail' or mould. The mould should be very lightly greased with lard.

Practice will be required in forcing the trellis evenly, the pipe should be raised, and the icing allowed to fall into position. Square or diamond trellis may be forced (the former shows defects more plainly) and the lines should be fairly close together to give strength. If forced directly on to the cake, pencil marks should be avoided. A few fine pinpricks will indicate the position of the trellis.

The trellis on a mould should be left in a warm place to dry, and should then be lifted carefully from the mould which should be warmed slightly by holding over a low light. The trellis should slip off easily, and can then be fixed in position with a little royal icing.

Basket work. Use a writing and a ribbon pipe, or a writing pipe only, as shown:

Method

1. Pipe a stay on to the basket mould, which is larded.
2. With ribbon or writing pipe, cross the stay making the lines long enough to come just under the next stay, and leaving spaces between equal to width of line or ribbon.
3. Pipe next stay over ends of lines just made.
4. Pipe as 2 in between first lines, and repeat.

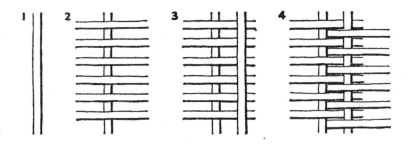

If care is taken to pipe just underneath the stays, the lines across will be joined so that the underside of the basket looks the same as the topside.

Note. Special basket moulds may be obtained; or patty pans, dariole moulds, etc can be used quite satisfactorily.

Star Pipes are used chiefly for borders and edges. In addition to stars they may be used for shells, scrolls, and curved lines, giving a pleasing variety. The centre of a star should not stand up in a point.

Star used as a shell – top and side views. Not as side view on right – too heavy

Petal Pipes are used chiefly for flower work. The thin edge of the pipe must always form the outer edge of the petal. To make roses: Force a small centre of icing on a piece of greaseproof or wax paper fixed to net nail with icing, then force each petal round it, starting from bottom of cone, and keeping each petal in an upright position.

Colouring. Flowers of uniform colour with little or no shading should be made in coloured icing (e.g. violets, primroses, forget-me-nots), but flowers such as roses can be made in white icing, and coloured afterwards, or in self colour and tinted later. Nearly all sugar flowers are improved by the addition of a little colour mixed with gum arabic solution, or with the solution only. It brightens and preserves the colour, and strengthens the flowers, etc. It is especially useful for glossy leaves and berries, such as holly. Vegetable colourings can be obtained from many chemists. The colours may be too strong, but may be toned down and softened by mixing as in water colour painting. When the desired colour is obtained, mix with a little gum arabic solution and apply with a small paint brush.

Gum arabic solution: 1oz gum arabic crystals 2½fl.oz water

Crush crystals if large. Put crystals and water in jar or small basin. Stand in pan of water, and heat, stirring occasionally till crystals are dissolved. Strain through hot wet muslin into jar or bottle. Keep corked.

Moulding. Used for decorations which are too large or unsuitable for piping. It can be carried out in marzipan or icing.

Marzipan. The best results are obtained from a boiled marzipan, which is pliable, not oily, and will be found useful and quite satisfactory.

Boiled Marzipan

½lb sugar (granulated, caster or lump)
6oz ground almonds
2½fl.oz water
1 white of egg
Pinch of cream of tartar

or –

1 teaspoon liquid glucose
1 teaspoon lemon juice
¼ teaspoon each vanilla, almond, ratafia essences

Dissolve sugar in water *without boiling*. Add cream of tartar or glucose. Boil to 238°F *without stirring*. Brush crystals from sides of pan with wet brush. When temperature is reached remove pan from heat. Stir in ground almonds all at once. Stir in white of egg unbeaten. Stir over gentle heat two to four minutes (according to size of white of egg). Add flavourings. Turn on to dish or formica board and work with wooden spoon till smooth and thick. If a small piece can be formed into a thin layer without sticking to the fingers, it is ready. Wrap in wax paper and a polythene bag when cold. Keep in a cool dry place. Colour and use as required.

Quickly-Made Marzipan

4oz icing sugar (sieved)
3oz ground almonds
White of egg
Flavourings as in boiled marzipan

Mix sugar and ground almonds. Add essences. Add enough unbeaten white of egg to make a smooth firm paste.

Moulding with Marzipan. When moulding leaves, copy the natural growth as far as possible, but do not colour a *dark* green. Natural colour is added later. Keep the edges very thin, and mark veins using the back of a knife. Put on a tin in a warm place to dry, curling leaves over small piece of wax paper if required. Leave some hours to dry, overnight if possible. When dry, paint with colour and gum arabic, and dry on a lightly larded tin in a warm place. Fix the leaves in position with a little royal icing. Leaves with outstanding veins on the back, such as primrose and syringa leaves, are useful in making marzipan leaves. Obtain a leaf of suitable size, form marzipan into the shape of the leaf, and then press on to the back of the natural leaf. Trim the edge, and peel off marzipan, which will show all the markings of the original leaf.

Precise directions for moulding flowers and other suitable decorations cannot be given in detail. Points to remember are accuracy in form and colour, correct proportions, and suitability. Some ingenious decorations are quite unsuitable for putting on the top of a cake.

Moulding in Icing. Icing is the most suitable medium for white and delicate flowers, such as apple blossom, wild rose, syringa, etc. Royal icing becomes too brittle to use satisfactorily alone, but can be used effectively when mixed with a little powdered gum tragacanth (obtainable at all chemists).

Method. Make royal icing in the usual way. To about 3oz icing sugar add a pinch of gum tragacanth (as much as can be put on a silver threepenny bit). Stir well. Leave to stand for several hours. Add more icing sugar if needed to make the icing of a moulding consistency. Make a small quantity only at one time.

Moulding Flowers, e.g. wild rose. Make each petal separately, and leave to dry. (They will dry quickly.) Fix petals together with royal icing to form the flower. When dry and firm, tint as required with paint mixed with gum arabic solution.

The calyx of the flower can be forced on to the back when dry with green icing in a writing pipe, No. 2 or 1. Put flower in desired position, and fix stalk (made of green marzipan or icing).

Stamens can be forced on to a larded tin with No. 0 or No. 00 writing pipe. Force a little soft icing on centre of flower, lift stamens with small forceps, and place in position.

Leaves may be made of icing, moulded in the same way as the flower, or preferably they may be made of marzipan as described previously.

The above directions may seem over-elaborate and intricate, but with practice and with all materials (pipes, bags, icing, marzipan, colourings, etc) ready, the worker will find she can produce a variety of suitable decorations in a short time.

In a short article it is impossible even to mention all that can be done with icing and marzipan. Methods of coating, forcing, and decorating have been given with hints which, it is hoped, may be useful to beginners. Decorations have been chiefly limited to flower-work, but with patience and ingenuity a wide variety of other decorations can be made. For many of these, a method called 'run-in' work is suitable, and can be briefly described.

Run-in Work. This method may be used for all kinds of designs, small animals, birds, figures, open-work, etc. They are made in soft royal icing, and put in position when set. The design is drawn on paper, or a printed illustration may be used. A piece of wax paper is placed over it, fixed with icing, and the design outlined with a writing pipe, No. 0, 1 or 2. Soft royal icing which will just find its level is then run into all parts which are to be filled in. A bag with the end cut off is used without a pipe. A paint brush is useful in getting the icing smoothly into corners.

The wax paper is then drawn off gently on to a flat tin, and left to dry in a warm place. A small piece will dry quickly, but large surfaces should be given two or three days to dry thoroughly.

The wax paper is then peeled off very carefully, and the design put in place with a little royal icing. A piece of open-work may be raised above the surface of the cake by forcing little supports on the surface before putting on the piece. A pretty effect may be obtained by painting the icing underneath with a colour which will show through the open-work.

An example of run-in work

CRYSTALLISED FLOWERS & CANDIED FRUITS

CRYSTALLISED FLOWERS

Crystallised flowers have become very popular as decoration for cakes, party sweets, etc. The method is simple and with care the flowers will last for months, keeping a fresh natural colour.

Method. Place 3 teaspoons of gum arabic (crystals not powder) in a small screw-top bottle, cover with 3 tablespoons of rose or orange water. Leave two or three days to dissolve into a sticky glue, shaking the bottle occasionally.

Using a small soft paint brush, cover the petals, calyx and as much stem as is needed of each flower with the gum arabic solution. Big loose flowers are best taken apart, each petal dealt with separately and the flowers made up again when wanted. The painting must be done very thoroughly, as bare spots shrivel and will not keep. Dredge lightly two or three times with caster sugar until each flower is well covered, and dry off in a warm place on muslin or grease-proof paper. Difficult flat blooms can be placed on the edge of a shelf, held down by something over their stems. Twenty-four hours in the linen cupboard is usually long enough for the flowers to become stiff and dry. Store in the dark, preferably in a cardboard box.

The following flowers crystallise well: Primroses, violets, forget-me-nots, mimosa, cowslips, plum and apple blossom, rose-leaves and sweet peas.

A little vegetable colouring in the gum arabic solution will give the flowers a more cheerful appearance, but care should be taken not to use too much or the result will be most unnatural.

Edible Frosting

Use the same gum arabic solution brush on a warm plate and dry off in a cool oven. The solution dries and chips off as frost for cake decorations.

CANDIED FRUITS

There are several methods of preparing candied fruits; the following is one of the more satisfactory. Pineapples, apricots, peaches, plums, greengages and cherries are the most successful fruits to use. Canned fruits are better than fresh fruits.

Different fruits should not be candied in the same syrup.

Method. Drain the syrup from the can or bottle in which about 1lb fruit has been preserved. Make the syrup up to ½ pint by adding water. Place the diluted syrup in a saucepan and add ½lb sugar. Heat, stirring thoroughly until the sugar has dissolved; bring to boiling point and then remove from the heat.

Place the fruit in a bowl and pour the syrup over it. There should be sufficient syrup to cover the fruit completely. Keep the fruit submerged by placing a saucer over the liquid.

Leave to stand for 24 hours.

At the end of this time pour off the syrup, add 2oz sugar to the syrup and heat gently until the sugar dissolves, then bring up to boiling point. Pour over the fruit again and leave to stand for 24 hours.

Repeat the process twice more adding 2oz sugar each time.

On the fifth day pour off the syrup and add 3oz sugar. Stir until the sugar dissolves, then add the fruit and boil for 3 or 4 minutes.

Return the fruit and the syrup to the bowl and leave for 48 hours.

Repeat this last process and if, when cool, the syrup is of the consistency of thick honey, leave the fruit to soak in it for 3 or 4 days.

If the syrup is of a thinner consistency, boil it again with a further 3oz sugar. Then leave the fruit in the syrup for another 3 or 4 days.

Drain off the syrup for the last time and place the fruit on a wire tray over a plate to drain and finally place the fruit in a very cool oven for about 3 days or on a warm tank or in an airing cupboard until dry.

Pack in boxes with waxed paper. Keep in a dark place.

SWEET-MAKING

The making of Home-made Sweets is an old-fashioned accomplishment which after a period of eclipse is now able to come into its own again.

Equipment

For the recipes in this leaflet, no special equipment is necessary, though to obtain consistently reliable results, a sugar thermometer is advisable. For home use, however, the methods of testing which follow should be successful.

Temperatures for Sweet-Making

Stage	Temperature	Method
Thread	230-234°F	Dip finger and thumb in cold water, then in syrup and back in cold water. Press together, then pull apart when a fine thread of syrup appears.
Soft Ball	235-245°F	Drop some syrup into cold water when a ball is formed which may be squashed flat when removed from the water.
Hard Ball	245-265°F	Test as for Soft Ball; in this case the ball will keep its shape.
Soft Crack	270-290°F	Drop a little syrup into cold water, separate and hard threads appear.
Hard Crack	300-310°F	Proceed as for soft crack; the threads are brittle and break easily.

Points to remember: Avoid stirring syrups unless the recipe specifically states that this should be done; a large thick pan must be used to avoid risk of burning the syrup.

The sides of the pan above the boiling syrup should be brushed continually with cold water. Alternatively the pan lid should be put on so that the steam is retained and sugar crystals do not form and spoil the texture of the sweetmeat. When the syrup has reached the required temperature, gently lift the pan and place it on a damp dish cloth; this avoids over-heating. For oiling tins use olive oil or melted unsalted butter.

PLAIN FUDGE

1lb granulated sugar   ¼ pint evaporated milk
2oz margarine   ¼ pint water
½ teaspoon essence

Using a large heavy saucepan, put all the ingredients, except the essence, in the pan. Heat gently until the fat is melted and sugar dissolved, then allow to boil. Stir and heat until 240°F (soft ball stage) is reached. Remove from heat, add essence and beat until almost set. Pour into an oiled tin. Leave until nearly set, then cut into one-inch squares.

CHOCOLATE FUDGE

1lb granulated sugar   2oz margaine
½oz cocoa   ⅛ teaspoon cream of tartar
2oz plain chocolate   ½ teaspoon vanilla essence
¼ pint evaporated milk   ¼ pint water

Dissolve the chocolate and cocoa in the milk, add the sugar and proceed as for Plain Fudge.

COFFEE AND WALNUT FUDGE

4oz coarsely chopped walnuts
1lb granulated sugar
½ pint evaporated milk
1 tablespoon fine coffee powder
1oz margarine
1 teaspoon vanilla essence

Dissolve coffee in milk, then proceed as for Plain Fudge, the walnuts being added when the 'soft ball' stage is reached.

269

ORANGE PASTILLES

¼ pint orange juice
4oz sugar
1oz powdered gelatine

6 tablespoons glucose
A little caster sugar

Dissolve sugar in the fruit juice. Cool. Add the gelatine and glucose and allow to dissolve. Pour into a wetted tin and leave to become firm. Remove from tin, cut into rounds and toss in caster sugar.

LEMON PASTILLES

1 pint sieved apple pulp
¾lb caster sugar
1½oz gelatine

Lemon essence
Yellow colouring
⅛ pint cold water

1 teaspoon cornflour *and* 1 teaspoon caster sugar mixed

Cook apples and sugar together until very thick. Dissolve the gelatine in water and add together with the flavouring and colouring. Pour the mixture into shapes and allow to set. Toss in the mixed cornflour and sugar.

RUM TRUFFLES

½lb plain chocolate
1 tablespoon condensed milk
A few drops of rum
Cocoa or powdered chocolate

Grate the chocolate or break into small pieces. Melt very slowly, add the milk and rum, stirring continuously. Beat very well and cool. Shape into small rounds and toss in the cocoa or powdered chocolate.

COFFEE TRUFFLES

¼lb fresh butter
½lb grated chocolate
6oz icing sugar

Coffee essence
Chocolate vermicelli

Cream the icing sugar and butter together, add the chocolate and essence, leave till firm and workable, shape into balls and toss in chocolate vermicelli.

CARAMELS

1lb granulated sugar
1lb golden syrup
essence

½ pint evaporated milk
1 tablespoon coffee

Put sugar, syrup and milk into a strong pan, cover, gently heat till the sugar is dissolved, then boil till 250°F (hard ball stage). Add the essence, do not beat. Pour into an oiled tin. When cool, mark into squares. Wrap in waxed or transparent paper to prevent the caramels becoming sticky. Store in an airtight container.

BUTTERED NUTS

8oz demerara sugar
2oz nuts
2oz margarine

¼ teaspoon cream of tartar
¼ pint water

Oil a tin and on it arrange the nuts about two inches apart, put to warm. Dissolve the sugar, margarine and cream of tartar in the water, heat to 280°F (soft crack stage). Pour a teaspoon of syrup over each nut. Leave to set.

CINDER TOFFEE

8oz sugar
¼ teaspoon cream of tartar
1 tablespoon golden syrup
⅛ pint cold water
¼ teaspoon bicarbonate of soda
1 teaspoon warm water

Heat the sugar, cream of tartar, golden syrup and water until the sugar is dissolved. Boil to 300°F (hard crack stage) without stirring. Put the bicarbonate of soda in the warm water and add to the mixture, which will froth. Stir and pour into an old tin. When cold break into pieces.

COOKED FONDANTS

¼ teaspoon cream of tartar   Flavourings and colourings
1lb granulated sugar   ¼ pint water

Gently heat the sugar and water. When sugar is dissolved, add the cream of tartar, heat to 240°F (soft ball stage). Damp a marble slab or enamel tray, pour the syrup on to it, cool slightly. Fold the edges of the syrup to the centre, repeat until it becomes whiter, when cool enough knead. Divide into portions, one for each colour and flavour. Add flavourings and colourings. Roll out on greaseproof paper, using icing sugar to prevent sticking. Cut into fancy shapes. Allow to dry on waxed paper.

UNCOOKED FONDANTS

1lb icing sugar

½ teaspoon lemon juice

Colourings if desired

White of 1 egg

Flavourings

Put the lemon juice to the sieved icing sugar, add white of egg to make a medium stiff mixture. Knead the fondant using sieved icing sugar to prevent any stickiness. Add the flavourings and colouring, knead thoroughly, roll out to a quarter of an inch thick and cut into fancy shapes, put on waxed paper to dry.

In the Parlour

TOYS

Stuffed toys appeal to young children for many reasons, one of the most important being the child's need to love. Most young children take something soft and cuddly to bed with them: a piece of blanket, a rag doll, a teddy bear are just three examples. These toys must stand up to hard wear, for young children will use them in expressing their feelings and will not only love and cuddle, but will beat them and throw them about. This is an important use of the toy for the child.

The age of the child should be considered when a toy is being made for him. Babies like to clasp things in their hands, therefore tiny stuffed toys three to four inches long are ideal; whereas children of four to five years old enjoy toys almost as big as themselves, particularly ones they can dress and undress. All the sizes in between are popular at different times and for different reasons.

New material is cheap and should be used in preference to old, although this is not essential; good parts of worn garments could be utilised. Material should be strong and firm in texture.

Suitable fabrics

Casement cloth, poplin, sailcloth – for plain soft toys.

Gingham – striped, checked or spotted – for patterned soft toys.

Jersey, celanese, locknit, calico – for dolls.

Fur fabric – for teddy bears and life-like animals.

Felt – for any toys.

Handknitted fabric knitted to shape – particularly for tiny toys about three inches long.

PATTERNS

Good patterns can be bought, or for a toy that is to be quite personal and original, they can be made. The shape should be simple and straightforward.

To Make a Pattern for a Toy Animal, e.g. a cat: Look at a cat and make a sketch in profile, or look at and copy a good picture of a cat, or get a child of seven years to draw the shape (this might result in the most successful animal). If necessary simplify the drawing. Cut four pieces: (1) one for the side, (2) one for the inside of legs and body, (3) one for the gusset for the top of the head, (4) and one for the ears.

The shape will appear more slender when stuffed so make the pattern big enough to allow for stuffing.

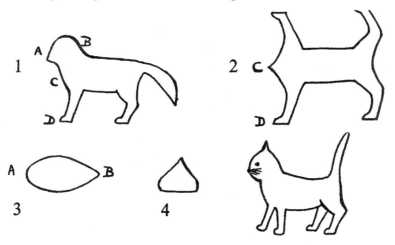

Cutting Out and Stitching

Pin the pattern on the chosen material. Cut out, allowing ¼ inch to ½ inch for seams, *or* draw round the pattern and then cut out, allowing for seams.

Some toys that are made from two pieces only, e.g. dolls, can be stitched before cutting out.

Use a strong cotton or thread. Backstitch by hand or stitch on the machine.

Stuffing

This must be done carefully. Kapok is best for soft cuddly toys and for tiny toys. Bits of latex foam are suitable if a firm, tightly stuffed toy is wanted. This stuffing is not easy to model but must be pushed in very tightly. Its use results in a toy which can be washed, put through a wringer and retains its shape. Wood straw is good for teddy bears and animals that need to be firm and keep their shape. The stuffing should be put into the toy in small bits and pushed to the extremities with a wooden stick or the knob end of knitting pin. There should be no spaces left, whatever the stuffing used. A certain amount of modelling can be achieved by pushing more stuffing where it is wanted, e.g. in the cheeks of a rag doll or animal. If the toy is really tightly stuffed these extra bits will stay in position. For further modelling, tiny almost invisible stitches can be made round the nose, in the eye sockets and mouth position, but this is only necessary in more elaborate toys. When making a toy, leave open suitable seams for the stuffing, e.g. the top of the head and a side

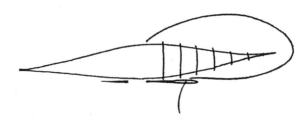

seam in a doll, the seam of the side and gusset in an animal. These seams can then be joined with ladder stitch which is pulled tight and becomes invisible.

Finishing

The toy when finished should be firm and light. All seams should be neat with no gaps between the stitches to allow stuffing to emerge. Fur fabric can be brushed up with a wire brush and will almost hide the seams. Hands, paws and feet are improved by stitching fingers, claws and toes when the toy is stuffed.

Leather shapes can be stitched to paws and feet. Eyes and mouth should be embroidered very simply, or pieces of felt applied. Refer to the animal or to pictures to get the correct shape for the features of an animal. If suitable colours are chosen, these can look very effective.

Glass eyes might be used. They are bought in pairs on one piece of wire. Cut the wire and bend over near the eye to make a firm loop. This wire loop should go right through the material into the head. Fasten it with strong thread tied tightly to the loop, then both ends of thread are taken right through the middle of the head, one at a time and again tied firmly in a reef knot which in turn is pushed inside the head.

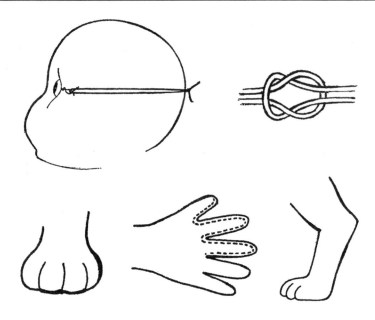

Glass eyes add a more professional finish to a toy but are a risk in that children might pull them off and swallow them. Embroidered eyes done carefully can be almost as effective and cannot be pulled out and eaten.

RAG DOLLS

These are a great favourite with young children and offer good scope for imaginative making and dressing.

Pattern

Cut the pattern from a folded piece of paper to get both sides alike. 8 inches by 12 inches makes a small doll, 12 inches by 16 inches makes a slightly larger doll.

278

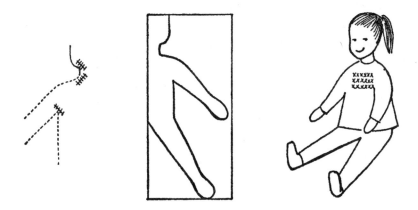

Making

Pin the pattern on to the fabric folded double – strong pink cotton, calico, or celanese. Draw or tack round pattern. Backstitch by hand or machine stitch – leave open top of head and one side of body. Cut out about ¼ inch from seam. Pay particular attention to points that need reinforcing, stitch across these several times.

Turn right side out. Stuff carefully with kapok or foam rubber, pushing the bits tightly down and leaving no spaces. Stuff the arms,

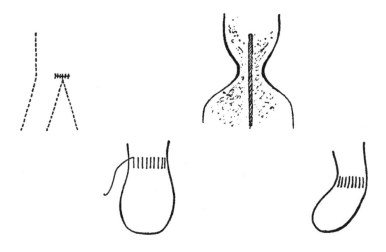

279

legs and body from the side seam, the neck and head from the top of head. If the head is to remain rigid and upright the neck will need some stiffening. A piece of plastic knitting pin will do for this purpose. It should be 2½ inches to 3½ inches long or according to the size of doll. It needs to reach from half-way into the head, through the neck down half-way into the chest. Bind it well with a strip of rag and make sure when it is inside the doll that it is well padded with stuffing all round.

The face can be made interesting by pushing the stuffing firmly into the cheeks and a bit extra for the nose. Stitch the seams with ladder stitch. Fingers and toes could be outlined. The foot can be made to turn up with a few strong stitches across the instep.

The Face

This is best done very simply. Cut out two eyes and a mouth in paper and place on the doll's face in order to get the right position. The features can be embroidered or appliqued. Red wax crayon or a little water colour gives added colour to the cheeks.

The Hair

Hair *(below left)* can be made from darning, knitting, rug or carpet wool, nylon stockings or raffia. Stitch it on with a matching cotton or thread or the same wool.

Clothes

The doll may be dressed in any way. If the clothes are to be taken off by the child they should have fastenings that can be managed easily, large buttons and buttonholes, press studs, elastic, etc. Usually the simpler the garments the nicer the doll appears.

ANIMAL TOYS

These may be dealt with in at least three different ways:

(1) *Straightforward natural shapes.* If these are intended to look like the actual animal it is best to buy a pattern unless the maker is good at drawing or design. Ideas for shape and colouring can be gained from studying real animals, domestic and at the zoo, looking at good pictures of them, for instance, in Puffin Picture Books, and at examples in museums.

(2) *Animal shapes treated decoratively.* In these the animal is used as a basis for decorative stitching. The shape should be made as simply as possible. Patterned fabrics are useful, checks, stripes, etc, make a background to which embroidery stitches are added to make the whole attractive.

(3) *Animals made like dolls.* The teddy bear is the best-known example of the animal that has taken a doll-like shape. Rabbits are also popular. Characters from stories that children enjoy are suitable subjects for this kind of toy, for instance, rabbits, bears, cats and mice.

GLOVE-MAKING

Glove-making is a traditional craft full of interest. A sound knowledge of plain sewing is a necessary foundation; then, with care, method and practice, gloves for every occasion may be made. No expensive tools are needed for this craft; those found in a well-equipped sewing-basket are all that are required – a small pair of really sharp shears, short betweens needles, sizes 5 to 8, and good thread. For the finer oversewn gloves, matching pure silk for sewing is the best to use if the finer cottons and threads are not available.

To choose a pattern measure, the hand tightly round the knuckles; the number of inches shown on the tape-measure indicates the size of pattern needed, e.g. 6¾ inches round the knuckles, get a 6¾ pattern. In a good pattern, the thumb-hole is wholly in the palm and the 'points' (tucks) on the back are evenly spaced with the centre point in a direct line with the cut between the long and third finger. The other points should converge from ¼ inch below the cuts between the other fingers to form an arrowhead at the base. A pattern consists of the trank, or main part of the glove, the thumb, fourchettes strip, or fourchettes with quirks.

Leathers. Choose firm leather of even thickness, dressed specially for glove-making and with a reasonable stretch across the skin. A firm chamois of a close even texture is suitable for a beginner. Do not attempt to make gloves with a soft skin that stretches every way.

Marking. 'Mark out' the pattern on the wrong side of the leather by closely spotting all round. Place a spot at each end of all straight lines and draw these lines with a ruler. Be sure to turn pattern over for the other glove of the pair.

Cutting. Cut through the spots down the sides and along the base of the trank; but cut in one large curve round the top of all fingers. Do not cut between the fingers until the points are sewn and the thumb is put in and then only cut between the fingers (shaping the tops) as each fourchette is put in. The thumb is cut out through the dots and when marking be sure to turn over for a pair.

The fourchettes (finger gussets) and the quirks (diamond-shaped pieces) are spotted and carefully cut with the stretch across. Note the way of the stretch in the quirk. Stitch with a stab-stitch. Stab-stitching looks like running stitches. There is no wrong side to the work; on both sides the stitches should be even, with the space between stitches the same size as the stitch. Make sure the cut edges lie closely together. Sew about one-sixteenth of an inch from the edge of the leather.

Method of Making

Points: Put pins into the spots at top and bottom of 'point' and crease on the line between the two pins, with the right side outside. With a single knot on end of thread pass needle from wrong to right side and stab-stitch to the top of points. Finish off by passing the thread on to the wrong side; run three little back-stitches into the fleshing and finish with a knot.

Thumbs and thumb-holes are numbered on the pattern to help in fitting together. Tie Nos. 1 to 1, 2 to 2, 3 to 3, with fine coloured silk. This is glover's tacking. Use two threads to sew in thumb. With one thread start at figure 1, sew to 2, to 3, and one inch beyond. Very neatly tuck in all corners. Fold the thumb as for wear and with a second needle and thread start at fold at top of thumb, sew round top and down the side and continue to the base of thumb-hole. Go back to the first needle, sew to meet the second needle, pass threads to wrong side of work and tie off with a reef-knot. Diagram 1.

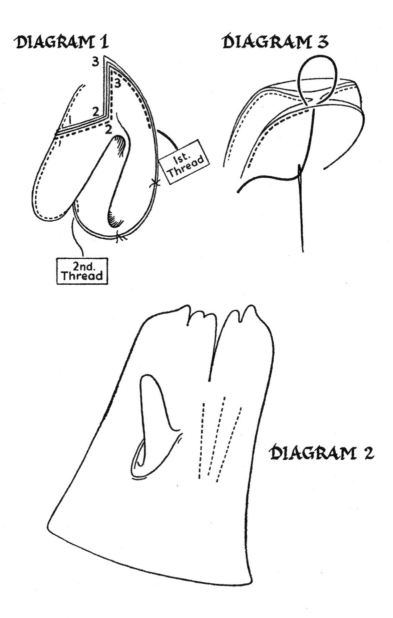

DIAGRAM 1

DIAGRAM 3

1st. Thread

2nd. Thread

DIAGRAM 2

Fourchettes: All fourchettes are cut, in the first place, the same length; long enough for the long finger, and each is reshaped during the making of the glove. All fourchettes are put into the back of the glove. Cut down between the first and long finger to the spot. See Diagram 2. Place the base of the fourchette snugly into the base of the cut, sew side of fourchette to side of finger for half-way up and then reshape the fourchette. To reshape, measure the fourchette against the finger. The fourchette should be about ¼ inch longer than the finger; cut off the surplus, place the pattern on the blunted fourchette and reshape exactly to pattern.

Quirks: These make for good fitting, good wear, and are in all the best makes of gloves. They are put into the base of the fourchette either with an ordinary stab-stitch seam, or if desired to be very flat, with a finely overlaid or flat seam. Before sewing in the quirk, be sure that the cut in the fourchette is as deep as the cut between the fingers in the palm but never alter cut on trank.

To close the glove: Fold as for wear. Tie together the back and palm of each finger-tip with fine silk thread, the base of the finger to the point of the quirk. Put one 'tie' in the centre of each side of each finger to hold fourchettes in place. Begin stitching at fold of first finger; with a single knot at end of the thread, draw through from wrong to right side and stab-stitch the palms of the fingers to the fourchettes and quirks, being careful that at the base of each finger the stitches flow evenly and firmly round. After closing the first and second finger it is advisable to have a new thread. The base of the cut between the long and the third finger is a convenient spot to put this join. Diagram 3 shows the neatening of the finger-tip.

To press the gloves, carefully fold the fourchettes smoothly inside the finger; with fine silk put two or three long tacking stitches to hold them in place. Fold the thumb to lie across the palm of the glove towards the base of the third finger. Place the gloves in white paper on a board under a moderate weight of books for a few days.

FUR GLOVES

Fur gloves are rather more complicated to make than ordinary slip-on leather gloves. The palms are made of leather, the backs of fur and the gloves must be lined with either fleecy lining (woollen stockinette), chamois or fur.

Choose good quality leather for the palms and use a good pattern. Two pelts are needed for the backs and these must be free from crackle and must match each other as much as possible.

Chamois leather is ideal for lining fur gloves – it is warm and supple but more expensive than fleecy lining. When fleecy lining is used, the fourchettes must be cut from silk stockinette, such as pieces from celanese underwear.

For warmth there is nothing to compare with fur lining although this tends to be very expensive, as four pelts are needed. Use chamois for the fourchettes for fur lining.

Use Kerr's Listre Thread No. 16 or 24 for stitching and betweens needles No. 6, 7 or 8-thread and needles must balance with the weight of the leather.

The palms, fourchettes and the two half thumbs must be cut in leather. Sew in the thumbs first, remembering that the straight edge of the thumb must be on the side of the thumb.

Join the fourchettes on the wrong side, starting at the long, pointed end and finishing at the short end. This is where the method of inserting fourchettes differs from inserting them in leather gloves. When making *fur gloves* sew the fourchettes on to the *palms* – the short side of the fourchette to the side of the finger on the palm. Measure and re-shape the fourchettes and complete each finger.

Elastic must now be sewn at the wrist of the glove. Draw a straight line across the palm about ½ inch below base of the thumb. Place the top edge of the elastic on this line and fasten the elastic securely as near the edge as possible, then herringbone – with the stitches practically touching each other – above and below the elastic, thus making a tunnel for it. Before securing the elastic at the opposite end, pull it fairly tightly to gather up the leather. Fasten the elastic firmly as near the edge as possible before cutting it. The palm is now ready for the fur.

Mark and cut the fur – the cutting to be done with a sharp knife or razor blade. The stroke of the fur *must* be towards the finger-tips. If there is a dark streak in the fur, place the pattern so that the streak runs down the back of the hand. Shake the fur well after cutting.

Tack the fur on to the wrong side of the palms by means of buttonhole stitches ¼ inch apart, pushing the fur inside all the time. Then oversew the fur on to the leather with firm oversewing, taking out the tacking stitches as you come to them.

Mark out and cut the lining – palms, half thumbs, backs and fourchettes. The lining must be made up into a complete glove by means of backstitching.

To attach the lining, place the back of the fingers on to the back of the fur, fold lining down the centre of fingers and sew a few stitches down. Care must be taken that the seams of the lining lie on the seams of the glove.

In order to turn the glove, push the tip of the thumb gently in, together with the lining, with the unsharpened end of a pencil. Repeat this with each finger, then push each one further until the whole fingers are through. Pull the glove right through and shake. Place your hand inside the glove and wriggle it so that the seams of the lining rest on the seams of the glove, thus removing any wrinkles in the lining. Pull the lining down so that it fits snugly, take the glove off and cut the surplus lining.

The cuff edge can be bound in the same way as a man's glove is bound with a narrow leather strip.

Lamb skins can be used for fur-backed gloves and are very attractive. It is easy to join lamb skins should the skins be too small. Another use for lamb skins is as a lining for leather or fur-backed gloves. Attractive little mittens can also be made from lamb skins.

With our Friends

MUSIC MAKING

WASSAIL SONG

GOD BLESS THE MASTER
From the 'Sussex Mummers' Carol

* When this number is sung alone start here

291

GLOVE PUPPETS

Glove Puppets are the natural outcome of doll and toy-making. A small child's baby doll or teddy bear is to him a living companion, who shares his joys and sorrows, his whole life in fact. How much better, therefore, if a favourite character can be made to move, to dance and above all to hold things. Many grown-ups are as fascinated as their children by these toys.

The body of a glove puppet is merely a sack-like shape, of a size to fit the hand of the manipulator, but varying in length from wrist to elbow. It is usually cut all in one with the arms, sleeves, wings or whatever is in-keeping with the character being made – raglan style. If, however, the arms are cut separately, with the front part cut away at the top and the armhole of the body is similarly shaped (Fig. 1), they will automatically extend forwards on the completed toy and greatly ease manipulation. Hands may be merely hollow extensions of the sleeve or may be stuffed and the fingers indicated by stitching. A piece of pipe cleaner pushed into each finger will allow the hand to be curled and shaped so that it may more easily grasp and hold objects.

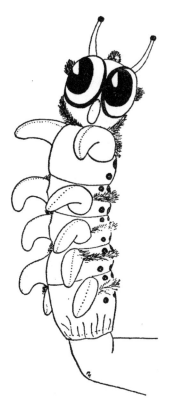

At the mention of glove puppets, the Punch and Judy of our British seasides, fairs, fêtes and Christmas parties inevitably spring to mind. Why such a wicked character as Punch, who beats his down-trodden wife, throws away his baby and emerges triumphant time and again, with only the casual remark 'What a pity!' should remain a national favourite, is difficult to imagine. It is all the more extraordinary, when one

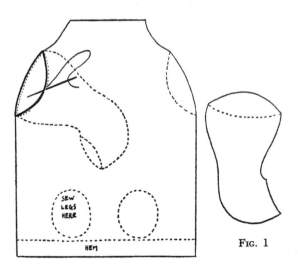

SEW LEGS HERE

HEM

FIG. 1

remembers that he is not even of British extraction but came to us from Italy, in the form of Pulcinello. Perhaps his redeeming feature is that he is never unkind to Dog Toby – British children would never put up with that! Today we seldom see a real Dog Toby, that patient, lovable character of former generations, but Mr Scaramouche, the doctor, the policeman and the hangman are still with us.

The most usual Punch and Judy puppets have gaily painted, hollow, papier-maché heads, easily made at home by modelling over a greased plasticine mould. For those nervous of their own capabilities, very inexpensive rubber or plastic heads are available today and only require painting. The needlewoman can make most effective heads by cutting two silhouettes in felt and joining them with a centre seam. The 'thickness' at the top is either achieved by a series of joined darts (Fig. 2) or a gusset extending from the top

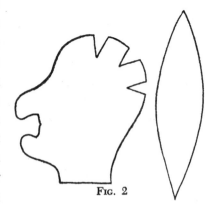

FIG. 2

FIG. 3

of the forehead to the nape of the neck. Features are embroidered or appliqued in bold, coloured felts (Fig. 3). The heads are stuffed, leaving room inside for a buckram or cardboard tube, which is inserted upwards from the neck, allowing the middle finger to manipulate the head (Fig. 4). Punch, himself, should be given the traditional hunch-back, and be dressed gaily, either in felt or in scraps left over from dressmaking! Most children enjoy making up plays and where no puppet theatre is available, will substitute the back of a couch or easy chair, with great effect.

FIG. 4

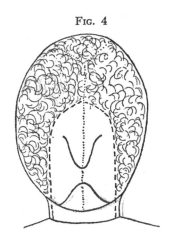

Some children who have no interest in the puppet theatre as such, will make a constant companion of a puppet animal, bird or sometimes a human or fairy figure – these are better described as glove toys.

It is usually best to cut the bodies of these toys on the large side, so that when finished they are loose on

FIG. 5

the hand, allowing for more flexibility. Two or three fingers are often used to manipulate the heads of these rather soft, cuddly puppets. As regards material, fur fabric is first choice, but should be adapted to the character of the animal, felt for an elephant for instance. The head of any favourite toy pattern can be adapted for this purpose, being made up in the usual way and joined to the sack-like puppet body, all round the neck. It is then stuffed firmly with Kapok, a central 'tube' being left for the fingers, which is lined by a small cotton bag sewn to the inside of the neck.

Appealing little creatures such as bears, kittens, dogs and ducks make enchanting glove toys and much character can be introduced by careful needle modelling of the faces, using a good picture as a guide. A long, fine, darning needle and strong matching thread is used, to take invisible stitches through the head from point to point, pulling tightly so as to form the characteristic dimples or puffiness of the animal in question. (Care should be taken not to sew through the finger tube!) Fig. 5 shows a white kitten whose face was modelled in this way.

Although glass eyes may be used, they give a rather staring, unnatural appearance and hand-made felt eyes add much to the charm of the puppet. Those of the kitten were in black, with a green iris, and black 'slit-like' pupil.

Circles, ovals, semi-circles and triangles of felt in various sizes and colours, build up to make most effective eyes and may be tried out by pinning to the toy, until a pleasing expression is produced

(Fig. 6). If they have a rather 'flat' appearance, each eye may be raised slightly, by pushing a small piece of stuffing underneath, when sewing to the head, and in the case of insects they should be made to bulge. A tiny highlight of white-stranded cotton, which will give the eye a lively 'shine,' is an improvement.

Puppets for use as toys will come to life more easily if they are given legs and tails where applicable. These are stuffed and ladder stitched firmly to the lower part of the body. For an animal character, turn up a narrow hem all round the base and insert elastic to fit the wrist snugly (Fig. 5). For a bird, sew a press stud on the inside of the hemline, so that the body fits tightly round the wrist in front and sticks out at the back to form a tail. Mouths and claws may be embroidered in stranded cotton and whiskers made from horsehair. An elbow-length green and yellow striped caterpillar is another amusing idea.

For those with a lively imagination, this craft presents an endless challenge and they will not only create the actual puppets, but write stories, plays and rhymes to go with them.

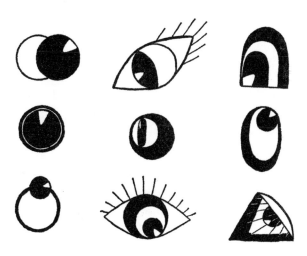

FIG. 6

ON BEING A COMMITTEE MEMBER

A committee may be set up in your village to run the flower show, or raise funds for re-roofing the hall, or the club or organisation to which you belong may ask you to stand for nomination to their committee. Though you may feel you do not know enough or have little to offer, accept the nomination if you can. Someone has had confidence in you or they would not have put your name forward. Bear in mind that nomination is not election and do not feel affronted if you are not elected, but be prepared to stand again.

As a committee member you should be prepared to attend meetings regularly and punctually: if you cannot attend a meeting, send an apology. Before the meeting you will receive the agenda and should study it so as to come ready with ideas on the matters to be discussed. You will be asked for your opinion and you may also be asked to undertake some special job – such as organising a sideshow or the selling of tickets or arranging the stewarding.

When doing a special job as a committee member, you must put your scheme before the committee and get sanction to put it into action. Remember you are one of a team and whether the committee on which you serve is in connection with the policy of an organisation, or the running of a flower show, the committee members must be prepared to give and take for the good of the 'whole'.

Some of the words and semi-technical terms used in committee work are given below. You will find that working to a certain recognised committee procedure makes for clarity and precision and so saves time and tempers.

In committee you should remember always to speak to the Chairman – this prevents the meeting breaking up into individual conversations. You should remember too that committee discussions are confidential. The decisions will be made known at the proper time. Committee work is often hard work but just as often very enjoyable and interesting.

Committee Terms

AD HOC means 'for this purpose'. An Ad Hoc sub-committee is one appointed to carry out one particular piece of work, such as arranging a money-raising effort. It functions in exactly the same way as a standing sub-committee, except that it automatically ceases to exist when its work is finished.

AFFILIATION means 'being united to'. To be affiliated is to be received into a society as a member organisation.

AGENDA. The agenda of a meeting is the programme of business which must be dealt with by that meeting, in the order in which it is to be considered. Every meeting should have an agenda. In the case of a committee, a copy of the agenda should be sent to every member before the meeting.

AMENDMENT. A proposal to alter the wording or details of a resolution without affecting the principle of the resolution. An amendment must be clearly worded to show exactly which part of the resolution it is proposed to alter. Amendments are voted upon before the resolution and, if passed, they at once become part of the resolution.

AUDITOR. A person appointed by an organisation to examine its accounts and to report as to whether or not they are correct.

BALLOT. A system of secret voting, by which voters mark their voting papers with a cross only, but do not sign them. Papers are then dropped into a box, and later, the votes are counted by the Tellers. A well-arranged secret ballot is an infallible way of arriving at the wishes of the majority.

BUDGET. A budget is an estimate of receipts and expenditure. The budget must be passed by the meeting.

BYE-LAW. A modification of the rules to suit local conditions.

CASTING VOTE. When a decision is being taken (either by written ballot or by a show of hands) and the result is a tie, it is usual for the chairman to have the deciding vote. This casting vote is in addition to her ordinary vote.

COMMITTEE. A smaller body elected from amongst the members of a larger body for the purpose of carrying out the policy laid down by the larger body. If any matter of policy is involved, no work must be done and no decision taken until the larger body has been consulted at an appropriate meeting, and has endorsed the recommendation of the committee.

CO-OPTION is the power given to a committee or sub-committee, to add a member or members (of its own choosing) to its number. This power is useful, especially if a member with special talent or ability is needed on a committee.

DELEGATE. A member elected to attend a meeting to vote according to the instructions of those who have elected her. It is the duty of the delegate to ensure that she knows the feelings and wishes of the body she represents so that she may express their views correctly. It is also her duty to take back a clear report of the meeting she has attended.

DEMOCRATIC. Applied to an organisation in which all members have the same rights and privileges, and where all decisions are taken by majority vote. The responsibility for the progress and well-being of a democratic movement rests on the shoulders of all and every member.

EXECUTIVE. An executive body is one which has the power to carry out business. In a democratic body this power is limited, as all-important matters must first be sanctioned by the majority.

EX-OFFICIO. The holder of a certain office is often entitled to be a member of some committee or other body by reason of her office. Anyone ceasing to hold office at once loses any ex-officio rights, as these belong not to any one person, but to the office itself.

FINANCIAL STATEMENT. A statement concerning the funds of an organisation, which should cover receipts and expenditure, and a comparison with the budget.

HONORARY. This describes unpaid officers and workers.

MAJORITY. The vote of the greater number in a ballot or a show of hands. A democratic movement is governed by the majority at all times, though the minority are encouraged to express their views and state their opinions.

MINUTES. The official record of the proceedings at a meeting of an organisation. Minutes should give detailed and accurate information regarding policy, decisions and resolutions. Minute books should be carefully preserved, so that they are available for reference.

NEM. CON. means 'no one voting against'. A resolution or decision is said to be carried nem. con. when no one has voted against it, but some have abstained from voting.

NOMINATION. The name of a person put forward as candidate for a particular position.

NOMINEE is the name given to a person nominated for a particular position, who has expressed her willingness to serve.

OFFICERS. Those who hold office, for example, president, vice-presidents, secretary, and treasurer.

POLICY. A course of action adopted by an organisation. This course of action must be within the constitution and rules of the organisation, and, in a democratic movement, is always decided upon by majority vote.

PROPOSER is the name given to a person who brings forward a resolution at meeting. It is her duty to state her case clearly and briefly, giving the reasons for the proposition.

QUESTION. Sometimes used in the same sense as Resolution or Motion. (See RESOLUTION below.)

To move that the question be now put: is to propose at a meeting that a vote be taken without further discussion. This motion can be made when either a substantive motion or an amendment is before a meeting. If this is carried, the proposer may be given her usual right of reply, but no other speakers are allowed. If this vote has been taken on an amendment, the discussion continues on the remaining amendments and the substantive motion.

To move that the meeting do now proceed to the next business: is to propose that the meeting pass on to the next business and no vote be taken on the question or subject under discussion, on the ground that it is at the time an unsuitable matter to vote on. It may be moved when a resolution or an amendment is being discussed. If this proposal is carried, there can be no further discussion of the resolution or of any amendments, and the meeting proceeds to the next item on the agenda. If this proposal is not carried, discussion on the resolutions and amendments continues.

QUORUM. The least number of members who must be present at a meeting in order that any decision taken may hold good. A Committee's standing orders should lay down the number necessary to form a quorum.

RECOMMENDATION. A proposal or suggestion put forward by a committee for endorsement and approval by the majority of the members. In the case of a sub-committee, recommendations are made to the main committee, who decide whether or not these recommendations should be endorsed at a meeting where the majority of members are present.

RECORD. The name given to the minutes of a meeting.

REFERRED BACK. If a committee does not agree with a recommendation made by a sub-committee, it is usual to 'refer it back.' This means that the recommendation in question is sent back to the sub-committee to be reconsidered.

RESOLUTION. A positive statement of opinion put forward for consideration at a meeting. A resolution calls for action, and should therefore deal with one subject only, and be clearly worded so that straight vote can be taken on it.

RIGHT OF REPLY. When a resolution has been fully discussed the mover has the right to reply. After the mover has made her reply no other member shall speak for or against the resolution. The mover of an amendment has not the right of reply, unless the amendment is passed and thus becomes the substantive resolution. When several amendments have been passed, the chairman decides to whom the right of reply shall be given.

RULING. An explanation, in cases of doubt, of what is the correct procedure in a certain case, or the exact meaning of some rule or regulation. Rulings are sought from higher authority.

SECONDER. The person who supports the proposer of a resolution. No resolution is valid, or may be voted upon, unless it is proposed and seconded.

STANDING ORDERS. The regulations drawn up by a meeting, defining its methods of work.

SUB-COMMITTEE. A subordinate body appointed by a committee to deal with all matters covered by its terms of reference, and to make recommendations for necessary action to the committee. No work may be undertaken by a sub-committee until such work has been approved by the committee. A sub-committee may hold no funds, but should submit a budget to the committee. If this is passed the treasurer will be authorised to pay bills up to the amount authorised, and to receive any money which is made as a result of the sub-committee's efforts.

TELLERS. Persons appointed to take charge of the arrangements at an election, to see that all is done in order, to count the votes, and to make out a list of those elected.

TERMS OF REFERENCE. The definition of the powers and duties of a committee or sub-committee, drawn up by the body which appoints it.

UNANIMOUSLY. A resolution or decision is said to be carried unanimously when everyone present has voted in favour of it, and no one has abstained from voting.

Local Festivals

'Bonfire Night' is really the first of the winter festivals with huge fires and fireworks exploding as the Guy Fawkes tradition is kept alive all over the country each November 5th.

In Sussex bonfire night is kept up with more than usual fervour; Lewes has eight societies of 'Bonfire Boys' who organise eight torchlight processions. Men, dressed as bishops, preside at the burning in effigy of Fawkes and Catesby below the Race Hill, and a blazing tar barrel is thrown into the River Ouse. Once ugly cries of 'No Popery' rang out, for dark memories of the burning of the Protestant Martyrs in 1557 still rankled, but now it is a cheerful night's entertainment. Fancy dresses are much in favour, many having been handed down from one generation to the next.

Battle and Rye also have similar excitements and the streets are thronged with revellers and more 'Bonfire Boys' collect for local charities. Rye W.I. has often won a prize for its tableau on these occasions.

While some are celebrating Guy Fawkes day, a strange ceremony of a very different kind is performed each year at Shebbear in Devon. They are 'turning the Devil's stone'. The great brown stone, measuring some 6ft by 4ft by 2ft thick, lying in the churchyard, is said to have been dropped by the Devil in his descent to hell. Tradition maintains that the stone must be turned each year or ill-luck will befall the parishioners, and so each year the evil spirits are challenged by the church bells being rung discordantly and the stone is turned over.

A medieval custom again associated with a stone is kept up at Dunchurch, Warwickshire, each St Martin's Day (November 11th) with the Payment of Wroth Silver. The custom is said to go back 1,000 years, and there are even 768 recorded occasions of the collection. The ceremony remains the same as in medieval times. The Duke of Buccleuch's representative, facing the east, reads out the Charter of Assembly, then calls upon the representatives of 26 parishes in the Hundred of Knightlow to pay their dues. In each case he is answered by the chink of coins being thrown into the hollowed-out centre of the weather-beaten wroth stone, said to be the base of a Saxon wayside cross, on Knightlow Hill.

After the ceremony, the party moves to the nearby Dun Cow Inn for breakfast, where the health of the Duke is drunk in traditional style in rum and milk.

Today the vast estates once held by the Duke of Buccleuch along the Fosse Way have all gone. The only piece of land he owns in the district is the small field where the Wroth Silver stone lies. But the parishes still obey the call to pay their dues, which amount to a grand total of 9s 4d.

A little time before Christmas, on December 10th, comes the big Beast Mart at Boston in Lincolnshire. By a charter granted by Elizabeth I in 1573 the Corporation of Boston were empowered to hold a Beast Mart or Cattle Fair. The Mart was formerly held in what has now become the playground of the Grammar School and although it has long been robbed of its former importance, it is still formally proclaimed there on December 10th of each year. On that day, in the presence of the Mayor, members of the Borough Council and the Headmaster, staff and boys of the school, the Town Clerk reads the traditional proclamation of the Mart.

After the Town Clerk has called for three cheers for the Sovereign, the Mayor and Corporation of Boston and the school, the Mayor speaks to the boys and ends by asking the Headmaster to grant them a half-holiday, symbolic of the times when the school had to be closed during the Mart.

A stained-glass window, installed in the School Hall to commemorate the fourth centenary of the foundation of the school by Philip and Mary in 1555, contains a panel depicting the proclamation ceremony and portraying the Mayor of 1955, the Town Clerk and the Headmaster.

Many local customs come with Christmas. In Berkshire at Sunningwell there is a Christmas Play which has been performed for generations, the words being handed down from father to son. The story is one of a hero, King George, slaying a dragon, with many other characters, all of whom are dressed in coats and cloth caps to which have been stitched long paper fringes. Another local variant is that many of the jokes are cracked by a woman, Mrs Finney, who, it is proclaimed, 'can cure a magpie with toothache in his heel'.

In Cheshire, the mummers play is called 'Soul-Caking'. Again the theme is based on an ancient ritual of death and resurrection. The men of Comberbach play the characters with such strange names as the 'Letter-in', King George, the Black Prince, the Old Woman, Quack Doctor, Dairy Dout, Beelzebub, Driver, and, not least, the Horse. For this a real horse's skull is used, the bones strung together so that the mouth works and the teeth can be snapped together. On All Hallow E'en, bands of children get together and go from door to door 'soul-caking' for pennies. Each band sings a different verse of which a sample is:

This night we come a-souling good nature to find,
And we hope you'll remember it's Soul Caking time.
Christmas is coming and the geese are getting fat,

Please put a penny in the old man's hat.
If you haven't got a penny, a ha'penny will do,
If you haven't got a ha'penny, God bless you.

After Christmas come the New Year festivities, which are perhaps more traditionally celebrated in the North. Durham, for example, has long adopted many Scots customs as well as those of the South. Christmas is celebrated as a family festival, while the New Year is given equal importance as an adult festival with Hogmanay.

The celebrations usually begin at midnight on New Year's Eve, when companies of friends meet before the town clock, or in the middle of the village, to welcome the New Year. After vociferous vocal greeting, the companies gather at the home of one of their members.

As it is accounted to be a sure forerunner of ill luck for the first to cross the threshold to be either a woman or a tall fair man, it is usually arranged for the first foot to enter the house to be that of a short dark man, who thus brings with him the deserved good fortune. To further ensure good luck, he is expected to bring with him a piece of greenery, a piece of coal, and wood for kindling, emblematically to provide food and firing for the coming year. His reward for so doing must be in silver. It is then that toasts are drunk, in wine or spirits. The party goes on to visit the home of each member, the last call being made at some pre-arranged home where a more solid breakfast has been prepared, after which all participants separate to their respective homes in the not-too-early morning.

Plough Monday – the first Monday after Twelfth Night – also used to be widely celebrated. Now it only occurs in a few villages such as those of Balsham and Swaffham Prior in Cambridgeshire. Plough Monday was the beginning of the agricultural season and the beginning of ploughing before it became common to do any winter sowing.

It used to be the custom for all the ploughmen and ploughboys to dress up and drag a wooden plough through the streets. One would be dressed as a Jack-in-the-Green, covered in evergreen and the others would put on any comic garments they could muster and most smeared their faces with burnt cork. They danced through the streets chanting songs, which were largely of a local variety and it was the custom to shout out 'A penny for the ploughboy!' If no pennies were forthcoming the plough boys would then proceed to either plough up one's cobbled path or put the share under the door-step and pull it up. In Cambridge the undergraduates would throw hot pennies from the upper storeys of the houses to the street below, where dancers from neighbouring villages were dancing through the town. It is on record that the landlord of the Pickerel Inn in Magdelene Street refused to pay and so they ploughed up the cobbled yard of the inn. Some of the wooden ploughs used are still to be found, as in the tower of Bassingbourn Church.

Another country ceremony, but of a very different nature, is the wassailling of the apple trees in Devon and Somerset. At Carhampton, Somerset, on January 17th each year up to 200 people may gather in the orchard behind the inn, and at about 8pm a local farm-hand who acts as master of ceremonies leads the way through the orchard with an oaken bucket filled with cider from one of the landlord's barrels. Near the chosen tree he sets down the bucket, and some of the party, including one or two men with accordions, form a ring round the tree. Stable lanterns carried by one of the wassaillers shed their light on the scene.

The master of ceremonies calls for the wassail song, and a local farmer steps forward and chants the lines. As he ends, a great cheer goes up, and two or three men with guns blaze off through the leafless branches of the tree. This and the shouting is supposed to frighten off the evil spirits and imps of mischief which may damage the crop prospects. Then – for the good spirits – the master of ceremonies places in a fork of the tree a piece of toast soaked in cider. The old belief was that these rites would ensure a bumper crop, and in days gone by when a party might wassail anything from 12 to 20 orchards, they would purposely avoid visiting those belonging to men who were not popular! After this ceremony the accordions break into popular airs and the crowd join in lustily until the cider is all gone, when they adjourn to the inn and carry on with the singing.

Wassailling of a different nature takes place in South Wales and is called the Mari Lwyd. This consists of a horse's skull draped with white cloth and decorated with rosettes, coloured tapes, papers and streamers and with eyes of bottle glass and cloth ears. The skull is fixed on a broomstick and carried by a man who, from beneath a sheet, is able to work the lower jaw. The Mari Lwyd is led from house to house at the head of a procession. In its full glory the party consisted of Mari, the Leader, Sergeant, Merryman, Punch and Judy – some of these characters being linked with medieval miracle plays. At each house a request of admittance and permission to sing is proffered in extempore verse following traditional rules. The occupants in the house reply in verse and a rhymed dialogue of a set type ensues, ending with the admission of the party. Health drinking was a part of the Mari Lwyd custom, the singers being provided with a wassail bowl which was passed round the company. In some parts of Glamorgan the wassail bowl was replaced by an ordinary bowl or even a bucket as the custom decayed. In Glamorgan and Monmouth the ceremony began on Christmas night and continued for two to four weeks. In other parts it was sometimes particularly associated with the New Year or Twelfth Night.

Another Welsh tradition is the throwing of hot halfpennies to the crowd each year after the January procession of the Anglesey Hunt at Beaumaris.

Local Skills

WELSH AND DURHAM QUILTING

Long ago it was discovered that warmth in bedclothing and garments was much increased if two layers of material were stitched together with a third layer of heat-conserving material between. For this, sheep's wool was found to be both economical and practical, being light, warm and excellent in the wash.

DESIGNS

The early quilters evolved decorative patterns by using nearby objects. Cups, plates and wine-glasses provided them with circles; ferns, flowers, leaves and shells with natural forms. These traditional

patterns increased in variety and complexity until a quilt became a masterpiece of original and beautiful design. In the quilts of the North Country (e.g. Durham, Northumberland) the designs are free and flowing and the traditional shapes include feathers, fans, waves, cables, tassels and wreaths. In Wales the designs tend to be more geometrical and circles, triangles and rectangles are frequently used as frames for spirals, palmettes, leaves and Tudor roses.

In the West Country such designs as have survived often show a naturalistic treatment derived from plant forms (e.g. ivy, oak, clover).

The design of a quilted article should exhibit decorative and orderly ornamentation with good spacing, but not more than two square inches should be left unquilted in order to prevent any movement of the filling. Choose one or more dominant shapes and ensure that they

stand out well enough against a subordinate background.

First design the central shape, next the borders and corners (which should fit accurately), then any secondary shapes that the size of the space to be filled may demand, lastly a contrasting background. In quilting, the lines of stitchery may be either close together (giving low relief), at a medium distance from each other (giving medium relief), or comparatively far apart (giving high relief). Harmony and balance in the proportion of these three types of relief are vital.

It is of the essence of the craft that no two quilted articles should ever be identical in design. The traditional motifs, so helpful to the designer, must always be arranged in accordance with individual taste. Through this union of tradition and novelty, quilting offers a unique opportunity for the ordinary person to create original work which combines utility with artistic merit.

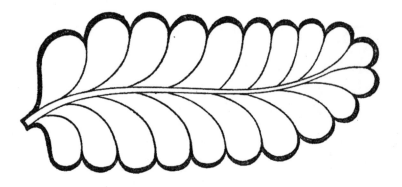

Equipment

Frame – indispensable.

Sheep's wool: 2 to 3lb needed for a large quilt. Unless bought already prepared, which is rather expensive, it must be washed, well teased or carded, and all dark grease spots removed. Old thin blankets could be used instead, but sheep's wool is softer to sew, lighter in weight and warmer in use. Cotton wadding may also be used but not cotton wool which mats easily, and is hard to sew.

Materials: Cotton poplin or any fine, pure cotton material, dull satin, fine sateen, Shanghai silk, shantung, tussore and similar materials are suitable. Taffeta, cheap satin and loaded silks should not be used. Always choose a plain (unpatterned) material, preferably light in colour and with a matt surface; very shiny materials, because of the highlights they give, detract from quilting designs.

Thread: Use cotton, No. 40, matching the material in tint, for all materials in preference to mercerised cotton.

Needles: Betweens, no more than $1\frac{1}{8}$ inches long.

Method

The full design should first be roughly sketched out on paper.

The frame should be set up.

Stitch firmly two separate pieces of material of the same size to the tape at the top edge of the frame. Stitch the underneath piece to the tape at the bottom edge of the frame.

Pin down the loose top layer of material to the tape at the bottom of the frame.

Shapes for design are usually cut out in stiff cardboard and are then called 'templates'. Many quilters possess templates – handed down for generations – of the different sizes of rose, feather, etc. Some of the simpler shapes can be obtained by the folding and cutting of paper.

In use, either place the template on the material and chalk round it with tailor's chalk, or rub round the edge of the template on the wrong side with chalk and press it firmly down on the material, thus leaving a firm chalk outline, or place the template on the material and scratch closely round the outline with a needle. The scratch mark should show clearly.

The whole of a small design may be marked out or, if large, a portion only (about 12 to 10 inches for the start). To mark background lines, if in patterns of squares or diamonds, rub a length of fine string in chalk, fix it with a pin at each end of the line to be made, and snap it sharply up and down; alternatively chalk along a ruler.

The details of the templates, e.g. veins of leaves, etc, are marked in as required. A pencil is never used for marking quilting designs since the marks would show after quilting.

Unpin top piece of material now marked with the design and turn it back. On lower piece lay one thickness of well-carded sheep's wool, spreading evenly so as to avoid lumps or thin places.

Bring top piece over and pin it securely down at bottom of frame.

Fasten the sides of the work with lengths of tape laced round the stretchers and pinned to the edges of the material. Tension should not be very tight.

To sew, make a knot in the cotton, insert the needle from underneath and pull the thread through. Give a small sharp jerk and the knot will come through the bottom layer but not through the top. Run two or three stitches at a time, holding the forefinger of the left hand under the frame and feeling the point of the needle each time that it goes through the three thicknesses. Note that this is a running stitch and not, as sometimes supposed, a stab stitch.

Running Stitch is used throughout and should be so regular that one cannot tell on which side the finished quilt has been worked. The needle must go right through all three thicknesses at every stitch. Stitches need not necessarily be very small but must be of even length both front and back, as must the spaces between them.

To fasten off, take one stitch half back over the last running stitch on the top, split this stitch, insert the needle through the top layer only, bring it out some way off, and cut the thread.

Finish

A bed quilt should have its edges turned in (making sure that the sheep's wool comes right to the edge) and run with two rows of running, about ½ inch apart, giving the appearance of another two rows of quilting. Cushion covers can well be finished with a neat piping in the same material. Knots and loose ends must never be allowed to show in the finished article.

Local Recipes

CHESHIRE PIGEON PIE

1 pigeon	Seasoning
½lb stewing veal	2 tablespoons stock
2oz bacon	1 dessertspoon flour
2oz chopped parsley	1 teaspoon chopped mushrooms

Cut up pigeon and veal into pieces. Dip in flour and fry lightly in a little dripping. Mix flour with remainder of dripping to a paste; add stock, boil a moment, then pour over remainder of ingredients in a casserole. Stew gently until meats are tender, put in a pie dish and cover with short pastry. Bake in a hot oven for about ½ hour.

ANGLESEY HARE PATE

Simmer some hare with vegetables and mixed herbs and garlic to taste for six hours.

Take hare off the bone, mince and add more pressed garlic if desired and a little stock. Also add a generous quantity of port. Return the mixture to the saucepan and stir well – the pate should not be too thick.

Pour into a dish and seal when cold with melted butter.

Index

Also published by Merlin Unwin Books

Wild Flowers of Britain Margaret Wilson

Wayside Medicine Julie Bruton-Seal & Matthew Seal

My Wood Stephen Dalton

Land's End to John O'Groats Helen Shaw & Bob Shelmerdine

A Job for all Seasons Phyllida Barstow

A Murmuration of Starlings Steve Palin

Mushrooming with Confidence Alexander Schwab

The Hare Jill Mason

Hedgerow Medicine Julie Bruton-Seal & Matthew Seal

The Byerley Turk Jeremy James

Venison: the game larder José Souto

Extraordinary Villages Tony Francis

Kitchen Medicine Julie Bruton-Seal & Matthew Seal